Deep Inside osCommerce
The Cookbook

Spice up your osCommerce website using
69 mouth-watering, ready-made recipes

Monika Mathé

PUBLISHING

BIRMINGHAM - MUMBAI

Deep Inside osCommerce: The Cookbook

First published: September 2006

Production Reference: 2210906

Published by Packt Publishing Ltd.
32 Lincoln Road
Olton
Birmingham, B27 6PA, UK.

ISBN 1-84719-090-1

www.packtpub.com

Cover Image by www.visionwt.com

Credits

Author

Monika Mathé

Reviewers

Carine Bruyndoncx

Jim Ekleberry

Karly Phillips

Development Editor

Louay Fatoohi

Assistant Development Editor

Nikhil Bangera

Technical Editor

Divya Menon

Editorial Manager

Dipali Chittar

Indexer

Mithil Kulkarni

Proofreader

Chris Smith

Layouts and Illustrations

Shantanu Zagade

Cover Designer

Shantanu Zagade

Foreword

osCommerce is more than simply an open-source e-commerce solution. For thousands and thousands of people, tweaking, adding, removing, and devising new and ingenious ways to enhance their online stores is not so much a chore as an engaging, fun, and above all, productive way of life.

Joining the osCommerce community means becoming part of a team of users and developers from all over the world who share a common passion for contributing to the project, or making use of it in any number of different ways. With a project like osCommerce that lends itself to such a wide variety of contributions, tools, tips, and tricks, it is important that you keep your finger on the pulse of the project.

Using the osCommerce website to discuss techniques and to share your ideas and solutions is part and parcel of being an active community member. It is also a great way to meet people with common ground, and help them with their projects or be helped in return; there is much to be learned from this medium.

I daresay, however, that there are few such members out there who have been *more* helpful and *more* supportive of osCommerce as whole than Monika — including helping me out, a while back!

It is really only fitting then that she has taken a step out of her normal online arena and written a book that mixes one part development experience with two parts fun to bring you an osCommerce cookbook to take delight in.

Good luck and have fun,

David Mercer

About the Author

Monika Mathé

Fascinated by being able to combine logic and creativity, it seems that destiny had finally found me when I became a software developer and Oracle Certified Database Administrator.

It was a tough call to decide in which field to work, but landing a position in a marketing agency and working with everything from Oracle to SQL Server and HTML, ASP, and JavaScript was a fabulous decision I still congratulate myself for! I learned more about marketing campaigns, e-commerce, CMS, and CRM than I had ever wanted to know, I mean, ever thought was possible!

I have been completely absorbed by the Open Source Community. I became an avid believer in PHP and in MySQL, and am definitely in a love affair with osCommerce. I believe almost anything can be done with it ... I challenge anyone to prove me wrong!

Being an active member of the osCommerce Online Community, I know preemptively which questions will arise in new shop creation. Presently, I am creating as many customized shops for clients as time permits; of course while urging them to add as many custom coded modules as I see fit ... that's dessert for me!

With special thanks to my family, my forum friends, and my clients all over the world. You are the spice of my life!

Monika Mathé
Architect
Oracle Certified Database Administrator (OCP DBA)
osCommerce Expert
http://www.monikamathe.com
osCommerce Profile Name: Monika in Germany
http://forums.oscommerce.com/index.php?showuser=56607

About the Reviewers

Carine Bruyndoncx

With a masters degree combining business, finance, and IT, it seems only natural that I have been working in IT, for almost a decade, purely for international financial companies and institutions. During these years, I have touched upon a lot of different systems, databases, and programming languages, and held a range of positions from analyst-programmer, DBA, quality assurance, and support as well as team-leading and project management.

This international working environment management allowed me to build a solid IT foundation. While living abroad and traveling extensively, I learned to appreciate the cultural differences, habits, and the nice weather (though mostly in other parts of the world).

In recent years, my focus has shifted away from finance towards CTI, CRM, and e-business systems. Having experience with Vantive, Siebel, and a SAP CRM eSales certification under my belt, it was time to start a new chapter in 2004. Following my mantra, "Think global, act local" I joined Keukenlust.be (my parents business) where among other responsibilites, I also handle the webshop (evidently based on osCommerce).

Since I can't stay away from computers, you might find me posting about osCommerce or other Open Source packages in my blog on the osCommerce forums, perhaps doing a little custom programming for clients, or troubleshooting complex problems, as time allows. I'm a perfectionist at heart; I like a good challenge; and guess what ... fruit salad is my favorite dessert !

Jim Ekleberry

Jim Ekleberry aka Jim Daemon from Tennessee, USA belongs to the top 20 list of osCommerce members and has been on the forums since January 2003. He likes meeting new people and making friends so working on this book as a technical reviewer was a great opportunity for him to show off his coding talents.

In his real life job, Jim works in his company Akoza which is a leading provider of Information Technology (IT) services and is an IT outsource partner for small and medium-sized businesses. He encourages all non-techie business people to spend their time on their business instead of their technology and have his company do the big business services for not-so-big companies.

His favorite quote is a clever remark by Albert Einstein, "Great spirits have always found violent opposition from mediocre minds. The latter cannot understand it when a man does not thoughtlessly submit to hereditary prejudices but honestly and courageously uses his intelligence." — a perfect mantra for a tech reviewer!

```
http://www.akoza.com
```

Karly Phillips

Working wonders in the kitchen is like work in life itself... the preparations for something exceptional and fulfilling keep us at it; keep us coming back again and again to try it in different ways to improve ourselves and our causes.

I am not a master chef; my dining room table has no Michelin stars, but the 1/7th of my life I spend passionately mucking about in my kitchen, I hope, will result in much more than well-prepared meals—to create fond memories, not unlike those I have of my own mother, for my children.

I am equally passionate about my work with To Love Children Educational Foundation International Inc., an NGO with special consultative status to the ECOSOC of the United Nations. TLC is making a difference in the poorest of the developing countries of our world.

Monika kindly allowed me to share in the work of her kitchen, even giving me permission to lick the spoon from time to time. Chapter 3, *Spice Up Your Infoboxes*, was so intriguing to me, as a non-osCommerce user, that I read front to back *Building Online Stores with osCommerce: Professional Edition* by David Mercer, registered a domain, and downloaded a copy to play with… just to better understand it. It is a wonderful tribute to her passion!

With my best wishes,

Karly Phillips

www.karlyphillips.com

www.tolovechildren.org

Table of Contents

Introduction

Dear fellow osCommerce community members, what's for dinner tonight?

Your good old stew recipe probably doesn't sound that appetizing anymore, and your customers probably share this view when they visit your website that hasn't been spiced up recently for added interest.

Let's whip up in our cuisine a donation module for that church, which prefers to collect alms not only during servicess, but also online these days. You may be an artist in need of an online showroom presenting courses, tutorials, and artwork in a content management system, with or without an added shopping-cart function as its backbone. Why not garnish your gift shop with a great solution for offering gift-wrapping choices during checkout.

osCommerce is a highly adaptable, fascinating piece of software that already offers most necessary ingredients to work with; yet you can compare it with a five-star restaurant where the secret trimmings and preparations make the unrivaled dishes.

Make your store truly yours by adding that special kick, which makes it stand out from the crowd of online shops. Just as you are willing to spend a dime on a fabulous five-star dinner prepared by the chef, you will find that your customers feel the same way, as your shop wins their favor due to your new custom code that enhances their shopping experience. Increased sales rates will show you just how much they really like those new treats.

With this book in your hands, you will find many inspiring ideas that will make you itch to dive into your code pages immediately. Some are only a few lines worth, some go knee-deep into core code changes, while others involve minor tackling of a lot of files with incredible outcomes. All will add that special flavor to your site that you have been looking for.

This step-by-step presentation of each tastefully prepared recipe will allow you to pick modules that you have always wanted to implement to finish off your store.

Your files are your ingredients; your brain is your equipment; add a bit of elbow grease, and your customers will be delighted to see the mouthwatering treats you cook up for them.

Just as a great cook can whip up an entire menu after a spoonful of that new gravy in his favorite restaurant, you too will be inspired to make changes similar to those in this book. You'll learn about code reading and the great pleasure of making that code yours. While I suggest making most changes manually, you can request a file set of each recipe from Packt's website by presenting a proof of purchase of this book. This will definitely come in handy with larger bits of code, when typing it all again could become messy.

But who cares about a bit of mess? Get out your apron and roll up your sleeves, and Bon appetit!

What This Book Covers

Chapter 1 equips you with a few, very easy, and very important changes to the basic design, which will make developing, and later modifying a whole new template a breeze.

Chapter 2 will help you modify your navigation to ensure a smoother shopping experience for your customers.

Chapter 3 covers infoboxes, and turns you into an expert in tweaking them to your needs.

Chapter 4 deals with one of the most important visual parts of your shop—the product display in the listings and the detail page.

Chapter 5 outlines different methods to make searching on your site a fun experience since you want your customers to use your search and to find the products you want to sell to them.

Chapter 6 highlights customizations of the checkout process, namely, the flow from the shopping cart to the shipping and payment pages up to the order email.

Chapter 7 talks about new shipping modules. You will learn how to adapt existing modules to create completely new rate systems for your shop.

Chapter 8 focuses on existing payment modules and how they can be tweaked.

Chapter 9 provides tips on efficiently using banners as a marketing tool.

Chapter 10 is a goody bag of extra special treats to indulge your sweet tooth.

Chapter 11 tackles changes in the admin area. You alone will be the keeper of these secret recipes hidden to the public eye.

What You Need for This Book

This book is for people who are already familiar with osCommerce. It presumes a working knowledge of PHP and HTML, as well as basic understanding of phpMyAdmin for database inserts.

How to Use This Book

As with any good cookbook, you can open this book in any chapter and start with the recipe that tantalizes your taste buds first. There is no need to first read the book cover to cover, as all individual recipes work as standalone modules to spice up your default osCommerce installation to suit your taste.

All recipes are sorted by topics into chapters and can be implemented in any order. Each recipe starts out with an **osCommerce 2.2 Milestone 2 Update 060817**, which has the latest security patches of August 2006 added to the core code. If you are using several recipes, make sure you mix and match carefully, so you won't break the code. Always take a backup of the files modified. For easier identification, mark the header part of the file with the recipe you are using in it.

Conventions

In this book, you will find a number of styles of text that distinguish between different kinds of information. Here are some examples of these styles, and an explanation of their meaning.

There are three styles for code. Code words in text are shown as follows: "Run the following SQL statement in your database to create the new columns `affiliate` and `affiliate_url` for the `products` table."

A block of code will be set as follows:

```
// the following cPath references come from application_top.php
    $category_depth = 'top';
    if (isset($cPath) && tep_not_null($cPath)) {
    $categories_products_query = tep_db_query("select count(*) as
total from
    " . TABLE_PRODUCTS_TO_CATEGORIES . " where categories_id = '" .
    (int)$current_category_id . "'");
```

When we wish to draw your attention to a particular part of a code block, the relevant lines or items will be made bold:

```
// the following cPath references come from application_top.php
$category_depth = 'top';
if (isset($cPath) && tep_not_null($cPath)) {

  $cPath_array = explode('_', $cPath);
  $stylesheet_test = $cPath_array[0];
  include(DIR_WS_MODULES . 'cat_driven_stylesheets.php');

  $categories_products_query =
      tep_db_query("select count(*) as total
      from " . TABLE_PRODUCTS_TO_CATEGORIES . "
      where categories_id = '" .
      (int)$current_category_id . "'");
}
```

New terms and **important words** are introduced in a bold-type font. Words that you see on the screen, in menus or dialog boxes for example, appear in our text like this: "clicking the **Next** button moves you to the next screen".

This sticky note box appears at the start of all recipes, and will tell you which **ingredients** to have ready before you get cooking.

 To make sure that your soup doesn't get too salty or burned, special tips are highlighted as **Chef's suggestion** in this format.

Reader Feedback

Feedback from our readers is always welcome. Let us know what you think about this book, what you liked or may have disliked. Reader feedback is important for us to develop titles that you really get the most out of.

To send us general feedback, simply drop an email to feedback@packtpub.com, making sure to mention the book title in the subject of your message.

If there is a book that you need and would like to see us publish, please send us a note in the SUGGEST A TITLE form on www.packtpub.com or email suggest@packtpub.com.

If there is a topic that you have expertise in and you are interested in either writing or contributing to a book, see our author guide on www.packtpub.com/authors.

Customer Support

Now that you are the proud owner of a Packt book, we have a number of things to help you to get the most from your purchase.

Downloading the Example Code for the Book

To obtain the code for this book, send a mail to service@packtpub.com. Your order will be verified and the code dispatched via email"

Errata

Although we have taken every care to ensure the accuracy of our contents, mistakes do happen. If you find a mistake in one of our books—maybe a mistake in text or code—we would be grateful if you would report this to us. By doing this you can save other readers from frustration, and help to improve subsequent versions of this book. If you find any errata, report them by visiting http://www.packtpub.com/support, selecting your book, clicking on the **Submit Errata** link, and entering the details of your errata. Once your errata have been verified, your submission will be accepted and the errata added to the list of existing errata. The existing errata can be viewed by selecting your title from http://www.packtpub.com/support.

Questions

You can contact us at questions@packtpub.com if you are having a problem with some aspect of the book, and we will do our best to address it.

1

Chop and Cream the Basic Design

Welcome to our cooking class! Your Chef is Monika—also known as **Monika in Germany** on the forums. There is no doubt about the fact that I absolutely love osCommerce, and thoroughly enjoy tweaking all parts of it to get the underlying code to perform at its best. In the following chapters, you will learn about all parts of the osCommerce structure and how to adapt them to your needs. Let's get cooking!

As starters, let's change a few design elements of the default osCommerce setup, namely, the stylesheet handling, and the three column layout, which is currently a bit inflexible.

In this chapter, we will see how to:

- Add easy top-category driven stylesheets
- Create flexible column definitions

1. Add Easy Top-Category Driven Stylesheets

This recipe allows you to personalize the look of your store with much more detail than one stylesheet alone could offer. You will be able to specify an extra stylesheet for use with any of your top categories. This will come in very handy for color driven categories like "Men's and Women's Perfumes", "Clothing", or "Food Groups". You can specify new stylesheets for all or only a few of your top categories; for all others the default stylesheet will be used. The new stylesheets are relevant for all product-related pages, which are:

- index.php
- product_info.php
- product_reviews.php
- product_reviews_info.php
- product_reviews_write.php
- tell_a_friend.php

Presentation

In our case, the three top categories of a default osCommerce installation are called **Hardware**, **Software**, and **DVD Movies**. We will have the following background colors assigned for easy referencing: **Hardware** is yellow, **Software** is red, and **DVD Movies** is blue.

Clicking on **Software** or any related subcategory shows the red background. As the rounded corners of the infoboxes are images and not stylesheet driven, they will be replaced by transparent images.

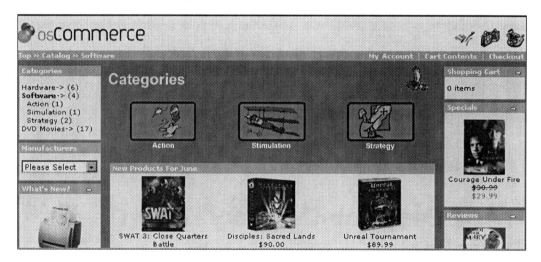

This is how the top category **DVD Movies** category will look:

Go fetch your butter, flour, and cream, and let's enrich your style!

Ingredients

New:

catalog/stylesheet_hardware.css
catalog/stylesheet_software.css
catalog/stylesheet_dvd.css
(these are modified versions of the stylesheet.css file)
catalog/includes/modules/cat_driven_stylesheets.php

Modified:

catalog/images/infobox/corner_left.gif
catalog/images/infobox/corner_right.gif
catalog/images/infobox/corner_right_left.gif
catalog/includes/functions/general.php
catalog/index.php
catalog/product_info.php
catalog/product_reviews.php
catalog/product_reviews_info.php
catalog/product_reviews_write.php
catalog/tell_a_friend.php

Cooking

1. Create transparent images for your infobox corners, and drop them in the `catalog/images/infobox` folder. Replace all three images `catalog/images/infobox/corner_left.gif`, `catalog/images/infobox/corner_right.gif`, and `catalog/images/infobox/corner_right_left.gif` with the new transparent image created in the same size while keeping the original filename.

2. Create new stylesheets in the `catalog` folder by copying `stylesheet.css` and naming them according to their intended use for easy referencing. For each category that has its own design colors (we will call these secondary stylesheets, determined by the `categories_id` used for that page), overwrite the default style parameters with new ones. Here our new files are called `stylesheet_hardware.css`, `stylesheet_software.css`, and `stylesheet_dvd.css`, as they will be used for **Hardware**, **Software**, and **DVD Movies** respectively.

Chef's suggestion:

A different naming convention could use the `categories_id` for naming the new stylesheets, so they would be called `stylesheet_cat_1.css`, `stylesheet_cat_2.css`, etc. If you are changing IDs often or are the visual type, using descriptive names is probably the better solution for you.

3. Make the changes in the new stylesheets for the desired new looks. Here only the style for BODY was assigned a new background color; so all other style classes were removed from the stylesheet files. The original code for the BODY class is defined as follows with the highlighted part changed for your secondary stylesheets files to assign new background colors:

```
BODY {
  background: #ffffff;
  color: #000000;
  margin: 0px;
}
```

4. Open `catalog/includes/functions/general.php`, and add the following new function before the closing `?>` tag, it will return the top category for a product, which will in turn decide on which stylesheet to add as a secondary stylesheet to your pages:

```
function tep_get_top_category_id($product_id) {

  $topcat_array = explode('_' ,
        tep_get_product_path($product_id));
  $top_cat = $topcat_array[0];

  return $top_cat;
}
```

Note that the built-in function of osCommerce, `tep_get_product_path`, only pulls one category for each product, which can prove tricky for linked products as those are assigned to several categories. If you have many linked products and want to change the category colors according to the current category, adding a clone of this function that takes `$current_category_id` as a second parameter may be an option for you. Another option would be to duplicate products so that they have their own `categories_id`; this is recommended only if you are not tracking stock.

Also remember that products set at top level will not show in your products listings and also not be able to use their own stylesheets.

5. Create the new file `cat_driven_stylesheets.php` in your `catalog/includes/modules` folder. It has the following code that assigns different stylesheets according to the `categories_id`:

```
<?php
/*
  $Id: cat_driven_stylesheets.php,
        v 1.00 2006/06/05 00:00:00 mm Exp $

  Module written by Monika Mathé
  http://www.monikamathe.com

  Module Copyright (c) 2006 Monika Mathé

  osCommerce, Open Source E-Commerce Solutions
  http://www.oscommerce.com

  Copyright (c) 2003 osCommerce

  Released under the GNU General Public License
*/
  switch ($stylesheet_test) {
    case '1':
      $stylesheet_add = 'hardware';
      break;
    case '2':
      $stylesheet_add = 'software';
```

```
        break;
     case '3':
        $stylesheet_add = 'dvd';
        break;
     default:
        $stylesheet_add = '';
        break;
  }
?>
```

6. Open the last six files of the ingredients list: `index.php`, `product_info.php`, `product_reviews.php`, `product_reviews_info.php`, `product_reviews_write.php`, and `tell_a_friend.php`, and find this line in each of them:

    ```
    <link rel="stylesheet" type="text/css" href="stylesheet.css">
    ```

    Directly below it, put on the following lines to add a secondary stylesheet if one was detected for the top category of the selected area:

    ```php
    <?php
    if ($stylesheet_add != '') {
       echo '<link rel="stylesheet"
              type="text/css" href="stylesheet_' .
              $stylesheet_add . '.css' . '">';
    }
    ?>
    ```

7. In `index.php`, find this code that deals with the different categories and their products:

    ```
    // the following cPath references come from application_top.php
    $category_depth = 'top';
    if (isset($cPath) && tep_not_null($cPath)) {
    $categories_products_query = tep_db_query("select count(*)
    as total from " . TABLE_PRODUCTS_TO_CATEGORIES .
    " where categories_id = '" . (int)$current_category_id . "'");
    ```

    Replace with the following code to fill the parameter `$stylesheet_test` with the top-level category ID if the selected category, and then call the file that decides which stylesheet to include as a secondary stylesheet:

    ```
    // the following cPath references come from application_top.php
    $category_depth = 'top';
    if (isset($cPath) && tep_not_null($cPath)) {

       $cPath_array = explode('_', $cPath);
       $stylesheet_test = $cPath_array[0];
       include(DIR_WS_MODULES . 'cat_driven_stylesheets.php');
    ```

```
$categories_products_query = tep_db_query("select count(*)
as total from " . TABLE_PRODUCTS_TO_CATEGORIES .
" where categories_id = '" .
(int)$current_category_id . "'");
```

8. In the other five product-related files, `product_info.php`,
   `product_reviews.php`, `product_reviews_info.php`,
   `product_reviews_write.php`, and `tell_a_friend.php`, find this:

   ```
   require('includes/application_top.php');
   ```

   Immediately below it, add the following two lines that check the top category
   ID by the current `products_id`, and then call the file that decides which
   stylesheet to include as a secondary stylesheet:

   ```
   $stylesheet_test =
     tep_get_top_category_id((int)$HTTP_GET_VARS['products_id']);
   include(DIR_WS_MODULES . 'cat_driven_stylesheets.php');
   ```

You've created a fantastically rich starter! Bon appetit!

2. Create Flexible Column Definitions

This recipe allows you to define and redefine column width and column layout,
and modify the traditional three column layout to any other combination including
asymmetrical designs, within seconds.

Presentation

You can completely remove the right column, freeing up all space taken up by it.

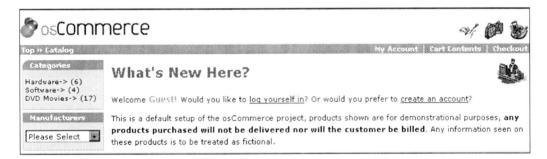

Or you may prefer to keep both columns, but use the right column for thumbnail
display only, as you have long category and manufacturer names, and need more
space on the left.

Let's take one of grandma's favorites and make it new!

Ingredients

Modified:

catalog/includes/application_top.php
All 38 files on root level in the catalog folder that have the right and left column.
catalog/includes/column_left.php
catalog/includes/column_right.php

Cooking

1. In catalog/includes/application_top.php find this:

```
// customization for the design layout
   define('BOX_WIDTH', 125);
// how wide the boxes should be in pixels (default: 125)
```

The default-box width is defined by this parameter. We divide the parameter into two using the left and right column respectively. Replace with this code:

```
// customization for the design layout
   define('BOX_WIDTH_LEFT', 125);
// how wide the boxes should be in pixels (default: 125)
   define('BOX_WIDTH_RIGHT', 125);
// how wide the boxes should be in pixels (default: 125)
```

This will set both columns at the same width, and will be your play area when the recipe is well done.

2. Find in `index.php` and the other root files (altogether 38) the following lines:

```
<td width="<?php echo BOX_WIDTH; ?>" valign="top">
  <table border="0" width="<?php echo BOX_WIDTH; ?>"
  cellspacing="0" cellpadding="2">
<!-- left_navigation //-->
<?php require(DIR_WS_INCLUDES . 'column_left.php'); ?>
<!-- left_navigation_eof //-->
  </table></td>
```

Replace this with the following lines, as we will be moving the column-cell definition directly into the column files:

```
<!-- left_navigation //-->
<?php require(DIR_WS_INCLUDES . 'column_left.php'); ?>
<!-- left_navigation_eof //-->
```

3. Repeat this for the right column, find:

```
<td width="<?php echo BOX_WIDTH; ?>" valign="top">
  <table border="0" width="<?php echo BOX_WIDTH; ?>"
  cellspacing="0" cellpadding="2">
<!-- right_navigation //-->
<?php require(DIR_WS_INCLUDES . 'column_right.php'); ?>
<!-- right_navigation_eof //-->
  </table></td>
```

Replace with this:

```
<!-- right_navigation //-->
<?php require(DIR_WS_INCLUDES . 'column_right.php'); ?>
<!-- right_navigation_eof //-->
```

4. For both columns, you have now removed the cell definition from the root files. This means that if the included file is empty, no additional cell will be added and the entire page width can be used for the site content.

The parts that were cut from the root files have to be added to the column files; so open `catalog/includes/column_left.php`, and add the following line at the very top, above the opening php tag:

```
<td width="<?php echo BOX_WIDTH_LEFT; ?>" valign="top">
  <table border="0" width="<?php echo BOX_WIDTH_LEFT; ?>"
  cellspacing="0" cellpadding="2">
```

Note how the new definition was used so that left and right columns can be defined independently. Add the following code after the closing php tag of `catalog/includes/column_left.php`:

```
  </table></td>
```

5. Repeat this procedure for the `catalog/includes/column_right.php` file using the column-right definition when replacing.

```
<td width="<?php echo BOX_WIDTH_RIGHT; ?>" valign="top">
  <table border="0" width="<?php echo BOX_WIDTH_RIGHT; ?>"
  cellspacing="0" cellpadding="2">
```

Add the following code after the closing php tag of `catalog/includes/column_right.php`:

```
</table></td>
```

If you'd now like to remove the whole column right without changing the underlying structure, so you can have it back as soon as you implement a new design, comment out everything in the file `catalog/includes/column_right.php`. You can add all boxes you'd like to keep to the left column.

Chef's suggestion:

This setup enables you to have more than three columns also (you may want to show a column for ads on your product pages); all it takes is a new include for the additional column in the relevant file and a new file created following this method for your `includes` folder, with its own width specified.

Just as easily, add a conditional statement at the top of the column file (close at bottom), so your right column only shows on certain pages.

Time to share a cup of tea with Grandma! You've done it! Bon appetit!

Summary

In this chapter, you have learned to add additional stylesheets for all top-category products that need a special flavor. You can now easily add more stylesheets and completely change the look of your sub-pages; they can use different colors and background images for each top-level category. In addition, you have learned to cut up your root files and take out the cell-definition part for your left and right columns, which allows you to make changes concerning the width of each column and allows you to remove one or both columns within seconds. Congratulations! You are now ready to tackle the next step in our culinary journey.

2

Serve them New Menus

In this chapter, we will whip up new navigation structures that will help your customers browse your pages with ease.

We will talk about how to:

- Show active subcategories only in your categories box
- Create separate boxes for each top category
- Simplify category box navigation by defining specific colors for each level
- Add extra links to your category box

3. Show Active Subcategories only in Your Category Box

In a default osCommerce setup, the category box holds your categories, and subcategories are displayed in the same box directly below the active category name. This recipe will use the category box for subcategories only while the main categories are displayed in a different menu.

By adding a navigation bar with your top categories at the top of the pages, the category box only needs to be visible if there are subcategories to a category. At all other times, the category box will be hidden to free up the space.

Presentation

In this setup a horizontal navigation bar was added at the very top of the page for the top categories of the shop, which are **Hardware**, **Software**, and **DVD Movies** in a default osCommerce installation. By clicking on the category **Software**, a subcategory box shows up, displaying all the subcategories that belong to **Software**. The box is still visible when you click on a subcategory from the box to show the subcategory product listing like here:

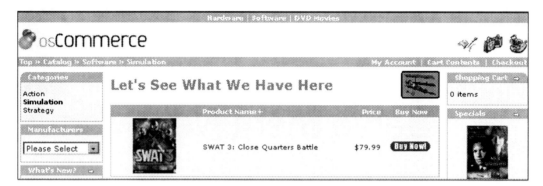

Chef's suggestion:

If your setup has five top categories with active subcategories and two top categories with products right on the first level, your top menu bar will show all seven top categories, but only the five that have subcategories will produce a category box with their subcategories when selected.

This one is very easy; so let's play—hide the pigs in blankets!

Ingredients

Modified:

```
catalog/includes/header.php
catalog/includes/boxes/categories.php
```

Cooking

1. Open `catalog/includes/header.php` and find this in line 51:

```
if ($messageStack->size('header') > 0) {
  echo $messageStack->output('header');
}
?>
```

Immediately below it, add the following code snippet to create the new top-category navigation bar. We are pulling all top categories from a query, lining them up horizontally as links to the respective `categories_id`, and displaying this string in a horizontal menu bar, cutting off the last characters used for separating menu items in the loop—the string `' | '`, which is 13 characters long:

```
<table border="0" width="100%" cellspacing="0" cellpadding="1">
  <tr class="headerNavigation">
    <td class="headerNavigation" align="center">
<?php
  $mylinks = '';
  $categories_query = tep_db_query("select c.categories_id,
    cd.categories_name, c.parent_id from " . TABLE_CATEGORIES .
    " c, " . TABLE_CATEGORIES_DESCRIPTION . " cd where
    c.parent_id = '0' and c.categories_id = cd.categories_id
    and cd.language_id='" . (int) $languages_id ."'
    order by sort_order, cd.categories_name");
  while ($categories = tep_db_fetch_array($categories_query))  {
    $mylinks .= '<a href="' . tep_href_link(FILENAME_DEFAULT,
    'cPath=' . $categories['categories_id']) . '"
    class="headerNavigation">' .
    $categories['categories_name'] . '</a> | ';
  }
  echo substr($mylinks, 0, strlen($mylinks)-13);
?>
    </td>
  </tr>
</table>
```

2. Open `catalog/includes/boxes/categories.php` and find the following code in line 16. This part of the function creates the category and subcategory levels when displaying the box:

```
for ($i=0; $i<$tree[$counter]['level']; $i++) {
  $categories_string .= "  ";
}

$categories_string .= '<a href="';

if ($tree[$counter]['parent'] == 0) {
  $cPath_new = 'cPath=' . $counter;
} else {
  $cPath_new = 'cPath=' . $tree[$counter]['path'];
}
```

```
$categories_string .= tep_href_link(FILENAME_DEFAULT,
                      $cPath_new) . '">';

if (isset($cPath_array) && in_array($counter, $cPath_array)) {
  $categories_string .= '<b>';
}

// display category name
$categories_string .= $tree[$counter]['name'];

if (isset($cPath_array) && in_array($counter, $cPath_array)) {
  $categories_string .= '</b>';
}

if (tep_has_category_subcategories($counter)) {
  $categories_string .= '-&gt;';
}

$categories_string .= '</a>';

if (SHOW_COUNTS == 'true') {
  $products_in_category =
    tep_count_products_in_category($counter);
  if ($products_in_category > 0) {
    $categories_string .= ' 
      (' . $products_in_category . ')';
  }
}
$categories_string .= '<br>';
```

Change to the new code. This will show rows only if it is a subcategory level or below, but not a top category:

```
if ($tree[$counter]['parent'] == 0) {
  $cPath_new = 'cPath=' . $counter;
} else {
  $cPath_new = 'cPath=' . $tree[$counter]['path'];
}

for ($i=0; $i<$tree[$counter]['level']; $i++) {
  $categories_string .=
    '<a href="' . tep_href_link(FILENAME_DEFAULT,
                  $cPath_new) . '">';
}

if (isset($cPath_array) && in_array($counter, $cPath_array)) {
  for ($i=0; $i<$tree[$counter]['level']; $i++) {
    $categories_string .= '<b>';
```

```
        }
    }

    // display category name
    $categories_string .= $tree[$counter]['name'];

    if (isset($cPath_array) && in_array($counter, $cPath_array)) {
      for ($i=0; $i<$tree[$counter]['level']; $i++) {
        $categories_string .= '</b>';
      }
    }

    if (!$tree[$counter]['parent'] == 0) {
      $categories_string .= '</a><br>';
    }
```

3. In this section, a new infobox heading will be created for categories, and
    the top-level category array is filled for display in the original box. Still in
    catalog/includes/boxes/categories.php, find the following code in
    line 61:

    ```
    new infoBoxHeading($info_box_contents, true, false);

    $categories_string = '';
    $tree = array();

    $categories_query = tep_db_query("select c.categories_id,
      cd.categories_name, c.parent_id from " .
      TABLE_CATEGORIES . " c, " . TABLE_CATEGORIES_DESCRIPTION .
      " cd where c.parent_id = '0' and
      c.categories_id = cd.categories_id and
      cd.language_id='" . (int) $languages_id ."'
      order by sort_order, cd.categories_name");
    while ($categories = tep_db_fetch_array($categories_query))  {
      $tree[$categories['categories_id']] = array(
        'name' =>$categories['categories_name'],
        'parent' => $categories['parent_id'],
        'level' => 0,
        'path' => $categories['categories_id'],
        'next_id' => false);
    ```

    Replace it with the following code; wrapping this whole section into an "if"
    statement, which checks whether we are indeed on subcategory level already.
    The query is adjusted to pull subcategories only from the current category.
    The category array has been removed as it is no longer needed:

    ```
    if (isset($cPath) && tep_not_null($cPath) &&
    tep_has_category_subcategories($cPath)) {
    ```

```
            new infoBoxHeading($info_box_contents, true, false);

            $categories_string = '';
            $tree = array();

            $categories_query = tep_db_query("select c.categories_id,
              cd.categories_name, c.parent_id from " .
              TABLE_CATEGORIES . " c, " . TABLE_CATEGORIES_DESCRIPTION .
              " cd where c.parent_id = '0' and
              c.categories_id = cd.categories_id and
              c.categories_id = '" . $cPath . "' and
              cd.language_id='" . (int)$languages_id ."'
              order by sort_order, cd.categories_name");
          while ($categories = tep_db_fetch_array($categories_query))  {
```

4. Almost at the bottom of the page, find the following in line 124, which displays the category box:

```
    new infoBox($info_box_contents);
```

Replace with the following code, closing the "if" statement created in step 3 after the categories box display is finished:

```
    new infoBox($info_box_contents);
  }
```

Good job getting those sausages in the cakes! Bon appetit!

4. Create Separate Boxes for Each Top Category

This recipe will create a category box for each of your top categories that have subcategories. To cover top categories that have products right in the next level without subcategories, a top navigation bar is added.

Presentation

Your navigation will look like the following screenshot, with top categories added in a bar at the very top of the page:

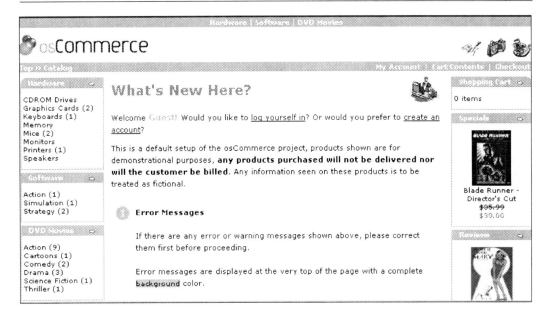

Chef's suggestion:

If your setup has five top categories with active subcategories and two top categories with products right on the first level, your infobox headers will show all seven top categories in the left column, but only five category boxes will show with subcategories obviously; the top categories that have no subcategories will show as links that direct to their product listing. See the Chef's suggestion below (at the end of the Cooking section) for a hack that only shows the box if there are subcategories for this top category.

Go grab your cookie cutters, and have fun hacking your code!

Ingredients

Modified:

```
catalog/includes/header.php
catalog/includes/boxes/categories.php
```

Cooking

1. Open `catalog/includes/header.php` and find this in line 51:

```
if ($messageStack->size('header') > 0) {
  echo $messageStack->output('header');
}
?>
```

Immediately below it, add the following code snippet to create the new top-category navigation bar. We are pulling all top categories from a query, lining them up horizontally as links to the respective `categories_id`, and displaying this string in a horizontal menu bar, cutting off the last characters used for separating menu items in the loop — the string `'  |  '`, which is 13 characters long:

```
<table border="0" width="100%" cellspacing="0" cellpadding="1">
  <tr class="headerNavigation">
    <td class="headerNavigation" align="center">
<?php
$mylinks = '';
$categories_query = tep_db_query("select c.categories_id,
  cd.categories_name, c.parent_id from " .
  TABLE_CATEGORIES . " c, " .
  TABLE_CATEGORIES_DESCRIPTION .
  " cd where c.parent_id = '0' and
  c.categories_id = cd.categories_id and
  cd.language_id='" . (int)$languages_id ."'
  order by sort_order, cd.categories_name");
while ($categories = tep_db_fetch_array($categories_query)) {
    $mylinks .= '<a href="' . tep_href_link(FILENAME_DEFAULT,
    'cPath=' . $categories['categories_id']) .
    '" class="headerNavigation">' .
    $categories['categories_name'] . '</a>  |  ';
}
echo substr($mylinks, 0, strlen($mylinks)-13);
?>
    </td>
  </tr>
</table>
```

2. Open `catalog/includes/boxes/categories.php` and find this in line 14, where the category tree is built, which in the default version holds all categories and subcategories:

```
global $tree, $categories_string, $cPath_array;

for ($i=0; $i<$tree[$counter]['level']; $i++) {
```

```
      $categories_string .= "  ";
}

$categories_string .= '<a href="';

if ($tree[$counter]['parent'] == 0) {
  $cPath_new = 'cPath=' . $counter;
} else {
  $cPath_new = 'cPath=' . $tree[$counter]['path'];
}

$categories_string .= tep_href_link(FILENAME_DEFAULT,
                  $cPath_new) . '">';

if (isset($cPath_array) && in_array($counter, $cPath_array)) {
  $categories_string .= '<b>';
}

// display category name
$categories_string .= $tree[$counter]['name'];

if (isset($cPath_array) && in_array($counter, $cPath_array)) {
  $categories_string .= '</b>';
}
```

Replace with the following code that will only display information about a specific category:

```
global $tree, $categories_string, $cPath_array, $cat_name;

$cPath_new = 'cPath=' . $tree[$counter]['path'];
$categories_string .= '<a href="';

$categories_string .= tep_href_link(FILENAME_DEFAULT,
                  $cPath_new) . '">';

if ($cat_name == $tree[$counter]['name']) {
  $categories_string .= '<b>';
}

// display category name
$categories_string .= $tree[$counter]['name'];

if ($cat_name == $tree[$counter]['name']) {
  $categories_string .= '</b>';
}
```

3. In this section, the category box is created in the default setup. Still in
catalog/includes/boxes/categories.php, find the following code in
line 64:

```
<!-- categories //-->
            <tr>
              <td>
<?php
  $info_box_contents = array();
  $info_box_contents[] = array('text' =>
                                      BOX_HEADING_CATEGORIES);

  new infoBoxHeading($info_box_contents, true, false);

  $categories_string = '';
  $tree = array();
  $categories_query = tep_db_query("select c.categories_id,
    cd.categories_name, c.parent_id from " .
    TABLE_CATEGORIES . " c, " .
    TABLE_CATEGORIES_DESCRIPTION . "
    cd where c.parent_id = '0' and
    c.categories_id = cd.categories_id and
    cd.language_id='" . (int)$languages_id ."'
    order by sort_order, cd.categories_name");
```

We want to create a category box for each top category; this section needs to
be wrapped into a loop, and the top-category name needs to be pulled into
the variable $cat_name, so it can be shown as the box heading. Replace the
previous code with the following, with the upper section being all new, and
with a few changes in the lower-loop part (important parts are highlighted).
Only the top box has a rounded corner, and the selection pulls in to each loop
only the subcategories of the relevant box:

```
<!-- categories //-->
<?php
  if (isset($cPath_array)) {
    for ($i=0, $n=sizeof($cPath_array); $i<$n; $i++) {
      $categories_query = tep_db_query("select categories_name
        from " . TABLE_CATEGORIES_DESCRIPTION .
        " where categories_id = '" . (int)$cPath_array[$i] .
        "' and language_id = '" . (int)$languages_id . "'");
      if (tep_db_num_rows($categories_query) > 0)
      $categories = tep_db_fetch_array($categories_query);
    }
    $cat_name = $categories['categories_name'];
  }
// display category name
```

```php
    $num = 0;

    $categories_box_query = tep_db_query("select c.categories_id,
      cd.categories_name, c.parent_id from " .
      TABLE_CATEGORIES . " c, " .
      TABLE_CATEGORIES_DESCRIPTION . " cd where c.parent_id = '0'
      and c.categories_id = cd.categories_id
      and cd.language_id='" . int)$languages_id ."'
      order by sort_order, cd.categories_name");
     while ($categories_box =
             tep_db_fetch_array($categories_box_query))  {
      $box_id = $categories_box['categories_id'];

//now loop through the box-cats and create extra boxes for them
?>
          <tr>
           <td>
<?php
  $info_box_contents = array();
  $info_box_contents[] = array(
    'text' => $categories_box['categories_name']);


    $num++;
    if ($num == 1) {
      new infoBoxHeading($info_box_contents, true, false,
        tep_href_link(FILENAME_DEFAULT,'cPath=' . $box_id),
        tep_href_link(FILENAME_DEFAULT,'cPath=' . $box_id));
    } else {
      new infoBoxHeading($info_box_contents, false, false,
        tep_href_link(FILENAME_DEFAULT,'cPath=' . $box_id),
        tep_href_link(FILENAME_DEFAULT,'cPath=' . $box_id));
      }
  if (tep_has_category_subcategories($box_id)) {
    $categories_string = '';
    $tree = array();

    $categories_query = tep_db_query("select c.categories_id,
      cd.categories_name, c.parent_id from " .
      TABLE_CATEGORIES . " c, " .
      TABLE_CATEGORIES_DESCRIPTION .
      " cd where c.parent_id = '" . (int)$box_id ."'
      and c.categories_id = cd.categories_id
      and cd.language_id='" . (int)$languages_id ."'
      order by sort_order, cd.categories_name");
```

4. Almost at the bottom of the page, find this in line 162:

```
new infoBox($info_box_contents);
?>
            </td>
        </tr>
```

This is where the default infobox is created. As we have many boxes, and have each of these boxes wrapped in its own table cell as seen in step 2, we need to close those cells, move one counter ahead in the loop, and free up the parameter $first_element so that only current-box data shows in each box. Replace with this:

```
new infoBox($info_box_contents);
?>
            </td>
        </tr>
<?php
  }
  unset($first_element);
}
?>
```

> **Chef's suggestion:**
>
> If you prefer to show the box only for categories that have subcategories, and are happy with the top-navigation bar for those categories that have products right on the next level, you only need to move one line in categories.php.
>
> Find the following code in line 85:
>
>
>
> ```
> if (tep_has_category_subcategories($box_id)) {
> ```
>
> Move it directly above line 77, which increases the $num parameter, so it looks like this:
>
> ```
> if (tep_has_category_subcategories($box_id)) {
>     $num++;
> ```
>
> Moving this row will exclude all categories that do not have subcategories from the box header creation loop, while the regular recipe code will display the header but no content if there are no subcategories.

They baked perfectly, right? Enjoy! Bon appetit!

5. Simplify Category Box Navigation by Defining Specific Colors for Each Level

In the default setup, all levels of categories have the same font color in the category box. If you'd like to color each level differently, this recipe will allow you to specify a stylesheet class for each category level.

Chef's suggestion:

Experiment using all the available class formatting options, not only colors. It may be the perfect choice for your store to show one of the levels in uppercase completely (with the first letter being bigger) using the parameter `font-variant: small-caps;`

Presentation

Your box could look like the one in this recipe. A second-level subcategory **Subcat level 2** was added for better demonstration:

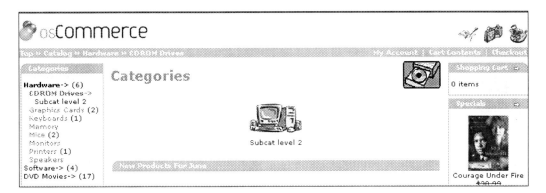

In this example, **Hardware** stays black, first-level subcategory **CDROM Drives** is red, and the added second-level subcategory is brown. The code presented here supports *four* levels of subcategories.

Chef's suggestion:

Keep in mind though that flat navigation structures are better for **SEO (Search Engine Optimization)**, as many search engines do not index very deep into trees (some only do two levels).

It will keep your customers far happier, though, if they do not have to click through a deep tree of categories to find the product they are looking for.

Need to add some food coloring to your mix? Go for it!

Ingredients

Modified:

```
catalog/stylesheet.css
catalog/includes/boxes/categories.php
```

Cooking

1. We will first need to include color definitions for subcategories in the stylesheet file that we can refer to when creating the category box. Open `catalog/stylesheet.css` and add anywhere in the file:

    ```
    /* begin styles for categories box, levels */
    A.cat {
      color: #000000;
      text-decoration: none;
    }
    A.subcat1 {
      color: #FF0000;
      text-decoration: none;
    }
    A.subcat2 {
      color: #5b0d0d;
      text-decoration: none;
    }
    A.subcat3 {
      color: #019901;
      text-decoration: none;
    }
    /* end styles for categories box, levels */
    ```

2. Open `catalog/includes/boxes/categories.php` and find this in line 20:

    ```
    $categories_string .= '<a href="';
    ```

Replace with the following code, which checks for the level the category is in and assigns the appropriate stylesheet class:

```
switch ($tree[$counter]['level']) {
  case 0:
    $class = 'cat';
    break;
  case 1:
    $class = 'subcat1';
    break;
  case 2:
    $class = 'subcat2';
    break;
  case 3:
    $class = 'subcat3';
    break;
  default:
    $class = '';
    break;
}
$categories_string .= '<a class="' . $class . '" href="';
```

A visually appealing dish, isn't it? Bon appetit!

6. Add Extra Links to Your Category Box

Depending on your layout and structure, you may benefit from adding important links directly to the bottom of your category box. You can use any links from your website that you want to put into easy reach. If you have added contributions that list all products, you can of course add a link to that page here also.

Presentation

In this example, direct links to the pages **Specials**, **What's New?**, and **Reviews** were added. Your screen will look like the following screenshot if you are adding this recipe; the links **Specials**, **What's New?**, and **Reviews** are added to your category box, separated by a line to make navigation even more intuitive:

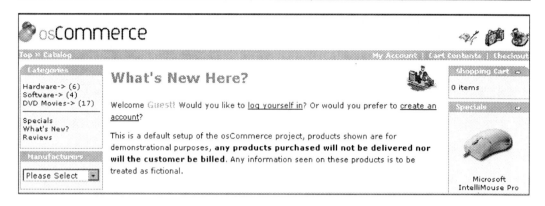

If you're looking for the cream of the cream, this is for you!

Ingredients

> **Modified:**
>
> `catalog/includes/boxes/categories.php`

Cooking

1. Open `catalog/includes/boxes/categories.php` and find this in line 132:

   ```
   $info_box_contents[] = array('text' => $categories_string);
   ```

   Add the following code right below it:

   ```
   $info_box_contents[] = array('text' => tep_draw_separator());

   $text2 = '';

   $text2 .= '<a href="' . tep_href_link(FILENAME_SPECIALS,
     BOX_HEADING_SPECIALS) . '">' . BOX_HEADING_SPECIALS .
     '</a><br>';

   $text2 .= '<a href="' . tep_href_link(FILENAME_PRODUCTS_NEW,
   BOX_HEADING_WHATS_NEW) . '">' . BOX_HEADING_WHATS_NEW .
   '</a><br>';

   $text2 .= '<a href="' . tep_href_link(FILENAME_REVIEWS,
   ```

```
    BOX_HEADING_REVIEWS)  .  '">'  .  BOX_HEADING_REVIEWS  .  '</a>';

    $info_box_contents[]  =  array('text'  =>  $text2);
```

Smoother than a great Béchamel! Bon appetit!

Summary

Having finished this chapter, you now have a full pantry of ideas to change your main navigating configuration. You can limit your category box to the active subcategories only and hide it when not in use. Alternatively, you can make the most of long category lists by dividing them into visually appealing single top-category boxes. Multi-level category boxes can be comfortably colored in different hues to provide visual diversity. Additional links to important pages can be added as eye catchers to the category box. As this chapter already deals with the most important infobox of all, the category box, in the following chapter we will take a look at infobox hacks in general.

3

Spice Up Your Infoboxes

Infoboxes can give your store a really distinct look and should be considered as design elements. This collection of recipes will show you a host of methods to embellish your infoboxes.

In this chapter we will discuss how to:

- Move your infobox header closer to content
- Make your infobox header taller
- Add a pop-up page from an infobox link
- Add images to infoboxes
- Add extra images to your columns without framing boxes
- Hide or show boxes driven by language choice
- Add boxes dedicated to specified countries
- Define box image size independent of product thumbs
- Show manufacturers' logos in the **Manufacturers** infobox
- Add double borders to boxes with background matting

7. Move Your Infobox Header closer to Content

This recipe is very useful when you only have a few lines in each box looking lost or wasting too much space, or when you have a number of boxes and need to make your columns shorter. You would then like to move the infobox content closer to its header. As you are amending the class for the infobox header, all infobox headers will be changed by only changing a single file.

Presentation

The following screenshot shows you the results of your cooking:

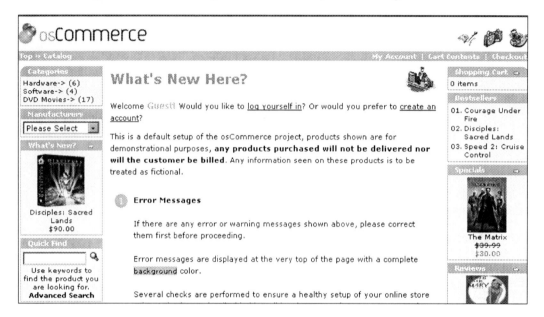

You will love this light and easy snack; so let's get going!

Ingredients

Modified:

`catalog/includes/classes/boxes.php`

Cooking

1. Open `catalog/includes/classes/boxes.php` and find the following in line 88:

```
$info_box_contents[] = array(array('text' =>
  tep_draw_separator('pixel_trans.gif', '100%', '1')));
```

This is a spacer row added between infobox header and content, therefore comment it out so that it looks like this (still all on one line):

```
// $info_box_contents[] = array(array('text' =>
  tep_draw_separator('pixel_trans.gif', '100%', '1')));
```

2. If you'd like to move the bottom border of the infobox closer to the content, just like on the screenshot, find a similar spacer further down in the same file in line 95:

```
$info_box_contents[] = array(array('text' =>
  tep_draw_separator('pixel_trans.gif', '100%', '1')));
```

Just as before, change it so that it is commented out and looks like this (still all on one line):

```
// $info_box_contents[] = array(array('text' =>
  tep_draw_separator('pixel_trans.gif', '100%', '1')));
```

Chef's suggestion:

What if you are interested in moving the infobox content away from its header? In that case, *do not* comment out those two lines, but change the third parameter of the function `tep_draw_separator`, which determines the height of the spacer row, from the value `1` to the distance you need, say `5`. The full line would then read:

```
$info_box_contents[] = array(array('text' =>
  tep_draw_separator('pixel_trans.gif',
                               '100%', '5')));
```

Did you enjoy it? Bon appetit!

8. Make Your Infobox Header Taller

This recipe shows you how to add height and impact to your infobox header while keeping the rounded colored images as infobox corners. This is extremely nice when you start playing with color and want to use a bit more of it on your page in well-defined spots. As you will be changing the box class used by all infoboxes, this modification will affect all infoboxes calling the class `infobox`. In a default osCommerce installation, all boxes in the left and right columns will be affected.

Presentation

Your infoboxes will look like those in the following screenshot:

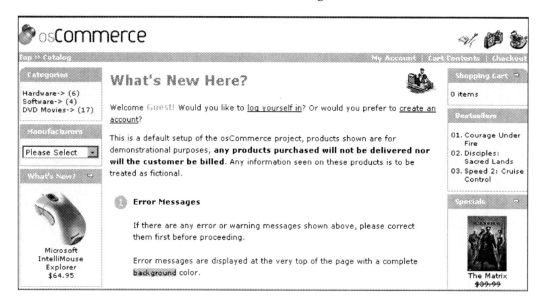

If your infoboxes have been waiting for that extra height all along, it's time to roll the dough for puff pastry!

Ingredients

> **Modified:**
>
> `catalog/includes/classes/boxes.php`

Cooking

1. Open `catalog/includes/classes/boxes.php` and find the following in line 121:

```
$info_box_contents[] = array(array('params' => 'height="14"
    class="infoBoxHeading"','text' => $left_corner),
                            array('params' => 'width="100%"
    height="14"class="infoBoxHeading"',
      'text' => $contents[0]['text']), array('params' =>
      'height="14" class="infoBoxHeading" nowrap','text' =>
      $right_corner));
```

Change it to the desired height. It is crucial that the images, which are no longer of the same height as the table cell, get aligned to the top, or the corners will not look rounded.

```
$info_box_contents[] = array(array('params' => 'height="20"
                                                valign="top"
         class="infoBoxHeading"','text' => $left_corner),
                       array('params' => 'width="100%"
                                                height="20"
         class="infoBoxHeading"','text' => $contents[0]['text']),
                       array('params' => 'height="20"
                                                valign="top"
         class="infoBoxHeading" nowrap','text' => $right_corner));
```

Chef's suggestion:

If you'd like to amend the headers of your content boxes in the main page, use the same technique to change the parameters in the same file, around line 149, for the class `contentBoxHeading`.

Those rose faster than the Pillsbury Doughboy! Bon appetit!

9. Add a Pop-Up Page from an Infobox Link

A nice-to-have feature is the option to have individually sized pop ups opened from your infoboxes. These can come in handy for sizing guides, info on international shipping, or any other page you'd like to show without leaving the underlying parent page.

Presentation

In this case, you copy the search help link to the search box from the `advanced_search.php` page. It will allow your customers to access **Search Help** from any page by clicking on the new link in the **Quick Find** infobox.

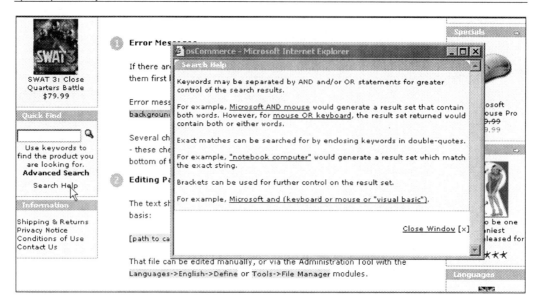

If you have sizing charts or other useful info to pop up, here you go!

Ingredients

Modified:

```
catalog/includes/languages/english/advanced_search.php
catalog/includes/languages/english.php
catalog/includes/categories.php
```

Cooking

1. Open `catalog/includes/languages/english/advanced_search.php` and
   move line 35, `define('HEADING_SEARCH_HELP', 'Search Help');`, from
   there into `catalog/includes/languages/english.php`, as it will now be
   used in several files. The main language files are loaded into all root files
   while the named files in the language folder are only loaded into the root file
   that has the same name as the language file. The best spot for the line will be
   right below the other search-box defines, which start in line 81. Your search-
   box-define section should look like this now:

   ```
   // quick_find box text in includes/boxes/quick_find.php
   define('BOX_HEADING_SEARCH', 'Quick Find');
   ```

```
define('BOX_SEARCH_TEXT', 'Use keywords to find the product you
                                    are looking for.');
define('BOX_SEARCH_ADVANCED_SEARCH', 'Advanced Search');
define('HEADING_SEARCH_HELP', 'Search Help');
```

Chef's suggestion:

Shop owners with multilingual shops need to copy and translate the changes done for english.php and all other language files, and drop them in the appropriate folders, for example the folder catalog/includes/languages/ french if you are using French and have modified french.php.

2. Open catalog/includes/boxes/search.php and add the following JavaScript code at the very top of the page, before the opening php tag. This code will open up a pop-up window when the **Search Help** link is clicked:

```
<script language="javascript"><!--
function popupWindowSearchhelp(url) {
  window.open(url,'popupWindow','toolbar=no,location=no,
      directories=no, status=no,menubar=no,scrollbars=yes,
      resizable=yes,copyhistory=no,width=450,height=280,
      screenX=150,screenY=150,top=150,left=150')
}
//--></script>
```

A bit further down, in line 28, find this code snippet:

```
$info_box_contents[] = array('form' =>
      tep_draw_form('quick_find',
      tep_href_link(FILENAME_ADVANCED_SEARCH_RESULT, '',
      'NONSSL', false),
    'get'),'align' => 'center','text' => tep_draw_input_field
    ('keywords', '', 'size="10" maxlength="30" style="width: ' .
    (BOX_WIDTH-30) . 'px"') . ' ' . tep_hide_session_id() .
    tep_image_submit('button_quick_find.gif',
    BOX_HEADING_SEARCH) .
  '<br>' . BOX_SEARCH_TEXT . '<br><a href="' .
  tep_href_link(FILENAME_ADVANCED_SEARCH) . '"><b>' .
  BOX_SEARCH_ADVANCED_SEARCH . '</b></a>');
```

Add immediately below it the array that creates a row holding the link to the **Search Help** pop up:

```
$info_box_contents[] = array('align' => 'center',
    'text' => '<a href="javascript:popupWindowSearchhelp
```

```
(\'' . tep_href_link(FILENAME_POPUP_SEARCH_HELP). '\')">' .
HEADING_SEARCH_HELP . '</a>');
```

Better than real popcorn, right? Bon appetit!

10. Add Images to Infoboxes

This recipe teaches you to add images to infoboxes. Potentially, there are three scenarios where you need an image in a box:

- You want to display an image in an existing box.
- You want to add a new box with an image.
- You want to display an image (either in an existing or a new box) that links to an internal or external page.

Presentation

Your screen will look similar to this one if you add an image to your shopping-cart infobox:

Let's whip up this one for you!

Ingredients

> **New:**
> `catalog/images/monika.jpg`
>
> **Modified:**
> `catalog/includes/boxes/shopping_cart.php`

Cooking

1. Open `catalog/includes/boxes/shopping_cart.php` and find this code in line 63:

   ```
   new infoBox($info_box_contents);
   ```

   Add directly above this line the following code, using your own image saved in the `images` folder:

   ```
   $info_box_contents[] = array('align' => 'center',
       'text' => tep_image(DIR_WS_IMAGES .       'monika.jpg',
                           'Monika Mathé', SMALL_IMAGE_WIDTH, ''));
   ```

That slid perfectly out of the mold! Bon appetit!

Variation #1

As mentioned above, you may prefer to create an additional box for your image. Your right column could look like this after adding an image-only box:

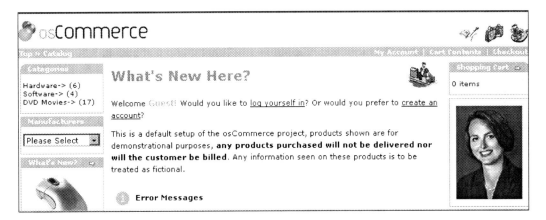

Ingredients

> **New:**
> `catalog/includes/boxes/photo.php`
>
> **Modified:**
> `catalog/includes/column_right.php`

Cooking

1. Create the new file `catalog/includes/boxes/photo.php` by copying the following code, and using your own image parameters:

```php
<?php
/*
  $Id: photo.php,v 1.00 2006/06/11 01:00:00 mm Exp $

  Module written by Monika Mathé
  http://www.monikamathe.com

  Module Copyright (c) 2006 Monika Mathé

  osCommerce, Open Source E-Commerce Solutions
  http://www.oscommerce.com

  Copyright (c) 2003 osCommerce

  Released under the GNU General Public License
*/
?>
<!-- photo //-->
          <tr>
            <td>
<?php
  $info_box_contents = array();

  $info_box_contents[] = array('align' => 'center',
                               'text' => tep_image(DIR_WS_IMAGES .
    'monika.jpg', 'Monika Mathé', SMALL_IMAGE_WIDTH, ''));

  new infoBox($info_box_contents);
?>
            </td>
          </tr>
<!-- photo_eof //-->
```

2. Open `catalog/includes/column_right.php` and find the following code in line 13:

```php
require(DIR_WS_BOXES . 'shopping_cart.php');
```

Add immediately below it the call for the new box:

```php
require(DIR_WS_BOXES . 'photo.php');
```

Variation #1 is the sweetest! Bon appetit!

Variation #2

If you'd like to have the image linked to a page, you can use the following recipe variation. In our case, we are linking to the `contact_us.php` page,

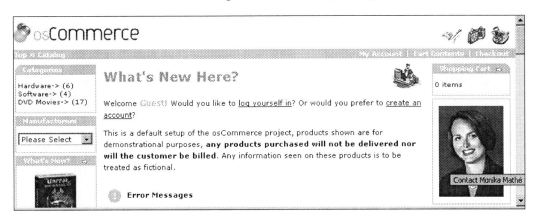

Ingredients

> **New:**
>
> `catalog/includes/boxes/photo_link.php`
> (this is a clone of the `catalog/includes/boxes/photo.php` file)
>
> **Modified:**
>
> `catalog/includes/column_right.php`

Cooking

1. Open the file `catalog/includes/boxes/photo.php`, modify, and save it as `catalog/includes/boxes/photo_link.php`, or create it anew if you haven't been following variation #1, with the following content:

    ```php
    <?php
    /*
      $Id: photo_link.php,v 1.00 2006/06/11 01:00:00 mm Exp $

      Module written by Monika Mathé
      http://www.monikamathe.com

      Module Copyright (c) 2006 Monika Mathé
    ```

```
        osCommerce, Open Source E-Commerce Solutions
        http://www.oscommerce.com

        Copyright (c) 2003 osCommerce

        Released under the GNU General Public License
*/
?>
<!--photo_link //-->
          <tr>
            <td>
<?php
  $info_box_contents = array();

  $info_box_contents[] = array('align' => 'center',
          'text' => '<a href="' . tep_href_link(FILENAME_
                                               CONTACT_US) .
          '">' . tep_image(DIR_WS_IMAGES . 'monika.jpg',
          'Contact Monika Mathé', SMALL_IMAGE_WIDTH, '')
          . '</a>');

  new infoBox($info_box_contents);
?>
            </td>
          </tr>
<!--photo_link_eof //-->
```

2. If you have been following variation #1, open `catalog/includes/column_right.php` and find this code in line 14:

    ```
    require(DIR_WS_BOXES . 'photo.php');
    ```

    Change it to:

    ```
    require(DIR_WS_BOXES . 'photo_link.php');
    ```

    If you do not have that line yet, add it below the shopping-cart-box code in line 13.

Variation #2 is the richest! Bon appetit!

11. Add Extra Images to Your Columns without Framing Boxes

There will be times when you'd like to add an image to your left or right column without an infobox. This could be the case for static banners leading to an external

site, in which case it's best to save that image to your `catalog/images` folder
(banners go to the subfolder `banners`), so you won't have to hide the box for secure
pages to prevent a security alert. You may also want to link to your **Contact** or
Shipping page to promote free shipping or a similar feature.

Presentation

This is how your screen will look when you add an image without a framing infobox
and link the image to a sub-page of your own site, in this case `contact_us.php`:

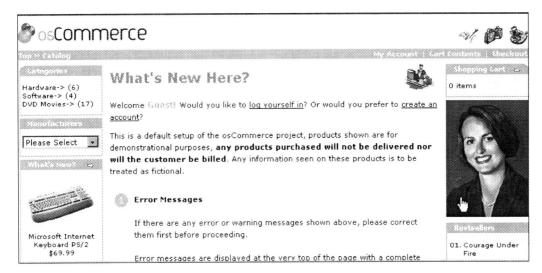

Let's throw this one together fast!

Ingredients

New:
`catalog/includes/boxes/photo_nobox.php`
`catalog/images/monika.jpg` (replace with your own image)

Modified:
`catalog/includes/column_right.php`

Cooking

1. Create a new file `catalog/includes/boxes/photo_nobox.php` with the following code, and using the parameters for your own image:

```php
<?php
/*
  $Id: photo_nobox.php,v 1.00 2006/06/12 00:00:00 mm Exp $

  Module written by Monika Mathé
  http://www.monikamathe.com

  Module Copyright (c) 2006 Monika Mathé

  osCommerce, Open Source E-Commerce Solutions
  http://www.oscommerce.com

  Copyright (c) 2003 osCommerce

  Released under the GNU General Public License
*/
?>
<!-- photo_nobox //-->
        <tr>
          <td>
<?php
 echo '<a href="' . tep_href_link(FILENAME_CONTACT_US) . '">' .
 tep_image(DIR_WS_IMAGES . 'monika.jpg', 'Contact Monika Mathé',
 BOX_WIDTH, '') . '</a>';
?>
          </td>
        </tr>
<!-- photo_nobox_eof //-->
```

2. Open `catalog/includes/column_right.php` and find this code in line 13:

```php
require(DIR_WS_BOXES . 'shopping_cart.php');
```

Immediately below this line, add the following call for your unframed image box:

```php
require(DIR_WS_BOXES . 'photo_nobox.php');
```

Happy cooking! Bon appetit!

12. Hide or Show Boxes Driven by Language Choice

This recipe is the right one for you if you'd like to show a special message in one language only, for a multi-language shop. This comes in handy if you do not speak other languages fluently enough for phone support, and therefore would prefer emails to phone support for those languages; you would not show your free helpline number to Spanish customers if you only speak Dutch. Another possibility would be showcasing certain awards or certificates that are difficult to translate, or are unknown outside of the country they were awarded in. The space freed up by not displaying information that is not relevant to a specific customer group can certainly be used more efficiently.

Presentation

This is an example for a free phone-support, **Special news** box, shown only when the site is viewed in English.

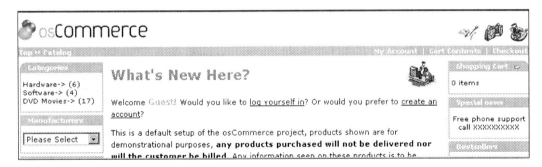

Let's get cracking on this one!

Ingredients

New:
catalog/includes/boxes/information_english_only.php
Modified:
catalog/includes/column_right.php

Cooking

1. Create a new file `catalog/includes/boxes/information_english_only.php` using the following code. This file will create a box to display your free-support helpline number. As this box will only show in English (or German, or French, etc.), this is an exception to our general approach of defining extra-language text for language files. Just type in the text you'd like to show in the appropriate language.

```php
<?php
/*
  $Id: information_english_only.php,
                      v 1.00 2006/06/12 00:00:00 mm Exp $

  Module written by Monika Mathé
  http://www.monikamathe.com

  Module Copyright (c) 2006 Monika Mathé

  osCommerce, Open Source E-Commerce Solutions
  http://www.oscommerce.com

  Copyright (c) 2003 osCommerce

  Released under the GNU General Public License
*/
?>
<!-- information_english_only //-->
        <tr>
          <td>
<?php
  $info_box_contents = array();
  $info_box_contents[] = array('text' => 'Special news');

  new infoBoxHeading($info_box_contents, false, false);

  $info_box_contents = array();
  $info_box_contents[] = array('align' => 'center',
                               'text' => 'Free phone support<br>
                                   call XXXXXXXXXX');

  new infoBox($info_box_contents);
?>
          </td>
        </tr>
<!-- information_english_only_eof //-->
```

2. Open `catalog/includes/column_right.php` and find this code in line 13:

```
require(DIR_WS_BOXES . shopping_cart.php');
```

Immediately below it add the call for your box, specifying the correct `languages_id` of your customer group in the "if" clause:

```
if ($languages_id == '1') include(DIR_WS_BOXES
                            .'information_english_only.php');
```

Chef's suggestion:

You can get the `languages_id` of the relevant language by navigating to **Administration | Localization | Languages** and highlighting the language you would like to use. The URL will change to something like `http://localhost/catalog/admin/languages.php?page=1&lID=1&action=edit` with the parameter for `lID`, in this case `lID=1`, holding the value you are looking for.

As easy as separating the yolk from the white! Bon appetit!

13. Add Boxes Dedicated to Specified Countries

This recipe is highly useful for displaying focused information to customers from a particular country. There is no need to bug customers from a different country about "free shipping over a certain amount" if they are not eligible for it; of course, you will have this information on your shipping page for everyone to view, just not as a box popping up annoyingly in their face.

Presentation

This **Free Shipping!** box will only show with a logged in customer from a particular country (we will use USA in our recipe). It is linked to the `shipping.php` page.

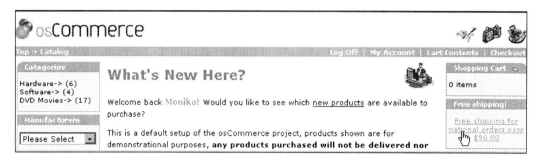

American Cheddar, French Brie, or Swiss Emmental, let's cheese it up!

Ingredients

New:

catalog/includes/boxes/information_usa_only.php

Modified:

catalog/includes/languages/english.php
catalog/includes/column_right.php

Cooking

1. In **Administration | Modules | Order Total**, click on **Shipping**, and edit the shipping module, so you offer free shipping for national orders only.

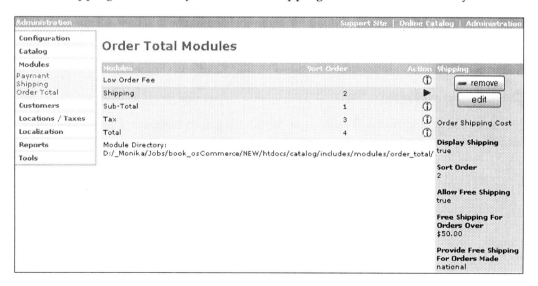

2. Add the following defines to your
   `catalog/includes/languages/english.php`:

   ```
   // usa box text in includes/boxes/information_english_only.php
   define('BOX_HEADING_USA', 'Free shipping!');
   define('BOX_USA_SHIPPING_TEXT',
                       'Free shipping for national orders over %s');
   ```

3. Create a new file `catalog/includes/boxes/information_usa_only.`
   `php` with the following code. It will create a new box with the heading
   Free Shipping, and we will set this box to be shown only to logged-in
   customers with USA as their country. The box text uses the configuration
   table parameter (`MODULE_ORDER_TOTAL_SHIPPING_FREE_SHIPPING_OVER`) to
   display the value for free shipping that was set in admin in step 1.

   ```php
   <?php
   /*
     $Id: information_usa_only.php,
                        v 1.00 2006/06/12 00:00:00 mm Exp $

     Module written by Monika Mathé
     http://www.monikamathe.com

     Module Copyright (c) 2006 Monika Mathé

     osCommerce, Open Source E-Commerce Solutions
     http://www.oscommerce.com

     Copyright (c) 2003 osCommerce

     Released under the GNU General Public License
   */
   ?>
   <!-- information_usa_only //-->
           <tr>
             <td>
   <?php
     $info_box_contents = array();
     $info_box_contents[] = array('text' => BOX_HEADING_USA);

     new infoBoxHeading($info_box_contents, false, false);

     $info_box_contents = array();
     $info_box_contents[] = array('align' => 'center',
                                  'text' => '<a href="' .
       tep_href_link(FILENAME_SHIPPING) . '">' . sprintf(
       BOX_USA_SHIPPING_TEXT, $currencies->format(
       MODULE_ORDER_TOTAL_SHIPPING_FREE_SHIPPING_OVER)) . '</a>');

     new infoBox($info_box_contents);
   ?>
   ```

```
            </td>
          </tr>
<!-- information_usa_only_eof //-->
```

4. Open `catalog/includes/column_right.php` and find the following code in line 13:

```
require(DIR_WS_BOXES . shopping_cart.php');
```

Immediately below it add the following call for your box, specifying the correct country code from the table countries:

```
if ((tep_session_is_registered('customer_id')) &&
    ($customer_country_id == '223')) include(DIR_WS_BOXES .
    'information_usa_only.php');
```

All cheesed out?! Log in as a customer from the USA, and check out your new box. Bon appetit!

14. Define Box-Image Size Independent of Product Thumbs

You will love this recipe if you have detailed product images that are shown fairly big in your product pages, but you have a limited box width in the columns. This recipe will allow you to keep larger product images while the images in the columns are calculated to their own size parameters.

Chef's suggestion:

Using the defined constant SMALL_IMAGE_WIDTH would automatically widen your column, which will mess up your site design.

Presentation

We are creating a new configuration table key to be used in product-displaying boxes like **Reviews, Specials, What's New?**, and **Manufacturer Info** instead of the default-image thumb key, SMALL_IMAGE_WIDTH.

Your screen will look like the one in this shot:

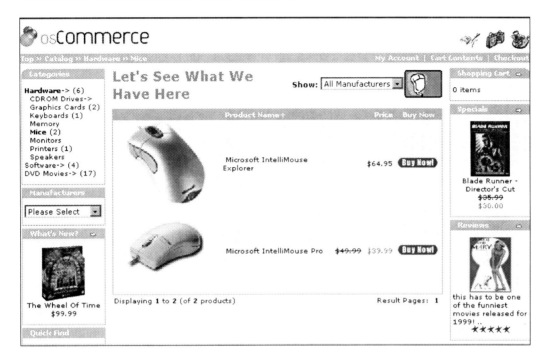

Make up a size and set new options. Ready to make it large?

Ingredients

New:

database.sql (to be run in phpMyAdmin)

Modified:

catalog/includes/boxes/whats_new.php
catalog/includes/boxes/specials.php
catalog/includes/boxes/reviews.php
catalog/includes/boxes/manufacturer_info.php

Cooking

1. Run the following SQL statement in your database to create two new configuration table keys for the images in your boxes:

```
INSERT INTO configuration (configuration_title, configuration_key,
configuration_value, configuration_description,
```

```
configuration_group_id, sort_order, date_added)
VALUES ('Columns Box Image Width', 'BOX_IMAGE_WIDTH', '100',
'The pixel width of small images in the columns',
                                        '4', '9', now());
INSERT INTO configuration (configuration_title, configuration_key,
configuration_value, configuration_description,
configuration_group_id, sort_order, date_added)
VALUES ('Columns Box Image Height', 'BOX_IMAGE_HEIGHT', '',
   'The pixel height of small images in the columns',
                                        '4', '10', now());
```

2. Navigate to **Administration | Configuration | Images**. You will find your new keys at the bottom of the list with the value for **Columns Box Image Height** left empty. This will ensure that the image has the correct width, but will not get squished. We want to display small images on products pages in more detail, so width is set here to **150**px, while for the boxes it is set at **100**px. **Calculate Image Size** is set to true, and the values for height are left empty to allow recalculation.

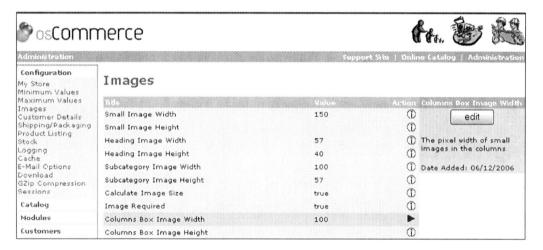

7. Modify the boxes one by one to use the new parameters, starting with catalog/includes/boxes/whats_new.php. Find the following in line 35:

```
$info_box_contents[] = array('align' => 'center',
  'text' => '<a href="' . tep_href_link(FILENAME_PRODUCT_INFO,
  'products_id=' . $random_product['products_id']) . '">' .
  tep_image(DIR_WS_IMAGES . $random_product['products_image'],
  $random_product['products_name'],
                   SMALL_IMAGE_WIDTH, SMALL_IMAGE_HEIGHT) .
  '</a><br>
  <a href="' . tep_href_link(FILENAME_PRODUCT_INFO,
```

```
                'products_id=' . $random_product['products_id']) . '">' .
                $random_product['products_name'] . '</a><br>' .
                                                    $whats_new_price);
```

Change to:

```
$info_box_contents[] = array('align' => 'center',
        'text' => '<a href="' . tep_href_link(FILENAME_PRODUCT_INFO,
        'products_id=' . $random_product['products_id']) . '">' .
        tep_image(DIR_WS_IMAGES . $random_product['products_image'],
        $random_product['products_name'],
                            BOX_IMAGE_WIDTH, BOX_IMAGE_HEIGHT) .
        '</a><br><a href="' . tep_href_link(FILENAME_PRODUCT_INFO,
        'products_id=' . $random_product['products_id']) . '">' .
        $random_product['products_name'] . '</a><br>' .
                                                    $whats_new_price);
```

3. Open `catalog/includes/boxes/specials.php`. Find the following in line 25:

```
$info_box_contents[] = array('align' => 'center',
        'text' => '<a href="' . tep_href_link(FILENAME_PRODUCT_INFO,
        'products_id=' . $random_product["products_id"]) . '">' .
        tep_image(DIR_WS_IMAGES . $random_product['products_image'],
        $random_product['products_name'],SMALL_IMAGE_WIDTH,
                                        SMALL_IMAGE_HEIGHT) .
        '</a><br>
        <a href="' . tep_href_link(FILENAME_PRODUCT_INFO,
        'products_id=' . $random_product['products_id']) . '">' .
        $random_product['products_name'] . '</a><br>
        <s>' . $currencies->display_price($random_product['products_
                                                        price'],
        tep_get_tax_rate($random_product['products_tax_class_id'])) .
        '</s><br>
        <span class="productSpecialPrice">' .
                                        $currencies->display_price
        ($random_product['specials_new_products_price'],
                                                tep_get_tax_rate
        ($random_product['products_tax_class_id'])) . '</span>');
```

Change to:

```
$info_box_contents[] = array('align' => 'center',
        'text' => '<a href="' . tep_href_link(FILENAME_PRODUCT_INFO,
        'products_id=' . $random_product["products_id"]) . '">' .
        tep_image(DIR_WS_IMAGES . $random_product['products_image'],
        $random_product['products_name'],
                        BOX_IMAGE_WIDTH, BOX_IMAGE_HEIGHT) .
```

```
'</a><br>
<a href="' . tep_href_link(FILENAME_PRODUCT_INFO,
    'products_id=' . $random_product['products_id']) . '">' .
    $random_product['products_name'] . '</a><br>
<s>' . $currencies->display_price($random_product['products_
    price'], tep_get_tax_rate($random_product['products_tax_
    class_id'])) . '</s><br>
<span class="productSpecialPrice">' .
    $currencies->display_price ($random_product['specials_
    new_products_price'], tep_get_tax_rate($random_
    product['products_tax_class_id'])) . '</span>');
```

4. Open `catalog/includes/boxes/reviews.php`. Find the following code in line 38:

```
$info_box_contents[] = array('text' =>
                            '<div align="center"><a href="' .
tep_href_link(FILENAME_PRODUCT_REVIEWS_INFO, 'products_id=' .
$random_product['products_id'] . '&reviews_id=' .
$random_product['reviews_id']) . '">' .
                            tep_image(DIR_WS_IMAGES .
$random_product['products_image'],
                            $random_product['products_name'],
SMALL_IMAGE_WIDTH, SMALL_IMAGE_HEIGHT) .
                            '</a></div><a href="' .
tep_href_link(FILENAME_PRODUCT_REVIEWS_INFO, 'products_id=' .
$random_product['products_id'] . '&reviews_id=' .
$random_product['reviews_id']) . '">' . $rand_review_text . '
..</a><br>
<div align="center">' . tep_image(DIR_WS_IMAGES . 'stars_' .
$random_product['reviews_rating'] . '.gif' ,
        sprintf(BOX_REVIEWS_TEXT_OF_5_STARS,
        $random_product['reviews_rating'])) . '</div>');
```

Change to:

```
$info_box_contents[] = array('text' =>
                            '<div align="center"><a href="' .
tep_href_link(FILENAME_PRODUCT_REVIEWS_INFO, 'products_id=' .
$random_product['products_id'] . '&reviews_id=' .
$random_product['reviews_id']) . '">' .
                            tep_image(DIR_WS_IMAGES .
$random_product['products_image'],
                            $random_product['products_name'],
BOX_IMAGE_WIDTH, BOX_IMAGE_HEIGHT) . '</a></div><a href="' .
tep_href_link(FILENAME_PRODUCT_REVIEWS_INFO, 'products_id=' .
$random_product['products_id'] . '&reviews_id=' .
```

```
$random_product['reviews_id']) . '">' . $rand_review_text . '
..</a><br>
<div align="center">' . tep_image(DIR_WS_IMAGES . 'stars_' .
$random_product['reviews_rating'] . '.gif' ,
sprintf(BOX_REVIEWS_TEXT_OF_5_STARS,
$random_product['reviews_rating'])) . '</div>');
```

5. In `catalog/includes/boxes/manufacturer_info.php`, there is a bit more work to be done, as the image sizes have not been defined there at all yet. This is an issue very commonly overlooked, and so many designs on live sites get messed up by manufacturers' logos that are not sized to match the column width.

    Find the following in line 28:

    ```
    if (tep_not_null($manufacturer['manufacturers_image']))
        $manufacturer_info_string .= '<tr><td align="center"
        class="infoBoxContents" colspan="2">' .
        tep_image(DIR_WS_IMAGES . $manufacturer['manufacturers_image'],
        $manufacturer['manufacturers_name']) . '</td></tr>';
    ```

    Change to:

    ```
    if (tep_not_null($manufacturer['manufacturers_image']))
        $manufacturer_info_string .= '<tr><td align="center"
        class="infoBoxContents" colspan="2">' .
        tep_image(DIR_WS_IMAGES . $manufacturer['manufacturers_image'],
        $manufacturer['manufacturers_name'],
                BOX_IMAGE_WIDTH, BOX_IMAGE_HEIGHT) . '</td></tr>';
    ```

Save your changes, navigate to your products pages, and enjoy! Bon appetit!

15. Show Manufacturers' Logos in the Manufacturers Infobox

A great recipe if your list of manufacturers is not too long and you have collected logos for all of them. Logos are highly recognizable for customers and will provide ease in navigation for a great shopping experience.

Presentation

Your **Manufacturers** box will look like the one in the following screenshot:

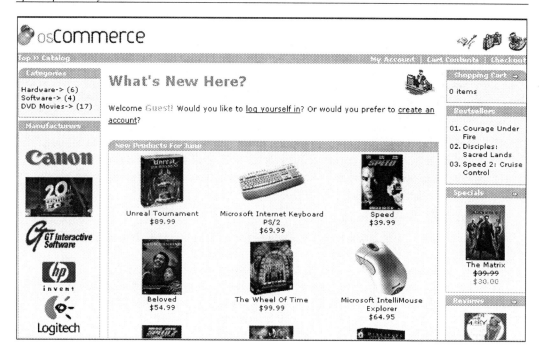

Roll up your sleeves, and let's get down to business!

Ingredients

Modified:

```
catalog/includes/boxes/manufacturers.php
```

Cooking

1. Make sure that your manufacturers' logos fit in the width of your box without being stretched. You can paste them on transparent gifs, centered, so all will look uniform.

2. Open `catalog/includes/boxes/manufacturers.php` and replace the code with the following new box code. Instead of just displaying the manufacturers' names and a link to their products, the logo pulled from the query is used to create the link.

    ```php
    <?php
    /*
    ```

```
$Id: manufacturers.php,v 1.00 2006/06/12 00:00:00 mm Exp $

osCommerce, Open Source E-Commerce Solutions
http://www.oscommerce.com

Copyright (c) 2003 osCommerce

Released under the GNU General Public License
*/

  $manufacturers_query = tep_db_query("select manufacturers_id,
    manufacturers_name, manufacturers_image from " .
          TABLE_MANUFACTURERS . " order by manufacturers_name");
  if ($number_of_rows = tep_db_num_rows($manufacturers_query)) {
?>
<!-- manufacturers //-->
            <tr>
              <td>
<?php
    $info_box_contents = array();
    $info_box_contents[] = array('text' =>
                                        BOX_HEADING_MANUFACTURERS);

    new infoBoxHeading($info_box_contents, false, false);

    $manufacturers_list = '';
    while ($manufacturers =
                  tep_db_fetch_array($manufacturers_query)) {

      $manufacturers_list .= '<a href="' .
                                  tep_href_link(FILENAME_DEFAULT,
      'manufacturers_id='
                . $manufacturers['manufacturers_id']) . '">' .
      tep_image(DIR_WS_IMAGES .
                      $manufacturers['manufacturers_image'],
      $manufacturers['manufacturers_name'],
                      SMALL_IMAGE_WIDTH) . '</a><br>';
    }

    $manufacturers_list = substr($manufacturers_list, 0, -4);

    $info_box_contents = array();
    $info_box_contents[] = array('align' => 'center',
                                  'text' => $manufacturers_list);

    new infoBox($info_box_contents);
  ?>
            </td>
```

```
            </tr>
<!-- manufacturers_eof //-->
<?php
   }
?>
```

Just like icing on the cake! Bon appetit!

16. Add Double Borders to Boxes with Background Matting

A lovely setting that makes your infoboxes really stand out and be noticed. Infobox headers and content flow together framed by a new border. Each box floats on a patterned matting.

Presentation

Your pages will look like the one in the following screenshot:

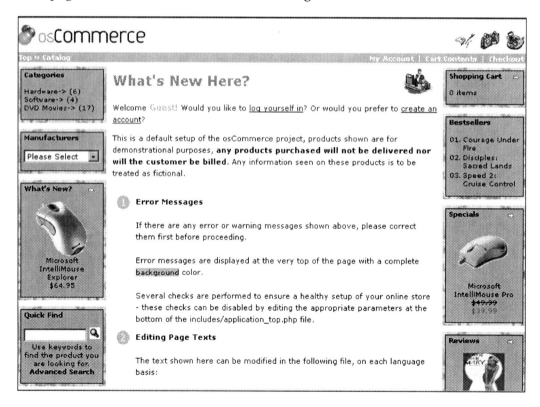

You want these, but you don't have a lot of experience in the kitchen? Forget that, apron up, and let's get cookin'!

Ingredients

New:
catalog/images/infobox/box_matting.gif

Modified:
catalog/images/infobox/corner_left.gif
catalog/images/infobox/corner_right.gif
catalog/images/infobox/corner_right_left.gif
All 38 files on root level in the catalog folder that have the right or left column, or both
catalog/includes/column_left.php
catalog/includes/column_right.php
(if you plan to follow the Chef's suggestion below)
catalog/stylesheet.css
All 15 boxes from the catalog/includes/boxes folder

Cooking

1. Create transparent images for your infobox corners, and drop them in the catalog/images/infobox folder. Replace all three images catalog/images/infobox/corner_left.gif, catalog/images/infobox/corner_right.gif, and catalog/images/infobox/corner_right_left.gif with the new transparent image created in the same size while keeping the original filename.

2. Create a background matting box_matting.gif for your infobox, and drop it in the catalog/images/infobox folder. The matting pattern should repeat vertically without a visible break for longer boxes.

3. Open all root files, and find the following line in each file that has the column left and right:

```
<td width="<?php echo BOX_WIDTH;
                        ?>" valign="top"><table border="0"
width="<?php echo BOX_WIDTH;
                        ?>" cellspacing="0" cellpadding="2">
```

You will find two occurrences of this in each file; modify both to look
as follows:

```
<td width="<?php echo BOX_WIDTH; ?>"
                    valign="top"><table border="0"
 width="<?php echo BOX_WIDTH; ?>"
                    cellspacing="0" cellpadding="4">
```

Increasing the `cellpadding` parameter will allow your box background to
peak through from under the box, which will then float on top. Experiment
with different values that suit your design best.

Chef's suggestion:

If you have used "Create Flexible Column Definitions" from
Chapter 1, this step will go rather fast for you as you only
have to make changes to `catalog/includes/column_`
`left.php` and `column_right.php` to adjust the column
table padding. If you have resisted the temptation to install
that recipe, do it now.

4. Open `catalog/stylesheet.css` and adjust the infobox colors. The
    backgrounds in the following three classes have to be the same: `.infobox`,
    `.infoBoxContents`, `TD.infoBoxHeading`. In the demo screenshot, the
    settings were as follows:

```
.infoBox {
  background: #FDA28D;
}

.infoBoxContents {
  background: #FDA28D;
  font-family: Verdana, Arial, sans-serif;
  font-size: 10px;
}

TD.infoBoxHeading {
  font-family: Verdana, Arial, sans-serif;
  font-size: 10px;
  font-weight: bold;
  background: #FDA28D;
  color: #000000;
}
```

5. Add the following two classes to `catalog/stylesheet.css` while specifying the infobox background matting and the color for the inner border you plan to use.

```
.matting {
  background-image:url('images/infobox/box_matting.gif');
}

TABLE.tableborder {
  border: solid; border-width: 1px;
  border-color: #000000;
}
```

    Note how `.matting` was used instead of `TD.matting` for the background image class, so that it has the flexibility to be reused as a table background if you decide to add the same image elsewhere on your site.

6. Open all boxes from your `catalog/includes/boxes` folder, and find this code snippet:

```
<tr>
  <td>
```

    Replace with the following code that creates a nested table with the matting background, having the regular box float on it with a border. This approach allows for the border to frame the whole box and not only the infobox header and content independently, which would create an extra line between header and content.

```
<tr>
  <td class="matting">
    <table class="tableborder" width="100%" cellspacing=
                                        "0" cellpadding="0">
<tr>
  <td>
```

7. In all box files still open, find the following code near the bottom of the file:

```
  </td>
</tr>
```

    Replace with the following code, closing the nested tables opened in the previous step and adding an extra separator row, so the boxes are set apart from each other for more impact.

```
      </td>
    </tr>
  </table>
  </td>
```

```
</tr>
<tr><td><?php echo tep_draw_separator('pixel_trans.gif',
                                          '100%', '1');
?></td></tr>
```

A little mess on your apron, and a great meal on the table, right? Bon appetit!

Summary

This chapter has prepared you with hacks to change the overall look of your infoboxes. You can now customize the header, content, and border, add special boxes, and hide or show boxes driven by parameters that are best suited to your customers. You can create individual pop ups for charts, and present your manufacturers as a list of logos rather than text. You learned that products' thumb sizes no longer determine image size in the column infoboxes; it can now be adjusted to fit your column width. We have added the same sizing to the manufacturers' infobox logos, which in a default installation don't resize. As we have touched the subject of displaying products here already, you'll enjoy learning a lot more about how to show them off in the next chapter.

4
Stuff Your Product Display

Presenting products in the best way is what will make your shop stand out. In this chapter, you can find a great collection of recipes customizing the following areas:

For your **Product Listing** page, you will learn how to:

- Add parent category in product listing
- Add top category in product listing
- Add a separator line in product listing
- Add a cell background and image border to product listing
- Sort product listing by date added
- Prepare a quick don't easy review system for product listing
- Whip up a top-category driven product listing
- Control manufacturer's image size

For your **Product Detail** page, we will discuss how to:

- Call a pop up from product description in product info
- Call unique code for a single product in product info
- Show a pop up with shipping options in product info
- Add an anchor for options in product info
- Integrate **Tell A Friend** into product info
- Offer an **Ask a Question about a Product** link on product info
- Sell affiliate products from your catalog

For the **Also Purchased Products** box, we will add new functionality so you can:

- Fill up Also Purchased Products search result

Also, in your **New Products** box you will be able to:

- Limit New Products to those with an image
- Set column count for New Products

17. Add Parent Category in Product Listing

This recipe displays the parent category along with the product name in product listing. This module is important if your customers find your products using the search function in most cases, and you want them to see the category of each product at a glance.

Presentation

Your screen will look like the following screenshot, with the parent category added to each product name, and separated by a dash:

You can easily hack this recipe to present category name first as shown in the variation later.

Are you ready to carve the roast?

Ingredients

Modified:

```
catalog/includes/functions/general.php
catalog/includes/modules/product_listing.php
```

Cooking

1. Open `catalog/includes/functions/general.php` and add the following function directly before the closing PHP tag to get the name of the parent category for a given product:

```php
function tep_get_category_name($product_id) {
  global $languages_id;

  $category_query =
              tep_db_query("select cd.categories_name from " .
  TABLE_CATEGORIES_DESCRIPTION . " cd,
  " . TABLE_PRODUCTS_TO_CATEGORIES . "
  p2c where p2c.products_id = '" . (int)$product_id . "' and p2c.
  categories_id = cd.categories_id and
  cd.language_id = '" . (int)$languages_id . "' limit 1");
  $category = tep_db_fetch_array($category_query);

  return $category['categories_name'];
}
```

2. Open `catalog/includes/modules/product_listing.php` and find this in line 95 where the content of the product-name column is defined:

```php
case 'PRODUCT_LIST_NAME':
  $lc_align = '';
  if (isset($HTTP_GET_VARS['manufacturers_id'])) {
    $lc_text = '<a href="' . tep_href_link(FILENAME_PRODUCT_INFO,
    'manufacturers_id=' . $HTTP_GET_VARS['manufacturers_id'] .
    '&products_id=' . $listing['products_id']) . '">' .
    $listing['products_name'] . '</a>';
  } else {
    $lc_text = ' <a href="' .
                        tep_href_link(FILENAME_PRODUCT_INFO,
    ($cPath ? 'cPath=' . $cPath . '&' : '') .
    'products_id=' . $listing['products_id']) . '">'
    . $listing['products_name'] . '</a> ';
  }
  break;
```

Replace with the following code, adding the parent-category name to the product-name column, separated by a dash:

```
case 'PRODUCT_LIST_NAME':
  $lc_align = '';
  if (isset($HTTP_GET_VARS['manufacturers_id'])) {
    $lc_text = ' <a href="' .
                           tep_href_link(FILENAME_PRODUCT_INFO,
    'manufacturers_id=' . $HTTP_GET_VARS['manufacturers_id'] .
    '&products_id=' . $listing['products_id']) . '">'
    . $listing['products_name'] . ' - '
    . tep_get_category_name($listing['products_id']) .
                                            '</a> ';
  } else {
    $lc_text = ' <a href="' .
                           tep_href_link(FILENAME_PRODUCT_INFO,
    ($cPath ? 'cPath=' . $cPath . '&' : '') .
    'products_id=' . $listing['products_id']) . '">'
    . $listing['products_name'] . ' - '
    . tep_get_category_name($listing['products_id']) .
                                            '</a> ';
  }
  break;
```

Variation

Alternatively, you can also show the parent category above the product name as seen in the following screenshot:

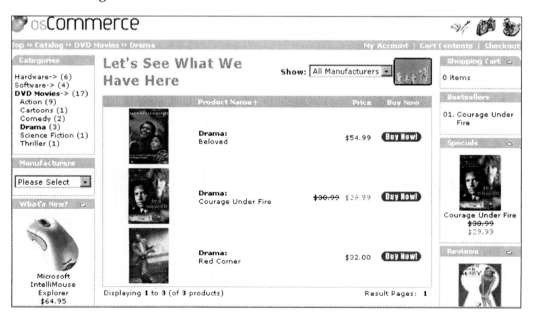

For this, you will have to modify the code in the earlier step 2 to the following:

```
case 'PRODUCT_LIST_NAME':
  $lc_align = '';
  if (isset($HTTP_GET_VARS['manufacturers_id'])) {
    $lc_text = ' <a href="' .
                            tep_href_link(FILENAME_PRODUCT_INFO,
    'manufacturers_id=' . $HTTP_GET_VARS['manufacturers_id'] .
    '&products_id=' . $listing['products_id']) . '">
    <b>' . tep_get_category_name($listing['products_id']) .
                                      ':</b><br> '
    . $listing['products_name']. '</a> ';
  } else {
    $lc_text = ' <a href="' .
                            tep_href_link(FILENAME_PRODUCT_INFO,
    ($cPath ? 'cPath=' . $cPath . '&' : '') .
    'products_id=' . $listing['products_id']) . '">
    <b>' . tep_get_category_name($listing['products_id']) .
                                      ':</b><br> '
    . $listing['products_name']. '</a> ';
  }
  break;
```

That sliced perfectly! Bon appetit!

18. Add Top Category in Product Listing

This recipe displays the top category along with the product name in product listing. This is a great alternative to the recipe shown before, especially when you have deeper category structures and want the category name to make clear which section each product belongs to. It is also a great help when you have products with the same name in different categories (and not being created as one product with different attributes), like movies offered in VHS and DVD format.

Presentation

Your screen will look like this with the top category of each product added before the product name:

Ready to try a roast alternative? Let's prime the rib!

Ingredients

Modified:

```
catalog/includes/functions/general.php
catalog/includes/modules/product_listing.php
```

Cooking

1. Open `catalog/includes/functions/general.php` and add this function directly before the closing `?>` PHP tag to get the top-category name for a given product:

```php
function tep_get_category_name($product_id) {
  global $languages_id;

  $topcat_array = explode('_' ,
                     tep_get_product_path($product_id));
  $top_cat = $topcat_array[0];

  $category_query =
           tep_db_query("select cd.categories_name from " .
```

```
        TABLE_CATEGORIES_DESCRIPTION .
                          " cd where cd.categories_id = '" .
        $top_cat . "' and cd.language_id = '" .
                                  (int)$languages_id . "'");
        $category = tep_db_fetch_array($category_query);

        return $category['categories_name'];
    }
```

2. Open `catalog/includes/modules/product_listing.php` and find the
following in line 95 where the content of the product-name column is defined:

```
    case 'PRODUCT_LIST_NAME':
      $lc_align = '';
      if (isset($HTTP_GET_VARS['manufacturers_id'])) {
        $lc_text = '<a href="' . tep_href_link(FILENAME_PRODUCT_INFO,
        'manufacturers_id=' . $HTTP_GET_VARS['manufacturers_id'] .
        '&products_id=' . $listing['products_id']) . '">' .
        $listing['products_name'] . '</a>';
      } else {
        $lc_text = ' <a href="' .
                              tep_href_link(FILENAME_PRODUCT_INFO,
        ($cPath ? 'cPath=' . $cPath . '&' : '') . 'products_id=' .
        $listing['products_id']) . '">' . $listing['products_name'] .
        '</a> ';
      }
      break;
```

Replace with this:

```
    case 'PRODUCT_LIST_NAME':
      $lc_align = '';
      if (isset($HTTP_GET_VARS['manufacturers_id'])) {
        $lc_text = ' <a href="' .
                              tep_href_link(FILENAME_PRODUCT_INFO,
        'manufacturers_id=' . $HTTP_GET_VARS['manufacturers_id'] .
        '&products_id=' . $listing['products_id']) . '">' .
        tep_get_category_name($listing['products_id']) .
                              '   <b>' .
        $listing['products_name'] . '</b></a> ';
      } else {
        $lc_text = ' <a href="' .
                              tep_href_link(FILENAME_PRODUCT_INFO,
        ($cPath ? 'cPath=' . $cPath . '&' : '') .
        'products_id=' . $listing['products_id']) . '">' .
        tep_get_category_name($listing['products_id']) .
                              '   <b>' .
```

```
$listing['products_name'] . '</b></a> ';
}
break;
```

Finger lickingly good! Bon appetit!

19. Add a Separator Line in Product Listing

This recipe shows you an option to add dividers between your products. It makes your product listing much clearer, and shopping at your store a pleasant experience.

Presentation

Your Product Listing page will look like the following screenshot with a light, gray separator line added between the rows of products:

Are you ready to separate the white meat from the dark?

Ingredients

Modified:

catalog/includes/modules/product_listing.php

Cooking

1. Open catalog/includes/modules/product_listing.php and find this code in line 137:

```
$list_box_contents[$cur_row][] = array('align' => $lc_align,
    'params' => 'class="productListing-data"',
    'text'   => $lc_text);
}
```

With this array, the content of each row is generated.

Immediately below it add the following code that will check how many rows you are actually showing and will set the colspan accordingly, creating a line that will be displayed after each product, and separating it from the last one:

```
if ($listing_split->number_of_rows > $rows) {
    $list_box_contents[][] = array(
      'params' => 'valign="middle" colspan="' .
                                    sizeof($column_list) . '"',
      'text'   => tep_draw_separator('pixel_silver.gif',
                                              '100%', '1') );
}
```

As fun as breaking the wishbone, right? Bon appetit!

20. Add a Cell Background and an Image Border to Product Listing

You can create great impact with this fun recipe. It will allow you to color any cell of your product listing, resulting in a vertical stripe effect, and also offers the option to frame each image with a border.

Presentation

To add even more focus to the images, a black border was added here, as you can see in the following screenshot:

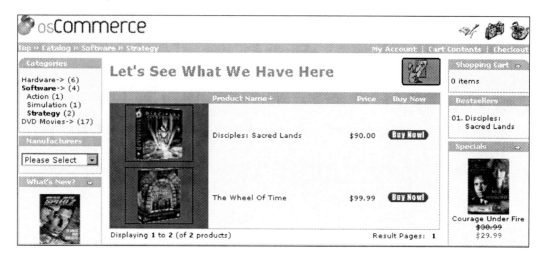

Let's sauce it up!

Ingredients

> **Modified:**
>
> ```
> catalog/includes/modules/product_listing.php
> catalog/stylesheet.css
> ```

Cooking

1. Open `catalog/includes/modules/product_listing.php` and find this in line 85, where the loop for creating the columns for your product listing starts:

   ```
   $cur_row = sizeof($list_box_contents) - 1;

   for ($col=0, $n=sizeof($column_list); $col<$n; $col++) {
     $lc_align = '';
   ```

   Immediately below it add the following line to define a variable. This will be used later to check if the default background should be used or a new one.

   ```
   $background = false;
   ```

2. In the same file, find the following in line 123 with the content of the image column:

```
case 'PRODUCT_LIST_IMAGE':
  $lc_align = 'center';
  if (isset($HTTP_GET_VARS['manufacturers_id'])) {
    $lc_text = '<a href="' . tep_href_link(FILENAME_PRODUCT_INFO,
    'manufacturers_id=' . $HTTP_GET_VARS['manufacturers_id'] .
    '&products_id=' . $listing['products_id']) . '">' .
    tep_image(DIR_WS_IMAGES . $listing['products_image'],
    $listing['products_name'], SMALL_IMAGE_WIDTH,
                                    SMALL_IMAGE_HEIGHT) .
    '</a>';
  } else {
    $lc_text = ' <a href="' .
                        tep_href_link(FILENAME_PRODUCT_INFO,
    ($cPath ? 'cPath=' . $cPath . '&' : '') . 'products_id=' .
    $listing['products_id']) . '">' . tep_image(DIR_WS_IMAGES .
    $listing['products_image'], $listing['products_name'],
    SMALL_IMAGE_WIDTH, SMALL_IMAGE_HEIGHT) . '</a> ';
  }
```

Replace with the following code, adding the stylesheet class `imageborder` for the `tep_image` function, which will allow us to define a border later. We also add the information that this cell is to use the new background by setting `$background = true;`

```
case 'PRODUCT_LIST_IMAGE':
  $lc_align = 'center';
  if (isset($HTTP_GET_VARS['manufacturers_id'])) {
    $lc_text = '<a href="' . tep_href_link(FILENAME_PRODUCT_INFO,
    'manufacturers_id=' . $HTTP_GET_VARS['manufacturers_id'] .
    '&products_id=' . $listing['products_id']) . '">' .
    tep_image(DIR_WS_IMAGES . $listing['products_image'],
    $listing['products_name'], SMALL_IMAGE_WIDTH,
                                    SMALL_IMAGE_HEIGHT,
    'class="imageborder"') . '</a>';
  } else {
    $lc_text = ' <a href="' .
                        tep_href_link(FILENAME_PRODUCT_INFO,
    ($cPath ? 'cPath=' . $cPath . '&' : '') . 'products_id=' .
    $listing['products_id']) . '">' . tep_image(DIR_WS_IMAGES .
    $listing['products_image'], $listing['products_name'],
    SMALL_IMAGE_WIDTH, SMALL_IMAGE_HEIGHT,
                                    'class="imageborder"') .
    '</a> ';
```

```
     }
   $background = true;
```

3. Also in the same file, find this in line 138 to create the row for each product:

```
$list_box_contents[$cur_row][] = array('align' => $lc_align,
  'params' => 'class="productListing-data"',
  'text'   => $lc_text);
  }
}

new productListingBox($list_box_contents);
```

Replace with the following snippet that checks for the cell you want to color:

```
if ($background == false) {
  $list_box_contents[$cur_row][] = array('align' => $lc_align,
  'params' => 'class="productListing-data"',
  'text' => $lc_text);
} else {
  $list_box_contents[$cur_row][] = array('align' => $lc_align,
  'params' => 'class="your_new_class"',
  'text' => $lc_text);
  }
 }
}
new productListingBox($list_box_contents);
```

4. In catalog/stylesheet.css, add the following class definitions to add a black border to the image and a red background to the image column:

```
.imageborder {
  border: #000000 1px solid;
}

.your_new_class {
  background: #c52a3a;
}
```

Smooth and colorful! Bon appetit!

21. Sort Product Listing by Date Added

This recipe shows you how to sort your product listing by date. If you often add products and have long lists, this will be useful to focus on new items.

Presentation

Your product listing will change from the default sorting done alphabetically by product name to sorting by the date on which each product was added:

Ready for some date pudding? Enjoy!

Ingredients

Modified:

`catalog/index.php`

Cooking

1. Open `catalog/index.php` and find the following code in line 191 where sorting is defined:

```
if ( (!isset($HTTP_GET_VARS['sort'])) || (!ereg('[1-8][ad]',
$HTTP_GET_VARS['sort'])) || (substr($HTTP_GET_VARS['sort'],
                                                      0, 1) >
sizeof($column_list)) ) {
  for ($i=0, $n=sizeof($column_list); $i<$n; $i++) {
    if ($column_list[$i] == 'PRODUCT_LIST_NAME') {
```

```
      $HTTP_GET_VARS['sort'] = $i+1 . 'a';
      $listing_sql .= " order by pd.products_name";
      break;
    }
  }
} else {
```

Replace with the following code, modifying the sort order so that the date a product was added on is the main sorting criterion:

```
if ( (!isset($HTTP_GET_VARS['sort'])) || (!ereg('[1-8][ad]',
  $HTTP_GET_VARS['sort'])) || (substr($HTTP_GET_VARS['sort'],
                                                        0, 1) >
  sizeof($column_list)) ) {
  for ($i=0, $n=sizeof($column_list); $i<$n; $i++) {
    if ($column_list[$i] == 'PRODUCT_LIST_IMAGE') {
      $HTTP_GET_VARS['sort'] = $i+1 . 'a';
      $listing_sql .= " order by products_date_added,
                                        pd.products_name";
      break;
    }
  }
} else {
```

Changing the check for the sorting to the unused header, PRODUCT_LIST_IMAGE, makes it possible to sort by all columns.

> **Chef's suggestion:**
>
> As **Advanced Search** uses a very similar structure to the category product listings setup, you can tweak this code to apply the new sorting there also. The relevant file to modify is advanced_search_result.php.

Lickety-split! Bon appetit!

22. Prepare a Quick 'n Easy Review System for Product Listing

It's likely that you're already bothered by the review stars only showing on the Product Detail page rather than offering an option for easy comparison in the Product Listing page.

With this recipe you will find a way to change this default behaviour in seconds, and your Product Listing page will show the review rating stars and links to add a new review.

Presentation

Your Product Listing page will look similar to the following screenshot after reviews have been added to it, with products not yet rated only showing the **Write Review** link:

Ready to spice it up? Use the code below!

Ingredients

> **Modified:**
>
> `catalog/includes/modules/product_listing.php`
> `catalog/includes/languages/english.php`

Cooking

1. Open `catalog/includes/modules/product_listing.php` and find the following code snippet in line 95. This is the section of your product listing where the product's name is defined.

   ```
   case 'PRODUCT_LIST_NAME':
   $lc_align = '';
   ```

```
if (isset($HTTP_GET_VARS['manufacturers_id'])) {
  $lc_text = '<a href="' . tep_href_link(FILENAME_PRODUCT_INFO,
  'manufacturers_id=' . $HTTP_GET_VARS['manufacturers_id'] .
  '&products_id=' . $listing['products_id']) . '">' .
  $listing['products_name'] . '</a>';
} else {
  $lc_text = ' <a href="' .
                           tep_href_link(FILENAME_PRODUCT_INFO,
  ($cPath ? 'cPath=' . $cPath . '&' : '') .
  'products_id=' . $listing['products_id']) . '">' .
  $listing['products_name'] . '</a> ';
}
```

Immediately below it add the following code to pull the appropriate average
rating for each product, display the stars if reviews have already been written, and add a link to those reviews. A **Write Review** link is displayed even if
no reviews are found.

```
$review_stars_query =
                  tep_db_query("select round(avg(reviews_rating))
as rating from " . TABLE_REVIEWS .
" where products_id = '" . $listing['products_id'] . "'");
$review_stars = tep_db_fetch_array($review_stars_query);
if ($review_stars['rating'] > 0) {
  $lc_text .= '<p> ' . tep_image(DIR_WS_IMAGES . 'stars_' .
$review_stars['rating'] . '.gif') . '   ';
  $lc_text .= '<a href="' .
                           tep_href_link(FILENAME_PRODUCT_REVIEWS,
  'products_id=' . $listing['products_id']) . '">' .
PL_TEXT_REVIEWS . '</a> | ';
} else {
  $lc_text .= '<p> ';
}
$lc_text .= '<a href="' .
                           tep_href_link(FILENAME_PRODUCT_REVIEWS_WRITE,
  'products_id=' . $listing['products_id']) . '">' .
PL_TEXT_WRITE_REVIEW . '</a>';
```

2. Add the following language defines to `catalog/includes/languages/
   english.php`:

```
define('PL_TEXT_REVIEWS', 'Reviews');
define('PL_TEXT_WRITE_REVIEW', 'Write review');
```

Chef's suggestion:

Note how we added the language defines to `english.php` and not `index.php`, in case you want to double this great recipe and apply it to your `advanced_search_results. php` file also. Both listings will be able to use the same language defines.

Tangy! Bon appetit!

23. Whip Up a Top-Category Driven Product Listing

This recipe is perfect if you need to display your product listing in a different way, determined by the top category. This would be an option if you'd like to display stock, or any other information, instead of the image for one of your top categories. You can also adjust the search-result count and previous/next navigation bar display. You could also use a completely new layout such as Product Listing in Columns for the additional product listing file.

Presentation

Here is a screenshot taken of a subcategory of **DVD Movies** with a new product-listing file for this top category:

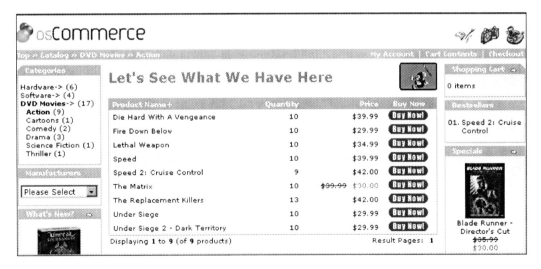

The new product-listing style is used for **DVD Movies** and **Software**, while **Hardware** still looks like this:

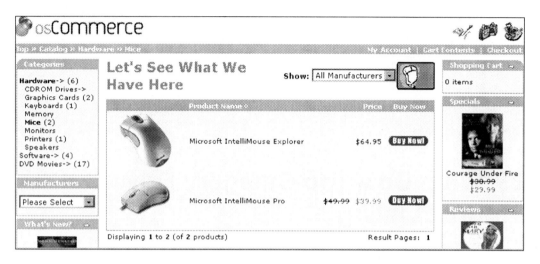

If this tantalizes your taste buds, get smacking!

Ingredients

New:

database.sql (to be run in phpMyAdmin)
catalog/includes/modules/product_listing_diff.php
(this is a clone of the catalog/includes/modules/product_listing.php file)

Modified:

catalog/includes/filenames.php
catalog/index.php

Cooking

1. Run the following SQL statement in phpMyAdmin to create a new configuration group #1234 (ensure that this ID is not already in use), duplicate the product-listing parameters, and add an option to define an extra search-result limit along with the top categories using this feature:

```
INSERT INTO configuration_group
VALUES ('1234', 'Product Listing Diff',
                      'Product Listing configuration
```

```
options for the second product listing file', '8', '1');

INSERT INTO configuration (configuration_title,
configuration_key, configuration_value,
configuration_description, configuration_group_id, sort_order,
date_added) VALUES ('Top categories',
'DIFFERENT_PRODUCT_LISTING', '',
'Comma separated list of top categories for
second product listing file',
'1234', '0', now());

INSERT INTO configuration (configuration_title,
configuration_key, configuration_value,
configuration_description, configuration_group_id,
sort_order, date_added) VALUES ('Search Results',
'MAX_DISPLAY_SEARCH_RESULTS_DIFF', '20',
'Amount of products to list', '1234', '0', now());

INSERT INTO configuration (configuration_title,
configuration_key, configuration_value,
configuration_description, configuration_group_id,
sort_order, date_added) VALUES ('Display Product Image',
'PRODUCT_LIST_IMAGE_DIFF', '1',
'Do you want to display the Product Image?',
'1234', '1', now());

INSERT INTO configuration (configuration_title,
configuration_key, configuration_value,
configuration_description, configuration_group_id,
sort_order, date_added) VALUES ('Display Product Manufaturer
Name','PRODUCT_LIST_MANUFACTURER_DIFF', '0',
'Do you want to display the Product Manufacturer Name?',
'1234', '2', now());
INSERT INTO configuration (configuration_title,
configuration_key, configuration_value,
configuration_description, configuration_group_id,
sort_order, date_added) VALUES ('Display Product Model',
'PRODUCT_LIST_MODEL_DIFF', '0',
'Do you want to display the Product Model?', '1234',
'3', now());

INSERT INTO configuration (configuration_title,
configuration_key, configuration_value,
configuration_description, configuration_group_id,
sort_order, date_added) VALUES ('Display Product Name',
'PRODUCT_LIST_NAME_DIFF', '2',
'Do you want to display the Product Name?', '1234', '4', now());
```

```
INSERT INTO configuration (configuration_title,
configuration_key, configuration_value,
configuration_description, configuration_group_id,
sort_order, date_added) VALUES ('Display Product Price',
'PRODUCT_LIST_PRICE_DIFF', '3',
'Do you want to display the Product Price', '1234', '5',
now());

INSERT INTO configuration (configuration_title,
configuration_key, configuration_value,
configuration_description, configuration_group_id,
sort_order, date_added) VALUES ('Display Product Quantity',
'PRODUCT_LIST_QUANTITY_DIFF', '0',
'Do you want to display the Product Quantity?', '1234',
'6', now());

INSERT INTO configuration (configuration_title,
configuration_key, configuration_value,
configuration_description, configuration_group_id,
sort_order, date_added) VALUES ('Display Product Weight',
'PRODUCT_LIST_WEIGHT_DIFF', '0',
'Do you want to display the Product Weight?', '1234',
'7', now());

INSERT INTO configuration (configuration_title,
configuration_key, configuration_value,
configuration_description, configuration_group_id,
sort_order, date_added) VALUES ('Display Buy Now column',
'PRODUCT_LIST_BUY_NOW_DIFF', '4',
'Do you want to display the Buy Now column?', '1234',
'1234', now());

INSERT INTO configuration (configuration_title,
configuration_key, configuration_value,
configuration_description, configuration_group_id,
sort_order, date_added) VALUES ('Display Category/
Manufacturer Filter (0=disable; 1=enable)',
'PRODUCT_LIST_FILTER_DIFF', '1', 'Do you want to display the
Category/Manufacturer Filter?', '1234', '9', now());

INSERT INTO configuration (configuration_title,
configuration_key, configuration_value,
configuration_description, configuration_group_id,
sort_order, date_added) VALUES ('Location of Prev/
Next Navigation Bar (1-top, 2-bottom, 3-both)',
'PREV_NEXT_BAR_LOCATION_DIFF', '2',
'Sets the location of the Prev/Next
Navigation Bar (1-top, 2-bottom, 3-both)', '1234', '10', now());
```

Chef's suggestion:

If you prefer to have your `configuration_group` table IDs lined up like ducks in a row and do not want to risk double entries, you can replace the defined ID value with `' '` using the autoincrement feature of MySQL, then select this last inserted value and use it for the matching configuration table entries instead of the hardcoded value. Look into the code like:

```
SELECT @pricelistid:=max(
                configuration_group_id)
                from configuration_group;
select @pricelistid;
```

2. Navigate to **Administration | Configuration | Product Listing Diff**. Your admin area will look like this after you edited the parameters to make the top categories with the IDs **2** (Software) and **3** (DVD Movies) use the new product-listing file:

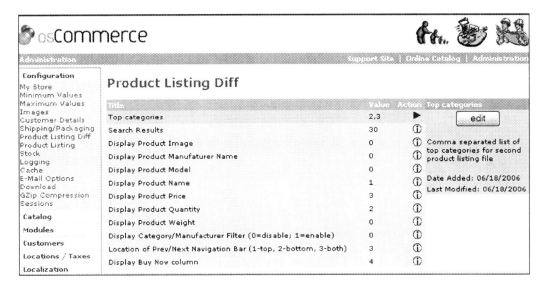

Chef's suggestion:

You can get the categories_id of each category by clicking on it in **Adminstration | Catalog | Categories/Products** and grabbing the value for `cID` in the URL. In the URL `http://localhost/catalog/admin/categories. php?cPath=&cID=1`, the `categories_id` is **1**.

3. Open `catalog/includes/filenames.php` and add the following define statement for the additional product-listing file:

```
define('FILENAME_PRODUCT_LISTING_DIFF',
                              'product_listing_diff.php');
```

4. Open `catalog/index.php` to set the switch for the two different product-listing files in use. Find this in line 129:

```
$define_list = array('PRODUCT_LIST_MODEL' => PRODUCT_LIST_MODEL,
                 'PRODUCT_LIST_NAME' => PRODUCT_LIST_NAME,
                 'PRODUCT_LIST_MANUFACTURER' =>
                                       PRODUCT_LIST_MANUFACTURER,
                 'PRODUCT_LIST_PRICE' => PRODUCT_LIST_PRICE,
                 'PRODUCT_LIST_QUANTITY' =>
                                       PRODUCT_LIST_QUANTITY,
                 'PRODUCT_LIST_WEIGHT' => PRODUCT_LIST_WEIGHT,
                 'PRODUCT_LIST_IMAGE' => PRODUCT_LIST_IMAGE,
                 'PRODUCT_LIST_BUY_NOW' => PRODUCT_LIST_BUY_NOW);
```

Replace with this:

```
$use_diff_pl = false;
$cPath_array = explode('_' , $cPath);
$diff_pl_array = explode(',' , DIFFERENT_PRODUCT_LISTING);
for ($i=0, $n=sizeof($diff_pl_array); $i<$n; $i++) {
 if ($diff_pl_array[$i] == $cPath_array[0]) $use_diff_pl = true;
}

if ($use_diff_pl == true) {
 $define_list = array('PRODUCT_LIST_MODEL' =>
                                       PRODUCT_LIST_MODEL_DIFF,
  'PRODUCT_LIST_NAME' => PRODUCT_LIST_NAME_DIFF,
  'PRODUCT_LIST_MANUFACTURER' =>
                                   PRODUCT_LIST_MANUFACTURER_DIFF,
  'PRODUCT_LIST_PRICE' => PRODUCT_LIST_PRICE_DIFF,
  'PRODUCT_LIST_QUANTITY' => PRODUCT_LIST_QUANTITY_DIFF,
  'PRODUCT_LIST_WEIGHT' => PRODUCT_LIST_WEIGHT_DIFF,
  'PRODUCT_LIST_IMAGE' => PRODUCT_LIST_IMAGE_DIFF,
  'PRODUCT_LIST_BUY_NOW' => PRODUCT_LIST_BUY_NOW_DIFF);
 $product_list_filter = PRODUCT_LIST_FILTER_DIFF;
 $filename_product_listing = FILENAME_PRODUCT_LISTING_DIFF;
} else {
 $define_list = array('PRODUCT_LIST_MODEL' => PRODUCT_LIST_MODEL,
  'PRODUCT_LIST_NAME' => PRODUCT_LIST_NAME,
  'PRODUCT_LIST_MANUFACTURER' => PRODUCT_LIST_MANUFACTURER,
  'PRODUCT_LIST_PRICE' => PRODUCT_LIST_PRICE,
  'PRODUCT_LIST_QUANTITY' => PRODUCT_LIST_QUANTITY,
  'PRODUCT_LIST_WEIGHT' => PRODUCT_LIST_WEIGHT,
```

```
          'PRODUCT_LIST_IMAGE' => PRODUCT_LIST_IMAGE,
          'PRODUCT_LIST_BUY_NOW' => PRODUCT_LIST_BUY_NOW);
      $product_list_filter = PRODUCT_LIST_FILTER;
      $filename_product_listing = FILENAME_PRODUCT_LISTING;
      }
```

5. In the same file, find this in line 257:

```
      if (PRODUCT_LIST_FILTER > 0) {
```

Replace with the following line that looks similar, but uses the new variable instead of the configuration key from the database to decide if the filter will be used:

```
      if ($product_list_filter > 0) {
```

6. Still in `catalog/index.php`, find this in line 302:

```
      <td><?php include(DIR_WS_MODULES .
                              FILENAME_PRODUCT_LISTING); ?></td>
```

Replace with the following code, again using the variable defined in step 3 to fill the parameter for the name of the file used for product listing instead of using the original database key:

```
      <td><?php include(DIR_WS_MODULES .
                              $filename_product_listing); ?></td>
```

7. Create a new file `catalog/includes/modules/product_listing_diff.php` as a clone of `catalog/includes/modules/product_listing.php`. Open the file and replace all *four* occurrences of the paging navigation bar, `PREV_NEXT_BAR_LOCATION`, two each in lines 15 and 154, with the parameter for the second product-listing file, `PREV_NEXT_BAR_LOCATION_DIFF`.

8. In the same new file, change the search-result count call in line 13 from `MAX_DISPLAY_SEARCH_RESULTS` to `MAX_DISPLAY_SEARCH_RESULTS_DIFF`.

Save all changes and check if all is lick-your-lips good! Bon appetit!

24. Control Manufacturer Image Size

This recipe should be very interesting for you if you have nice subcategory images of one size and manufacturer logos of a different size. Your `index.php` file that uses the middle block of the file for showing subcategory or manufacturer product listings only uses one set of sizing, which is `HEADING_IMAGE_WIDTH` and `HEADING_IMAGE_HEIGHT`. You will be able to define manufacturer image size independent of category image size.

Presentation

The default size of **57** for HEADING_IMAGE_WIDTH and **40** for HEADING_IMAGE_HEIGHT looks fine for the subcategory images, as you can see in the following screenshot:

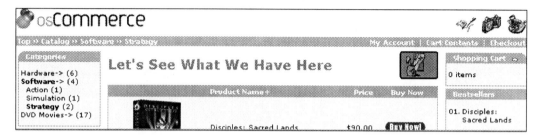

However, it often makes the logos too small and turns them into hard-to-read blobs, as in this screenshot:

The solution is to offer different sizing for logos and subcategory images so that the logo will not be squished, but will show the way it should.

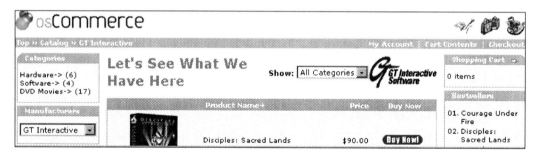

Choose the pan that best fits your loaf, and get baking!

Ingredients

New:

`database.sql` (to be run in phpMyAdmin)

Modified:

`catalog/index.php`

Cooking

1. Run the following SQL statement in your database to create two new keys for the images in your boxes:

```
INSERT INTO configuration (configuration_title,
configuration_key, configuration_value,
configuration_description, configuration_group_id,
sort_order, date_added) VALUES ('Manufacturer Image Width',
'MANU_IMAGE_WIDTH', '100', 'The pixel width of small images in
index.php for manufacturers', '4', '0', now());

INSERT INTO configuration (configuration_title,
configuration_key, configuration_value,
configuration_description, configuration_group_id,
sort_order, date_added) VALUES ('Manufacturer Image Height',
'MANU_IMAGE_HEIGHT', '', 'The pixel height of small images in
index.php for manufacturers', '4', '0', now());
```

2. Navigate to **Administration | Configuration | Images**. You will find your new keys at the top of the list. The value for **Manufacturer Image Height** is left empty; this will ensure that the image has the correct width and will not get squished. We want to display the manufacturer image in its original size, so width is set here to **100**px (which is the width of all manufacturers' images in default osCommerce), while for the categories it is set to **57**px. **Calculate Image Size** is set to **true** as the value for height is left empty to allow recalculation.

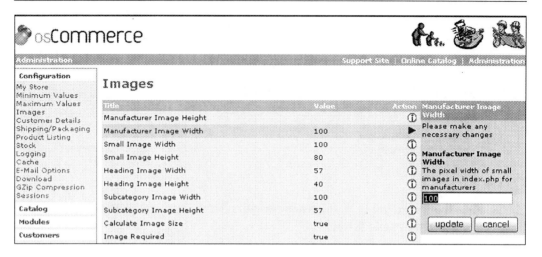

3. Open `catalog/index.php` and find this in line 260 where the image display is defined, choosing a category image or manufacturer's image respectively:

```
// Get the right image for the top-right
    $image = DIR_WS_IMAGES . 'table_background_list.gif';
    if (isset($HTTP_GET_VARS['manufacturers_id'])) {
      $image = tep_db_query("select manufacturers_image from " .
      TABLE_MANUFACTURERS . " where manufacturers_id = '" .
      (int)$HTTP_GET_VARS['manufacturers_id'] . "'");
      $image = tep_db_fetch_array($image);
      $image = $image['manufacturers_image'];
    } elseif ($current_category_id) {
      $image = tep_db_query("select categories_image from " .
      TABLE_CATEGORIES . " where categories_id = '" .
      (int)$current_category_id . "'");
      $image = tep_db_fetch_array($image);
      $image = $image['categories_image'];
    }
?>
<td align="right"><?php echo tep_image(DIR_WS_IMAGES . $image,
HEADING_TITLE, HEADING_IMAGE_WIDTH, HEADING_IMAGE_HEIGHT);
                                                    ?></td>
```

Here the correct image is selected and then called, using the same size parameters in both cases. Change it to the following, to specify separate sizing for category and manufacturer images:

```
// Get the right image for the top-right
    $image = DIR_WS_IMAGES . 'table_background_list.gif';
    if (isset($HTTP_GET_VARS['manufacturers_id'])) {
```

```
        $image = tep_db_query("select manufacturers_image from " .
        TABLE_MANUFACTURERS . " where manufacturers_id = '" .
        (int)$HTTP_GET_VARS['manufacturers_id'] . "'");
        $image = tep_db_fetch_array($image);
        $image = $image['manufacturers_image'];
        $width = MANU_IMAGE_WIDTH;
        $height = MANU_IMAGE_HEIGHT;
    } elseif ($current_category_id) {
        $image = tep_db_query("select categories_image from " .
        TABLE_CATEGORIES . " where categories_id = '" .
        (int)$current_category_id . "'");
        $image = tep_db_fetch_array($image);
        $image = $image['categories_image'];
        $width = HEADING_IMAGE_WIDTH;
        $height = HEADING_IMAGE_HEIGHT;
    }
?>
<td align="right"><?php echo tep_image(DIR_WS_IMAGES . $image,
                    HEADING_TITLE, $width, $height); ?></td>
```

Let it cool before you serve! Bon appetit!

25. Call a Pop Up from Product Description in Product Info

This recipe shows you how to call a pop up from within your product-description text, which is extremely useful for sizing charts, color swatches, or any other information of your product that customers would need to see. It is especially practical for blocks that are reusable, and therefore can be added to multiple products.

Presentation

Here is an example of a pop up added to the description of the product; it lets customers know to which countries heavier items can be shipped.

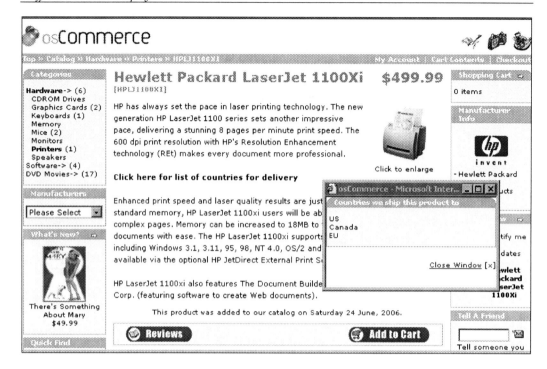

Ready for a toasty treat? Here's your code!

Ingredients

> **New:**
>
> `catalog/popup_shipto.php`
> (this is a clone of the `catalog/popup_search_help.php` file)
>
> **Modified:**
>
> `catalog/includes/languages/english/product_info.php`
> `catalog/product_info.php`

Cooking

1. Make a clone of `catalog/popup_search_help.php` and save it as `catalog/popup_shipto.php`.

2. Open your new file and change line 3 to reflect the new file name, so it looks like the following:

```
$Id: popup_shipto.php,v 1.00 2006/06/17 00:00:00 mm Exp $

Module written by Monika Mathé
http://www.monikamathe.com

Module Copyright (c) 2006 Monika Mathé
```

3. In line 22, find this:

   ```
   require(DIR_WS_LANGUAGES . $language . '/' .
                               FILENAME_ADVANCED_SEARCH);
   ```

   Add immediately below it the call for the language file of the Product Detail page:

   ```
   require(DIR_WS_LANGUAGES . $language . '/' .
                               FILENAME_PRODUCT_INFO);
   ```

   We are retaining the language file for **Advanced Search** page as it has the **Close Window** text define statement. Alternatively, that text could be shifted to `english.php`.

4. In the next two sections, we will customize the box to show shipping details instead of search information. In line 36, find the following code for the box heading:

   ```
   $info_box_contents[] = array('text' => HEADING_SEARCH_HELP);
   ```

   Change to:

   ```
   $info_box_contents[] = array('text' => HEADING_SHIPTO);
   ```

5. In line 41, find the code for the box content:

   ```
   $info_box_contents[] = array('text' => TEXT_SEARCH_HELP);
   ```

   Change to:

   ```
   $info_box_contents[] = array('text' => TEXT_SHIPTO);
   ```

6. Add the following defines to your `catalog/includes/languages/english/product_info.php` file:

   ```
   define('HEADING_SHIPTO', 'Countries we ship this product to');
   define('TEXT_SHIPTO', 'US<br>Canada<br>EU');
   ```

7. Open `catalog/product_info.php` and add the function to call your pop up to the header part at line 31:

   ```
   function popupWindowShipto(url) {

   window.open(url,'popupWindow','toolbar=no,location=no,
   directories=no,status=no,menubar=no,scrollbars=no,resizable=yes,
   copyhistory=no,width=250,height=130,screenX=150,screenY=150,
   ```

```
        top=150,left=150')
    }
```

You can specify the pop-up size to match the content you'd like to display.

8. Open the **Product Description** in edit mode for the product you want to add the pop up to, and add the following code (using your own URL) at the spot you want to display the link for your pop-up file:

```
<a href="javascript:popupWindowShipto
('http://localhost/catalog/popup_shipto.php')"><b>Click here
for list of countries for delivery</b></a><br><br>
```

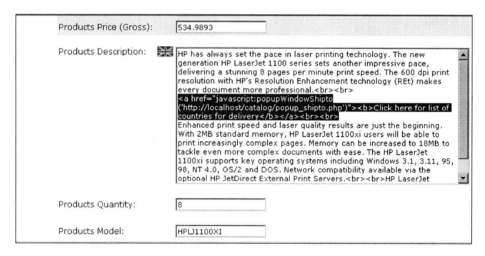

Nothing's sweeter than Pop-Tarts®! Bon appetit!

26. Call Unique Code for a Single Product in Product Info

There may be situations where you'd like to add some very special information to one product only, but do not want to add an entirely new column system for the `products` table in database and admin. This quick recipe shows you how to deal with this special situation elegantly.

Presentation

For this screenshot, the following situation was created: All customers logged in with the first name **Mary** will see, only for the product **There's Something About Mary**, a nice message displayed. Should you have a contribution with gift vouchers installed, this would be a perfect spot to show a "MARY" voucher code say for 10% off for this DVD. There are countless possibilities to modify this hack, which in our situation looks like this:

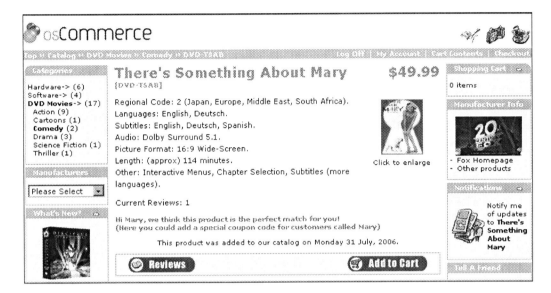

Chef's suggestion:

This recipe is not a one size fits all template that you will be able to use for your site. Carefully adjust the configuration table headings and condition statements to match your own requirements.

Serving special guests? Then this dish is for you!

Ingredients

New:

database.sql (to be run in phpMyAdmin)

Modified:

catalog/includes/languages/english/product_info.php
catalog/product_info.php

Cooking

1. Run the following SQL statement in your database to create two new keys for the images in your boxes (ensure that the new group ID is not in use yet):

```
INSERT INTO configuration_group
VALUES ('23456', 'Unique product', 'Unique product', '20', '1');

INSERT INTO configuration (configuration_title,
configuration_key, configuration_value,
configuration_description, configuration_group_id,
sort_order, date_added) VALUES ('Condition product name',
'UNIQUE_IF_ONE', '', 'A search term from the products name',
'23456', '1', now());

INSERT INTO configuration (configuration_title,
configuration_key, configuration_value,
configuration_description, configuration_group_id,
sort_order, date_added) VALUES ('Condition customer firstname',
'UNIQUE_IF_TWO', '', 'A search term from the customer firstname',
'23456', '2', now());
```

2. Navigate to your new configuration group **Administration | Configuration | Unique product**. Set the customer's first name parameter to **Mary** as we want to check the first name of your customer for the word **Mary**, and set the the product name for the expression **Something about Mary**. Setting up these kinds of keys is helpful when, for example, you decide to have a Fathers' Day promotion done in a similar way.

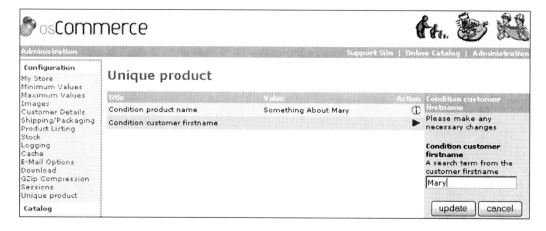

3. Open `catalog/includes/languages/english/product_info.php` and add the following define, which you need to modify to suit your requirements. In this case, we call the customer by first name using the `sprintf` function later in the PHP code:

```
define('TEXT_UNIQUE', 'Hi %s, we think this product is
the perfect match for you!<p>(Here you could add a special
coupon code for customers called Mary)');
```

4. Open `catalog/product_info.php` and find this block of code in line 181:

```
if (tep_not_null($product_info['products_url'])) {
?>
  <tr>
   <td class="main"><?php echo sprintf(TEXT_MORE_INFORMATION,
   tep_href_link(FILENAME_REDIRECT, 'action=url&goto=' .
   urlencode($product_info['products_url']),
                                    'NONSSL', true, false)); ?>
   </td>
  </tr>
  <tr>
   <td><?php echo tep_draw_separator('pixel_trans.gif',
                                        '100%', '10');
    ?></td>
  </tr>
<?php
}
```

Add the following immediately below it, adding another "if" block this time
to check the name of your customer:

```
if ((stripos($product_info['products_name'],
                              UNIQUE_IF_ONE) !== false)
&& (stripos($customer_first_name, UNIQUE_IF_TWO) !== false)) {
?>
  <tr>
    <td class="uniqueProduct"><?php echo sprintf(TEXT_UNIQUE,
    $customer_first_name); ?>
    </td>
  </tr>
  <tr>
    <td><?php echo tep_draw_separator('pixel_trans.gif',
                                        '100%', '10'); ?>
    </td>
  </tr>
<?php
}
```

Chef's suggestion:

To maintain php4 compatability the `strpos` function can be used instead of the new `stripo` function:

```
if ((strpos(strtolower
    ($product_info['products_name']),
    strtolower(UNIQUE_IF_ONE)) !== false) &&
    (strpos(strtolower($customer_first_name),
    strtolower(UNIQUE_IF_TWO)) === 0)) {
?>
<tr>
  <td class="uniqueProduct"><?php echo
sprintf(TEXT_UNIQUE, $customer_first_name); ?>
  </td>
</tr>
<tr>
  <td><?php echo tep_draw_separator
    ('pixel_trans.gif', '100%', '10'); ?>
  </td>
</tr>
<?php
}
```

5. Open `catalog/stylesheet.css` and add the following new class:

```
TD.uniqueProduct {
  font-family: Verdana, Arial, sans-serif;
  font-size: 10px;
  color: #ff0000;
  font-weight : bold;
}
```

Change your first name to **Mary** for testing!

Pleasing to your guests, isn't it? Bon appetit!

27. Show a Pop Up with Shipping Options in Product Info

This recipe allows you to show all shipping options for a product in a pop up opening from the Product Detail page. Default osCommerce offers shipping options only after logging in during the checkout procedure. This module is suitable for you, if you do not have heavily zone-based shipping options, or if your shipping options have clear names to distinguish between zones.

Presentation

Your page will look like this with the new link, **View delivery options**, added below the product's model:

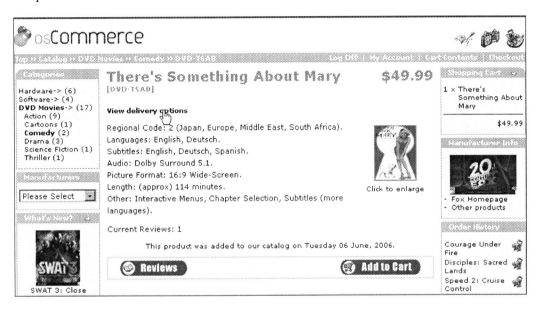

When clicking the **View delivery options** link, the following pop up opens:

Boiled, Deviled, Fried, Poached, and Scrambled!

Ingredients

> **New:**
>
> ```
> catalog/view_delivery.php
> ```
>
> **Modified:**
>
> ```
> catalog/includes/languages/english/product_info.php
> catalog/includes/languages/english/checkout_shipping.php
> catalog/product_info.php
> ```

Cooking

1. Create the new pop-up file `catalog/view_delivery.php` using the following code. Most parts of the code come from the Checkout Shipping page and are reused to display shipping options before entering the checkout loop:

```php
<?php
/*
  $Id: view_delivery.php,v 1.00 2006/06/21 00:00:00 mm Exp $

  Module written by Monika Mathé
  http://www.monikamathe.com

  Module Copyright (c) 2006 Monika Mathé

  osCommerce, Open Source E-Commerce Solutions
  http://www.oscommerce.com

  Copyright (c) 2003 osCommerce

  Released under the GNU General Public License
*/

require('includes/application_top.php');

$product_info_query = tep_db_query("select p.products_id,
pd.products_name, p.products_model from " .
TABLE_PRODUCTS . " p, " .
TABLE_PRODUCTS_DESCRIPTION . " pd where p.products_status = '1'
and p.products_id = '" . (int)$HTTP_GET_VARS['products_id'] . "'
and pd.products_id = p.products_id
and pd.language_id = '" . (int)$languages_id . "'");
$product_info = tep_db_fetch_array($product_info_query);

if (tep_not_null($product_info['products_model'])) {
  $products_name = $product_info['products_name'];
```

```
  } else {
    $products_name = $product_info['products_name']; }

// load all enabled shipping modules
require(DIR_WS_CLASSES . 'shipping.php');
$shipping_modules = new shipping;

if ( defined('MODULE_ORDER_TOTAL_SHIPPING_FREE_SHIPPING') &&
(MODULE_ORDER_TOTAL_SHIPPING_FREE_SHIPPING == 'true') ) {
  $pass = false;

  switch (MODULE_ORDER_TOTAL_SHIPPING_DESTINATION) {
   case 'national':
    if ($order->delivery['country_id'] == STORE_COUNTRY) {
      $pass = true;
    }
     break;
   case 'international':
    if ($order->delivery['country_id'] != STORE_COUNTRY) {
      $pass = true;
    }
     break;
   case 'both':
     $pass = true;
     break;
  }

  $free_shipping = false;
  if ( ($pass == true) && ($order->info['total'] >=
  MODULE_ORDER_TOTAL_SHIPPING_FREE_SHIPPING_OVER) ) {
    $free_shipping = true;

    include(DIR_WS_LANGUAGES . $language .
    '/modules/order_total/ot_shipping.php');
  }
} else {
  $free_shipping = false;
 }

// get all available shipping quotes
$quotes = $shipping_modules->quote();

require(DIR_WS_LANGUAGES . $language . '/' .
                                   FILENAME_CHECKOUT_SHIPPING);

$breadcrumb->add(NAVBAR_TITLE_1,
```

```
    tep_href_link(FILENAME_CHECKOUT_SHIPPING, '', 'SSL'));
    $breadcrumb->add(NAVBAR_TITLE_2,
    tep_href_link(FILENAME_CHECKOUT_SHIPPING, '', 'SSL'));?>
    <!doctype html public "-//W3C//DTD HTML 4.01 Transitional//EN">
    <html <?php echo HTML_PARAMS; ?>>
    <head>
    <meta http-equiv="Content-Type" content="text/html;
     charset=<?php echo CHARSET; ?>">
    <title><?php echo TITLE; ?></title>
    <base href="<?php echo (($request_type == 'SSL') ?
     HTTPS_SERVER : HTTP_SERVER) . DIR_WS_CATALOG; ?>">
    <link rel="stylesheet" type="text/css" href="stylesheet.css">
    </head>
    <body marginwidth="0" marginheight="0"
    topmargin="0" bottommargin="0"
    leftmargin="0" rightmargin="0">
    <!-- body //-->
    <table border="0" width="100%" cellspacing="3" cellpadding="3">
     <tr>
    <!-- body_text //-->
      <td width="100%" valign="top"><table border="0" width="100%"
       cellspacing="0" cellpadding="0">

    <table width="98%" border="0" align="center" cellpadding="0"
     cellspacing="0">
     <tr>
      <td class="main" align="left" valign="middle">
       <b><?php echo SHIPPING_OPTIONS; ?></b></td>
     </tr>
     <tr>

      <td colspan="2"> </td>
     </tr>

     <tr>
      <td><?php echo tep_draw_separator('pixel_trans.gif',
                                        '100%', '10'); ?></td>
     </tr>
     <tr>
      <td colspan="2"><h1 class=
              "pageHeading"><?php echo $products_name; ?></h1></td>
     </tr>
    <?php
     if (tep_count_shipping_modules() > 0) {
    ?>
```

```
<tr>
  <td><table border="0" width="100%" cellspacing=
                                    "1" cellpadding="2">
    <tr>
     <td><table border="0" width="100%" cellspacing=
                                    "0" cellpadding="2">
<?php
  if ($free_shipping == true) {
?>
 <tr>
   <td><?php echo tep_draw_separator('pixel_trans.gif',
                                    '10', '1'); ?></td>
   <td colspan="2" width="100%"><table border="0" width="100%"
    cellspacing="0" cellpadding="2">
 <tr>
  <td width="10"><?php echo tep_draw_separator('pixel_trans.
                                    gif', '10', '1'); ?></td>
  <td class="main" colspan="3"><li><b><?php echo
                                    FREE_SHIPPING_TITLE;
  ?></b></li> <?php echo $quotes[$i]['icon']; ?></td>
  <td width="10"><?php echo tep_draw_separator('pixel_trans.
                                    gif', '10', '1'); ?></td>
 </tr>
 <tr>
  <td width="10"><?php echo tep_draw_separator('pixel_trans.
                                    gif', '10', '1'); ?></td>
  <td class="main" width="100%">
  <?php echo sprintf(FREE_SHIPPING_DESCRIPTION,
   $currencies->format(
    MODULE_ORDER_TOTAL_SHIPPING_FREE_SHIPPING_OVER)); ?></td>
  <td width="10"><?php echo tep_draw_separator('pixel_trans.
                                    gif', '10', '1'); ?></td>
 </tr>
   </table>
   </td>
   <td><?php echo tep_draw_separator('pixel_trans.gif',
                                    '10', '1'); ?></td>
 </tr>
<?php
  } else {
    for ($i=0, $n=sizeof($quotes); $i<$n; $i++) {
?>
 <tr>
  <td><?php echo tep_draw_separator('pixel_trans.gif',
                                    '10', '1'); ?></td>
  <td colspan="2"><table border="0" width="100%" cellspacing="0"
```

```
    cellpadding="2">
  <tr>
   <td width="10"><?php echo tep_draw_separator('pixel_trans.
                            gif', '10', '1'); ?></td>
   <td class="main" colspan="3"><li><b><?php echo
                            $quotes[$i]['module'];
   ?></b></li> <?php if (isset($quotes[$i]['icon']) &&
   tep_not_null($quotes[$i]['icon']))
                        { echo $quotes[$i]['icon']; } ?></td>
   <td width="10"><?php echo tep_draw_separator('pixel_trans.
                            gif', '10', '1'); ?></td>
  </tr>
<?php
    if (isset($quotes[$i]['error'])) {
?>
  <tr>
   <td width="10"><?php echo tep_draw_separator('pixel_trans.
                            gif', '10', '1'); ?></td>
   <td class="main" colspan="3"><?php echo $quotes[$i]['error']; ?>
   </td>
   <td width="10"><?php echo tep_draw_separator('pixel_trans.
                            gif', '10', '1'); ?></td>
  </tr>
<?php
    } else {
      for ($j=0, $n2=sizeof($quotes[$i]['methods']);
                            $j<$n2; $j++) {
?>
  <tr>
   <td width="10"><?php echo tep_draw_separator('pixel_trans.
                            gif', '10', '1'); ?></td>
   <td class="main" width="75%">
   <?php echo tep_draw_separator('pixel_trans.gif',
      '15', '1') . $quotes[$i]['methods'][$j]['title']; ?></td>
<?php
    if ( ($n > 1) || ($n2 > 1) ) {
?>
   <td class="main">
   <?php echo $currencies->format(tep_add_tax(
      $quotes[$i]['methods'][$j]['cost'],
      (isset($quotes[$i]['tax']) ? $quotes[$i]['tax'] : 0))); ?>
   </td>
   <td class="main" align="right"> 
   </td>
<?php
```

```
        } else {
?>
  <td class="main" align="right" colspan="2">
  <?php echo $currencies->format(tep_add_tax($quotes[$i]
                    ['methods'][$j]['cost'],
                    $quotes[$i]['tax'])); ?></td>
<?php
        }
?>
  <td width="10"><?php echo tep_draw_separator('pixel_trans.
                            gif', '10', '1'); ?></td>
  </tr>
<?php
      }
    }
?>
  </table></td>
  <td><?php echo tep_draw_separator('pixel_trans.gif',
                            '10', '1'); ?></td>
 </tr>
<?php
  }
  }
?>
  </table></td>
 </tr>
  </table></td>
 </tr>
 <tr>
  <td><?php echo tep_draw_separator('pixel_trans.gif',
                            '100%', '10'); ?></td>
 </tr>
 <tr>
  <td colspan="2" align="right" style="padding-bottom: 5px;">
  <a href="javascript:window.close()
  ;" title="<?php echo TEXT_CLOSE;
  ?>"><strong><?php echo TEXT_CLOSE; ?></strong></a>
  </td>
 </tr>
<?php
 }
?>
  </table></td>
<!-- body_text_eof //-->
 </tr>
```

```
        </table>
        <!-- body_eof //-->

        </body>
        </html>
        <?php require(DIR_WS_INCLUDES . 'application_bottom.php'); ?>
```

2. Add the following language defines to `catalog/includes/languages/english/checkout_shipping.php`:

```
define('SHIPPING_OPTIONS', 'Delivery options');
define('TEXT_CLOSE', 'Close window');
```

3. Add the following language define to `catalog/includes/languages/english/product_info.php`:

```
define('TEXT_VIEW_DELIVERY_OPTIONS', 'View delivery options');
```

4. Open `catalog/product_info.php` and find this JavaScript pop-up function in line 28:

```
function popupWindow(url) {
  window.open(url,'popupWindow','toolbar=no,location=no,
  directories=no,status=no,menubar=no,scrollbars=no,
  resizable=yes,copyhistory=no,width=100,height=100,screenX=150,
  screenY=150,top=150,left=150')
}
```

Add immediately below it, the function for the pop up of the delivery information:

```
function popupWindowDelivery(url) {

  window.open(url,'popupWindow','toolbar=no,location=no,
  directories=no,status=no,menubar=no,scrollbars=yes,
  resizable=yes,copyhistory=no,width=400,height=300,screenX=150,
  screenY=150,top=150,left=150')
}
```

5. Still in `catalog/product_info.php`, find in line 86 this code defining the product's name and model:

```
if (tep_not_null($product_info['products_model'])) {
  $products_name = $product_info['products_name'] . '<br>
  <span class="smallText">[' .
            $product_info['products_model'] . ']</span>';
} else {
$products_name = $product_info['products_name'];
  }
```

Immediately below it add the call for the pop up:

```
$products_name .= "<p><span class=\"smallText\">
<a href=\"javascript:popupWindowDelivery('" .
tep_href_link('view_delivery.php',
'products_id=' . $HTTP_GET_VARS['products_id']) . "')\">" .
TEXT_VIEW_DELIVERY_OPTIONS . "</a></span>";
```

A dime a dozen! Bon appetit!

28. Add an Anchor for Options in Product Info

This recipe is great for those of you who have to choose from long descriptions and options for your products. It's important for customers to be able to view product options quickly, and here they can jump directly to the relevant spot. This link will only display if there are existing options to choose from.

Presentation

Your Product Detail page will look like this:

After clicking on the link, your customer jumps directly to the options offered, as shown here:

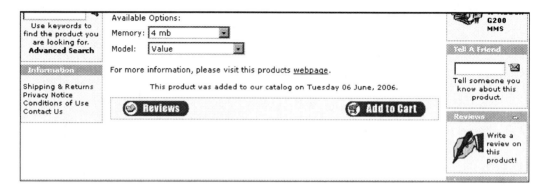

Have your eyes on the fries? Help yourself!

Ingredients

Modified:

```
catalog/includes/languages/english/product_info.php
catalog/product_info.php
```

Cooking

1. Add the following language define statement to `catalog/includes/languages/english/product_info.php`:

   ```
   define('TEXT_VIEW_OPTIONS', 'View Options');
   ```

2. Open `catalog/product_info.php` and find the following code in line 83 where the product name and model are defined:

   ```
   if (tep_not_null($product_info['products_model'])) {
     $products_name = $product_info['products_name'] . '<br>
     <span class="smallText">[' .
                   $product_info['products_model'] . ']</span>';
   } else {
     $products_name = $product_info['products_name'];
   }
   ```

Add immediately below it the following link for the anchor; it will be displayed only if there are options to jump to. For this check, we need to move the query for attributes up to this position.

```
//Check here if we have options
$products_attributes_query =
                tep_db_query("select count(*) as total from " .
TABLE_PRODUCTS_OPTIONS . " popt, " . TABLE_PRODUCTS_ATTRIBUTES .
" patrib where patrib.products_id='" .
                             (int)$HTTP_GET_VARS['products_id'] .
"' and patrib.options_id = popt.products_options_id and
popt.language_id = '" . (int)$languages_id . "'");
$products_attributes =
                tep_db_fetch_array($products_attributes_query);
if ($products_attributes['total'] > 0) {
  $products_name .= '<p><span class="smallText">
  <a href="' . tep_href_link(basename($PHP_SELF),
  tep_get_all_get_params()) . '#options">' .
  TEXT_VIEW_OPTIONS . '</a></span>';
}
```

3. Still in `catalog/product_info.php`, find the attribute query in line 129:

```
<?php
$products_attributes_query =
                tep_db_query("select count(*) as total from " .
TABLE_PRODUCTS_OPTIONS . " popt, " . TABLE_PRODUCTS_ATTRIBUTES .
" patrib where patrib.products_id='" .
                             (int)$HTTP_GET_VARS['products_id'] .
"' and patrib.options_id = popt.products_options_id
and popt.language_id = '" . (int)$languages_id . "'");
$products_attributes =
                tep_db_fetch_array($products_attributes_query);
  if ($products_attributes['total'] > 0) {
?>
  <table border="0" cellspacing="0" cellpadding="2">
  <tr>
  <td class="main" colspan="2"><?php echo
                                TEXT_PRODUCT_OPTIONS; ?>
  </td>
  </tr>
```

Replace with the following code, now only displaying the options as the query was moved up in step 2:

```
<?php
  if ($products_attributes['total'] > 0) {
?>
```

```
                <table border="0" cellspacing="0" cellpadding="2">
            <tr>
            <td class="main" colspan="2"><?php echo
                    TEXT_PRODUCT_OPTIONS; ?><a name="options"></a></td>
        </tr>
```

Faster than take-away! Bon appetit!

29. Integrate Tell a Friend into Product Info

This recipe is a treat if you intend to get rid of as many infoboxes as possible while keeping their function. We will look at adding **Tell a Friend** as a link or as a button.

Presentation

Your Product Detail page will look like this if you add **Tell a Friend** as a link for variation #1:

If you prefer to use a button centered between **Reviews** and **Add to Cart**, try out variation #2 and your screen will look like this:

Will you offer fresh ground pepper or parmesan?

Variation #1

This variation of the theme will add a **Tell a Friend** link right above the product description.

Ingredients

> **Modified:**
>
> ```
> catalog/includes/column_right.php
> catalog/includes/languages/english/product_info.php
> catalog/product_info.php
> ```

Cooking

1. Open `catalog/includes/column_right.php` and comment out the call for the Tell a Friend box in line 36. Change it from this:

   ```
   if (basename($PHP_SELF) != FILENAME_TELL_A_FRIEND)
   include(DIR_WS_BOXES . 'tell_a_friend.php');
   ```

   To this:

   ```
   // if (basename($PHP_SELF) != FILENAME_TELL_A_FRIEND)
   // include(DIR_WS_BOXES . 'tell_a_friend.php');
   ```

2. Open `catalog/includes/languages/english/product_info.php` and add the following language define statement (you may want to shorten the text to fit in the space you want to use):

```
define('TEXT_TELL_A_FRIEND', 'Tell a friend about this product');
```

3. Open `catalog/product_info.php` and find the call for the product's description in line 127:

```
<p><?php echo stripslashes($product_info[
                          'products_description']); ?></p>
```

Add immediately above it the link to the **Tell a Friend** page:

```
<p><span class="smallText"><?php echo '<b>
  <a href="' . tep_href_link(FILENAME_TELL_A_FRIEND,
  tep_get_all_get_params()) . '">' .
  TEXT_TELL_A_FRIEND . '</a></b>'; ?>
</span></p>
```

The pasta's all peppered up! Bon appetit!

Variation #2

This variation adds a new **Tell a Friend** button link in the button bar, centered between **Reviews** and **Add to Cart**.

Ingredients

New:

```
catalog/includes/languages/english/images/buttons/
                          button_tell_a_friend_text.gif
```
(using `extras/button_template/button_template.psd` as a template)

Modified:

```
catalog/includes/column_right.php
catalog/product_info.php
```

Cooking

1. Open `catalog/includes/column_right.php` and comment out the call for the Tell a Friend box in line 36. Change it from this:

```
if (basename($PHP_SELF) != FILENAME_TELL_A_FRIEND)
include(DIR_WS_BOXES . 'tell_a_friend.php');
```

To this:

```
// if (basename($PHP_SELF) != FILENAME_TELL_A_FRIEND)
// include(DIR_WS_BOXES . 'tell_a_friend.php');
```

2. Using `extras/button_template/button_template.psd`, create a new button **Tell a Friend**, and save as `catalog/includes/languages/english/images/buttons/button_tell_a_friend_text.gif`.

3. Open `catalog/product_info.php` and find the code for the button bar in line 210:

```
<tr>
 <td width="10"><?php echo tep_draw_separator('pixel_trans.gif',
                                              '10', '1'); ?></td>
 <td class="main">
 <?php echo '<a href="' . tep_href_link(FILENAME_PRODUCT_REVIEWS,
 tep_get_all_get_params()) . '">' .
                            tep_image_button('button_reviews.gif',
                            IMAGE_BUTTON_REVIEWS) . '</a>'; ?></td>
  <td class="main" align="right">
  <?php echo tep_draw_hidden_field('products_id',
  $product_info['products_id']) .
                            tep_image_submit('button_in_cart.gif',
                            IMAGE_BUTTON_IN_CART); ?></td>
 <td width="10"><?php echo tep_draw_separator('pixel_trans.gif',
                                              '10', '1'); ?></td>
</tr>
```

Replace with this, adding a new button centered between the two default buttons:

```
<tr>
 <td width="10"><?php echo tep_draw_separator('pixel_trans.gif',
                                              '10', '1'); ?></td>
 <td class="main">
 <?php echo '<a href="' .
                            tep_href_link(FILENAME_PRODUCT_REVIEWS,
 tep_get_all_get_params()) . '">' .
                            tep_image_button('button_reviews.gif',
                            IMAGE_BUTTON_REVIEWS) . '</a>'; ?></td>
 <td class="main" align="center">
 <?php echo '<a href="' . tep_href_link(FILENAME_TELL_A_FRIEND,
 tep_get_all_get_params()) . '">' .
 tep_image_button('button_tell_a_friend_text.gif',
 IMAGE_BUTTON_TELL_A_FRIEND) . '</a>'; ?></td>
 <td class="main" align="right">
 <?php echo tep_draw_hidden_field('products_id',
```

```
$product_info['products_id']) .
                        tep_image_submit('button_in_cart.gif',
                        IMAGE_BUTTON_IN_CART); ?></td>
    <td width="10"><?php echo tep_draw_separator('pixel_trans.gif',
                        '10', '1'); ?></td>
    </tr>
```

Sweet parmesan! Bon appetit!

30. Offer an Ask a Question about a Product Link on Product Info

This recipe creates a link to the **Contact Us** page, with information about the product already added as a reference.

Presentation

Your Product Detail page will look like this if you add **Ask a question about this product** as a link for variation #1:

If you prefer to use a button centered between **Reviews** and **Add to Cart**, your screen will look like this in variation #2:

In both variations, the link takes you to the **Contact Us** page, which will look like this screenshot:

Ready to dish out what your guests really want?

Variation #1

This variation on the topic will add an **Ask a question about this product** link right after the product description.

Ingredients

> **Modified:**
> ```
> catalog/includes/languages/english/product_info.php
> catalog/includes/languages/english/contact_us.php
> catalog/product_info.php
> catalog/contact_us.php
> ```

Cooking

1. Open `catalog/includes/languages/english/product_info.php` and add the following define statement:

   ```
   define('TEXT_ASK_A_QUESTION',
                            'Ask a question about this product');
   ```

2. Open `catalog/includes/languages/english/contact_us.php` and add the following define statement:

   ```
   define('TEXT_ASK_A_QUESTION', 'I have a question about %s:');
   ```

3. Open `catalog/product_info.php` and find the reviews query in line 164:

   ```
   <?php
     $reviews_query = tep_db_query("select count(*) as count from " .
     TABLE_REVIEWS .
     " where products_id = '" .
                         (int)$HTTP_GET_VARS['products_id'] . "'");
     $reviews = tep_db_fetch_array($reviews_query);
     if ($reviews['count'] > 0) {
   ?>
   ```

   Add immediately above it the new link to the **Contact Us** page carrying over information about the product's name and model:

   ```
   <tr>
     <td class="main"><?php echo '<b>
   ```

```
<a href="' . tep_href_link(FILENAME_CONTACT_US,
                                       'products_name=' .
$product_info['products_name'] . '&products_model=' .
$product_info['products_model']) . '">' .
                      TEXT_ASK_A_QUESTION . '</a></b>';?></td>
</tr>
<tr>
  <td><?php echo tep_draw_separator('pixel_trans.gif',
                                 '100%', '10'); ?></td>
</tr>
```

4. Open `catalog/contact_us.php` and find the input field for the message in line 126:

```
<td><?php echo tep_draw_textarea_field('enquiry',
                                 'soft', 50, 15); ?></td>
```

Change to the following code, prefilling the message box with the information about the product pulled from the link URL:

```php
<?php
$infotext = '';
if (isset($HTTP_GET_VARS['products_name']))
$infotext .= $HTTP_GET_VARS['products_name'];
if (isset($HTTP_GET_VARS['products_model']))
$infotext .= ' [' . $HTTP_GET_VARS['products_model'] . ']';
if ($infotext != '')
$infotext = sprintf(TEXT_ASK_A_QUESTION, $infotext);
?>
<td><?php echo tep_draw_textarea_field('enquiry', 'soft',
 50, 15, $infotext);
?></td>
```

Makes clean up faster, right? Bon appetit!

Variation #2

This variation adds a new **Ask a Question** button link in the button bar, centered between **Reviews** and **Add to Cart**.

Ingredients

New:

```
catalog/includes/languages/english/images/buttons/
                              button_ask_a_question.gif
(using extras/button_template/button_template.psd as a template)
```

Modified:

```
catalog/includes/languages/english.php
catalog/includes/languages/english/contact_us.php
catalog/product_info.php
catalog/contact_us.php
```

Cooking

1. Open `catalog/includes/languages/english.php` and add the following define statement:

    ```
    define('IMAGE_BUTTON_ASK_A_QUESTION', 'Ask a Question');
    ```

2. Open `catalog/includes/languages/english/contact_us.php` and add the following define statement:

    ```
    define('TEXT_ASK_A_QUESTION', 'I have a question about %s:');
    ```

3. Using `extras/button_template/button_template.psd`, create a new button **Ask a Question**, and save as `catalog/includes/languages/english/images/buttons/button_ask_a_question.gif`.

4. Open `catalog/product_info.php` and find the code for the button bar in line 210:

    ```
    <tr>
     <td width="10"><?php echo tep_draw_separator('pixel_trans.gif',
                                        '10', '1');?></td>
     <td class="main">
     <?php echo '<a href="' .
                          tep_href_link(FILENAME_PRODUCT_REVIEWS,
     tep_get_all_get_params()) . '">' .
     tep_image_button('button_reviews.gif',
                          IMAGE_BUTTON_REVIEWS) . '</a>'; ?></td>
     <td class="main" align="right">
     <?php echo tep_draw_hidden_field('products_id',
     $product_info['products_id']) .
       tep_image_submit('button_in_cart.gif', IMAGE_BUTTON_IN_CART);
       ?></td>
    ```

```
<td width="10"><?php echo tep_draw_separator('pixel_trans.gif',
                                            '10', '1');?></td>
</tr>
```

Replace with the following code, adding the new button centered between the default buttons:

```
<tr>
 <td width="10">
 <?php echo tep_draw_separator('pixel_trans.gif', '10', '1');
 ?></td>
 <td class="main">
 <?php echo '<a href="' .
                        tep_href_link(FILENAME_PRODUCT_REVIEWS,
 tep_get_all_get_params()) . '">' .
                        tep_image_button('button_reviews.gif',
 IMAGE_BUTTON_REVIEWS) . '</a>';
 ?></td>
 <td class="main" align="center">
 <?php echo '<a href="' . tep_href_link(FILENAME_CONTACT_US,
 'products_name=' . $product_info['products_name'] .
 '&products_model=' . $product_info['products_model']) . '">' .
 tep_image_button('button_ask_a_question.gif',
 IMAGE_BUTTON_ASK_A_QUESTION) .
 '</a>';
 ?></td>
 <td class="main" align="right">
 <?php echo tep_draw_hidden_field('products_id',
 $product_info['products_id']) .
                        tep_image_submit('button_in_cart.gif',
 IMAGE_BUTTON_IN_CART);
 ?></td>
 <td width="10"><?php echo tep_draw_separator('pixel_trans.gif',
 '10', '1');
 ?></td>
</tr>
```

5. Open `catalog/contact_us.php` and find the input field for the message in line 126:

```
<td><?php echo tep_draw_textarea_field('enquiry',
                                        'soft', 50, 15); ?></td>
```

Change to the following code, adding information about the product from the URL:

```
<?php
 $infotext = '';
 if (isset($HTTP_GET_VARS['products_name']))
```

```
$infotext .= $HTTP_GET_VARS['products_name'];
if (isset($HTTP_GET_VARS['products_model']))
$infotext .= ' [' . $HTTP_GET_VARS['products_model'] . ']';
if ($infotext != '') $infotext = sprintf(TEXT_ASK_A_QUESTION,
                                         $infotext);?>
<td><?php echo tep_draw_textarea_field('enquiry', 'soft',
50, 15, $infotext);?></td>
```

Chef's suggestion:

If you'd like to see at a glance the topic of each question in your email folder, add the parameters for the product's name and model to the subject of the email.

They'll be asking for seconds! Bon appetit!

31. Sell Affiliate Products from Your Catalog

This recipe is fabulous if you want to comfortably link to affiliate sites to make a margin on products sold, and integrate their products into your catalog, so your own products and theirs have the same look and feel. In this example, we do not carry the DVD, **There's Something About Mary**, ourselves, rather we offer a link to Amazon where it will be logged when a sale is made. This sale tracking will result in a percentage being paid to us by Amazon.

Presentation

As you can see in the following screenshot, this product is presented with the same look and feel, with no change to design and layout apart from using the button **Buy Now** instead of **Add to Cart**:

Clicking on **Buy Now** opens a new window with the affiliate's website and the product selected; in this case, the DVD, **There's Something About Mary**. The URL used, `http://www.amazon.com/exec/obidos/ASIN/6305499136/monikamathece-20/...`, has been specified in admin and allows Amazon to track sales (see the affiliate code `monikamathece-20`; the last part of the URL is Amazon's session ID).

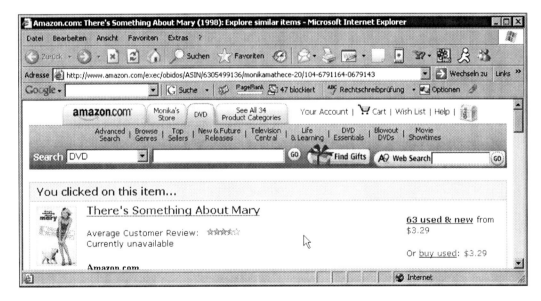

Even the best cooks offer baker's bread at their table!

Ingredients

New:

database.sql (to be run in phpMyAdmin)
catalog/includes/languages/english/images/buttons/
                                        button_affiliate.gif
(using extras/button_template/button_template.psd as a template)
catalog/admin/includes/languages/english/categories.php
catalog/admin/categories.php
catalog/includes/languages/english.php
catalog/product_info.php

Cooking

1. Run the following SQL statement in your database to create the new columns affiliate and affiliate_url for the products table:

    ```
    ALTER TABLE products
    ADD affiliate INT NOT NULL DEFAULT 0 AFTER products_id ,
    ADD affiliate_url VARCHAR( 255 ) NULL AFTER affiliate ;
    ```

2. Open catalog/admin/includes/languages/english/categories.php and add the following define statements:

    ```
    define('TEXT_AFFILIATE', 'Affiliate:');
    define('TEXT_AFFILIATE_URL', 'Affiliate URL:');
    ```

3. Open catalog/admin/categories.php and find this in line 215 to fill the array for inserting products:

    ```
    $sql_data_array = array(
    'products_quantity' =>
    tep_db_prepare_input($HTTP_POST_VARS['products_quantity']),
    'products_model' =>
    tep_db_prepare_input($HTTP_POST_VARS['products_model']),
    'products_price' =>
    tep_db_prepare_input($HTTP_POST_VARS['products_price']),
    ```

    Add immediately below it:

    ```
    'affiliate' =>
    tep_db_prepare_input($HTTP_POST_VARS['affiliate']),
    'affiliate_url' =>
    tep_db_prepare_input($HTTP_POST_VARS['affiliate_url']),
    ```

4. Find this in line 290, in the copy-product section:

```
} elseif ($HTTP_POST_VARS['copy_as'] == 'duplicate') {
$product_query = tep_db_query("select products_quantity,
products_model, products_image, products_price,
products_date_available, products_weight,
products_tax_class_id, manufacturers_id from " .
TABLE_PRODUCTS . " where products_id = '" .
(int)$products_id . "'");
$product = tep_db_fetch_array($product_query);

tep_db_query("insert into " . TABLE_PRODUCTS .
" (products_quantity, products_model,products_image,
products_price, products_date_added,
products_date_available, products_weight, products_status,
products_tax_class_id, manufacturers_id) values ('" .
tep_db_input($product['products_quantity']) . "', '" .
tep_db_input($product['products_model']) . "', '" .
tep_db_input($product['products_image']) . "', '" .
tep_db_input($product['products_price']) . "',  now(), " .
(empty($product['products_date_available']) ? "null" : "'" .
tep_db_input($product['products_date_available']) . "'") .
                                        "', '" .
tep_db_input($product['products_weight']) . "', '0', '" .
(int)$product['products_tax_class_id'] . "', '" .
(int)$product['manufacturers_id'] . "')");
```

Replace with the following code, again adding the two new columns:

```
} elseif ($HTTP_POST_VARS['copy_as'] == 'duplicate') {
$product_query = tep_db_query("select affiliate, affiliate_url,
products_quantity, products_model, products_image,
products_price, products_date_available, products_weight,
products_tax_class_id, manufacturers_id from " .
TABLE_PRODUCTS . " where products_id = '" .
(int)$products_id . "'");
$product = tep_db_fetch_array($product_query);

tep_db_query("insert into " . TABLE_PRODUCTS .
" (affiliate, affiliate_url, products_quantity, products_model,
products_image, products_price, products_date_added,
products_date_available, products_weight, products_status,
products_tax_class_id, manufacturers_id)
values ('" . tep_db_input($product['affiliate']) . "', '" .
tep_db_input($product['affiliate_url']) . "', '" .
tep_db_input($product['products_quantity']) . "', '" .
tep_db_input($product['products_model']) . "', '" .
```

```
tep_db_input($product['products_image']) . "', '" .
tep_db_input($product['products_price']) . "', now(), " .
(empty($product['products_date_available']) ? "null" : "'" .
tep_db_input($product['products_date_available']) . "'") .
                                                    "', '" .
tep_db_input($product['products_weight']) . "', '0', '" .
(int)$product['products_tax_class_id'] . "', '" .
(int)$product['manufacturers_id'] . "')");
```

5. Find this in line 358 where the `$parameters` variable is defined:

```php
<?php
 if ($action == 'new_product') {
  $parameters = array('products_name' => '',
             'products_description' => '',
             'products_url' => '',
             'products_id' => '',
             'products_quantity' => '',
             'products_model' => '',
```

Add immediately below it:

```
'affiliate' => '',
'affiliate_url' => '',
```

6. Still in `catalog/admin/categories.php`, find the products query in line 381:

```
$product_query = tep_db_query("select pd.products_name,
pd.products_description, pd.products_url, p.products_id,
p.products_quantity, p.products_model, p.products_image,
p.products_price, p.products_weight, p.products_date_added,
p.products_last_modified, date_format(p.products_date_available,
'%Y-%m-%d') as products_date_available, p.products_status,
p.products_tax_class_id, p.manufacturers_id from " .
TABLE_PRODUCTS . " p, " . TABLE_PRODUCTS_DESCRIPTION .
" pd where p.products_id = '" . (int)$HTTP_GET_VARS['pID'] . "'
and p.products_id = pd.products_id and pd.language_id = '" .
(int)$languages_id . "'");
```

Replace with this:

```
$product_query = tep_db_query("select p.affiliate,
p.affiliate_url, pd.products_name, pd.products_description,
pd.products_url, p.products_id, p.products_quantity,
p.products_model, p.products_image, p.products_price,
p.products_weight, p.products_date_added,
p.products_last_modified, date_format(p.products_date_available,
'%Y-%m-%d') as products_date_available, p.products_status,
```

```
p.products_tax_class_id, p.manufacturers_id from " .
TABLE_PRODUCTS . " p, " . TABLE_PRODUCTS_DESCRIPTION .
" pd where p.products_id = '" . (int)$HTTP_GET_VARS['pID'] . "'
and p.products_id = pd.products_id and pd.language_id = '" .
(int)$languages_id . "'");
```

7. Find the manufacturers array in line 392:

```
$manufacturers_array = array(array('id' => '',
                                   'text' => TEXT_NONE));
$manufacturers_query = tep_db_query("select manufacturers_id,
manufacturers_name from " . TABLE_MANUFACTURERS .
" order by manufacturers_name");
while ($manufacturers =
                  tep_db_fetch_array($manufacturers_query)) {
  $manufacturers_array[] = array('id' =>
                            $manufacturers['manufacturers_id'],
     'text' =>$manufacturers['manufacturers_name']);
}
```

Immediately below it add the new array for your affiliates:

```
$affiliate_array = array(array('id' => '0',
                               'text' => TEXT_NONE));
$affiliate_array[] = array('id' => '1', 'text' => 'Amazon');
```

Chef's suggestion:

Here you can specify as many affiliate partners as you need. If you have a lot, it may be worth it to create an extra table and use a query for IDs/affiliate names.

8. Find the following in line 492:

```
<tr>
  <td class="main"><?php echo TEXT_PRODUCTS_DATE_AVAILABLE; ?>
  <br><small>(YYYY-MM-DD)</small>
  </td>
  <td class="main"><?php echo tep_draw_separator(
                  'pixel_trans.gif', '24', '15') . ' '; ?>
  <script language="javascript">dateAvailable.writeControl();
  dateAvailable.dateFormat="yyyy-MM-dd";</script></td>
</tr>
<tr>
```

```
      <td colspan="2"><?php echo tep_draw_separator('pixel_trans.
                                  gif', '1', '10'); ?></td>
   </tr>
```

Add immediately below it your new fields for adding affiliates with the
drop-down using the array you have defined in step 7:

```
   <tr>
      <td class="main"><?php echo TEXT_AFFILIATE; ?>
      </td>
      <td class="main"><?php echo tep_draw_separator(
            'pixel_trans.gif', '24', '15') . ' ' .
            tep_draw_pull_down_menu('affiliate', $affiliate_array,
            $pInfo->affiliate); ?></td>
   </tr>
   <tr>
      <td class="main"><?php echo TEXT_AFFILIATE_URL; ?>
      </td>
      <td class="main"><?php echo tep_draw_separator(
            'pixel_trans.gif', '24', '15') . ' ' .
            tep_draw_input_field('affiliate_url',
            $pInfo->affiliate_url); ?></td>
   </tr>
   <tr>
      <td colspan="2"><?php echo tep_draw_separator(
            'pixel_trans.gif', '1', '10'); ?></td>
   </tr>
   <tr>
```

9. Find this query that pulls info about one product, in line 621:

```
   $product_query = tep_db_query("select p.products_id,
   pd.language_id, pd.products_name, pd.products_description,
   pd.products_url, p.products_quantity, p.products_model,
   p.products_image, p.products_price, p.products_weight,
   p.products_date_added, p.products_last_modified,
   p.products_date_available, p.products_status,
   p.manufacturers_id  from " . TABLE_PRODUCTS . " p, " .
   TABLE_PRODUCTS_DESCRIPTION .
   " pd where p.products_id = pd.products_id and p.products_id = '"
   . (int)$HTTP_GET_VARS['pID'] . "'");
```

Replace with:

```
   $product_query = tep_db_query("select p.affiliate,
   p.affiliate_url, p.products_id, pd.language_id,
   pd.products_name, pd.products_description, pd.products_url,
   p.products_quantity, p.products_model, p.products_image,
   p.products_price, p.products_weight, p.products_date_added,
```

```
p.products_last_modified, p.products_date_available,
p.products_status, p.manufacturers_id  from " .
TABLE_PRODUCTS . " p, " .
TABLE_PRODUCTS_DESCRIPTION .
" pd where p.products_id = pd.products_id
and p.products_id = '" . (int)$HTTP_GET_VARS['pID'] . "'");
```

10. Navigate to **Administration | Catalog** and seach for the product you want to set up for an affiliate program. Choose the name of the affiliate (here **Amazon**) and enter the URL containing your affiliate tracking identifier (here `http://www.amazon.com/exec/obidos/ASIN/6305499136/ monikamathece-20.`)

Chef's suggestion:

Make sure you enter the full URL as you see it in your browser, complete with the `http://` part, or your links will not work.

11. Open `catalog/includes/languages/english.php` and add the following define statement:

```
define('IMAGE_BUTTON_AFFILIATE', 'Buy from Affiliate');
```

12. Using `extras/button_template/button_template.psd`, create a new
    button **Buy Now**, and save as `catalog/includes/languages/english/`
    `images/buttons/button_affiliate.gif`.

13. Open `catalog/product_info.php` and find the query for the products table
    in line 72:

```
$product_info_query = tep_db_query("select p.products_id,
pd.products_name, pd.products_description, p.products_model,
p.products_quantity, p.products_image, pd.products_url,
p.products_price, p.products_tax_class_id,
p.products_date_added, p.products_date_available,
p.manufacturers_id from " . TABLE_PRODUCTS . " p, " .
TABLE_PRODUCTS_DESCRIPTION .
" pd where p.products_status = '1' and
p.products_id = '" . (int)$HTTP_GET_VARS['products_id'] . "'
and pd.products_id = p.products_id and
pd.language_id = '" . (int)$languages_id . "'");
```

Replace with the following code, adding the new columns for affiliates:

```
$product_info_query =
              tep_db_query("select p.affiliate, p.affiliate_url,
    p.products_id, pd.products_name, pd.products_description,
    p.products_model, p.products_quantity, p.products_image,
    pd.products_url, p.products_price, p.products_tax_class_id,
    p.products_date_added, p.products_date_available,
    p.manufacturers_id from " . TABLE_PRODUCTS . " p, " .
    TABLE_PRODUCTS_DESCRIPTION . " pd where p.products_status = '1'
    and p.products_id = '" . (int)$HTTP_GET_VARS['products_id'] . "'
    and pd.products_id = p.products_id and
    pd.language_id = '" . (int)$languages_id . "'");
```

14. Find the submit button in the button bar, line 213:

```
<td class="main" align="right">
<?php echo tep_draw_hidden_field('products_id',
$product_info['products_id']) .
                      tep_image_submit('button_in_cart.gif',
IMAGE_BUTTON_IN_CART); ?>
</td>
```

Replace with this new code that replaces the regular button with an affiliate
link for affiliate products:

```
<td class="main" align="right">
<?php
 if ($product_info['affiliate'] > 0) {
   echo '<a target="_blank" href="' .
```

```
                              $product_info['affiliate_url'] . '">' .
     tep_image_button('button_affiliate.gif',
                              IMAGE_BUTTON_AFFILIATE) . '</a>';
     } else {
       echo tep_draw_hidden_field('products_id',
                              $product_info['products_id']) .
       tep_image_submit('button_in_cart.gif', IMAGE_BUTTON_IN_CART);
     }
   ?>
   </td>
```

Sometimes, it's all in the bread! Bon appetit!

32. Fill Up Also Purchased Products Search Result

This recipe allows you to show a determined number of products in the Also Purchased Products box even when sales have not been made yet. This module checks for sales and the number you'd like to display, and if the number generated by the regular Also Purchased Products query is too low, random products are added. This is a very important feature for new shops or shops already using the Also Purchased Products box for design purposes, and not wanting it to look different on different product pages.

Presentation

Your screen will look like this screenshot with your Also Purchased Products box filled to the brim (defined in admin to show six products):

Think this is hot stuff? Grab your oven gloves!

Ingredients

> **Modified:**
>
> catalog/includes/modules/also_purchased_products.php

Cooking

1. Open catalog/includes/modules/also_purchased_products.php and find this in line 14:

    ```
    $orders_query = tep_db_query("select p.products_id,
    p.products_image from " . TABLE_ORDERS_PRODUCTS .
    " opa, " . TABLE_ORDERS_PRODUCTS . " opb,
    " . TABLE_ORDERS . " o, " . TABLE_PRODUCTS .
    ```

```
" p where opa.products_id = '" .
(int)$HTTP_GET_VARS['products_id'] . "'
and opa.orders_id = opb.orders_id and
opb.products_id != '" . (int)$HTTP_GET_VARS['products_id'] .
"' and opb.products_id = p.products_id and
opb.orders_id = o.orders_id and p.products_status = '1' group by
p.products_id order by o.date_purchased desc limit
" . MAX_DISPLAY_ALSO_PURCHASED);
$num_products_ordered = tep_db_num_rows($orders_query);
if ($num_products_ordered >= MIN_DISPLAY_ALSO_PURCHASED) {
```

Replace with the following code that fills an array with the products that
were in fact purchased, and compares the product count to the number of
products you would like to display. Should this value be lower than needed,
random products are added to the array to fill up the box:

```
$orders_query_sql = "select p.products_id from " .
TABLE_ORDERS_PRODUCTS . " opa, " .
TABLE_ORDERS_PRODUCTS . " opb, " .
TABLE_ORDERS . " o, " . TABLE_PRODUCTS .
" p where opa.products_id = '" .
                    (int)$HTTP_GET_VARS['products_id'] . "'
and opa.orders_id = opb.orders_id and
opb.products_id != '" .
                    (int)$HTTP_GET_VARS['products_id'] . "' and
opb.products_id = p.products_id and opb.orders_id =
o.orders_id and p.products_image <> '' and p.products_status =
'1' group by p.products_id order by o.date_purchased desc limit
" . MAX_DISPLAY_ALSO_PURCHASED;
$orders_query = tep_db_query($orders_query_sql);
$num_products_ordered = tep_db_num_rows($orders_query);

//adding 0 to have at least one value for implode
$prod_array[] = '0';
while ($orders = tep_db_fetch_array($orders_query)) {
 $prod_array[] = $orders['products_id'];
}

if ((sizeof($prod_array) - 1) < MAX_DISPLAY_ALSO_PURCHASED) {
 $add_query_sql = "select p.products_id from
 " . TABLE_PRODUCTS .
 " p where p.products_status = '1' and
 p.products_id not in ('" . implode("', '", $prod_array) . "') and
 p.products_image <> '' order by rand() limit " .
 (MAX_DISPLAY_ALSO_PURCHASED - sizeof($prod_array) + 1);
 $add_query = tep_db_query($add_query_sql);
 while ($add = tep_db_fetch_array($add_query)) {
```

```
    $prod_array[] = $add['products_id'];
  }
}
$orders_query = tep_db_query("select distinct pd.products_name,
m.manufacturers_name, p.products_image, p.products_id,
p.manufacturers_id, p.products_price, p.products_tax_class_id,
IF(s.status, s.specials_new_products_price, NULL) as
specials_new_products_price,
IF(s.status, s.specials_new_products_price, p.products_price)
as final_price from  " . TABLE_PRODUCTS . " p left join  " .
TABLE_SPECIALS . " s on p.products_id = s.products_id,  " .
TABLE_PRODUCTS_DESCRIPTION . " pd,  " .
TABLE_MANUFACTURERS . " m where p.products_status = '1' and
pd.products_id = p.products_id and pd.language_id = '1' and
p.products_id in ('" . implode("', '", $prod_array) . "')
limit " . MAX_DISPLAY_ALSO_PURCHASED);
```

2. Find at the bottom of the file, in line 58:

```
<!-- also_purchased_products_eof //-->
<?php
    }
  }
?>
```

Replace with the following code that closes the only unclosed "if" statement:

```
<!-- also_purchased_products_eof //-->
<?php
    }
?>
```

Soup's on! Bon appetit!

33. Limit New Products to Those with an Image

This recipe is very important when most of your products have images, but some do not. As soon as new products are added, they appear in the list of the New Products box and will distort the look of the box, even when you have set **Image required** to false in **Administration | Configuration | Images**.

Presentation

Products without images or with an image placeholder (which is an image telling the customer that there is no image) will be removed from the selection if you use this query.

Otherwise, your screenshot would have looked like this, where you allow products with no image specified to be shown:

No beef in the fridge, but stew's on the menu? Hack your code!

Ingredients

Modified:

`catalog/includes/modules/new_products.php`

Cooking

1. Open `catalog/includes/modules/new_products.php` and find this in line 20, which runs the queries for new products depending on a category selected:

```
if ( (!isset($new_products_category_id)) ||
    ($new_products_category_id == '0') ) {
  $new_products_query = tep_db_query("select p.products_id,
  p.products_image, p.products_tax_class_id,
  if(s.status, s.specials_new_products_price, p.products_price)
  as products_price from " . TABLE_PRODUCTS . " p left join " .
  TABLE_SPECIALS . " s on p.products_id = s.products_id where
  products_status = '1' order by p.products_date_added desc
  limit " . MAX_DISPLAY_NEW_PRODUCTS);
} else {
  $new_products_query = tep_db_query("select distinct
  p.products_id, p.products_image, p.products_tax_class_id,
  if(s.status, s.specials_new_products_price, p.products_price)
  as products_price from " . TABLE_PRODUCTS . " p left join " .
  TABLE_SPECIALS . " s on p.products_id = s.products_id, " .
  TABLE_PRODUCTS_TO_CATEGORIES . " p2c, " . TABLE_CATEGORIES .
  " c where p.products_id = p2c.products_id and
  p2c.categories_id = c.categories_id and
  c.parent_id = '" . (int)$new_products_category_id . "' and
  p.products_status = '1' order by p.products_date_added desc
  limit " . MAX_DISPLAY_NEW_PRODUCTS);
}
```

Replace with the following code, using your own placeholder image name (here, `noimage.gif`):

```
if ( (!isset($new_products_category_id)) ||
    ($new_products_category_id == '0') ) {
  $new_products_query = tep_db_query("select p.products_id,
  p.products_image, p.products_tax_class_id,
  if(s.status, s.specials_new_products_price, p.products_price)
  as products_price from " . TABLE_PRODUCTS . " p left join " .
  TABLE_SPECIALS . " s on p.products_id = s.products_id where
  products_status = '1' and p.products_image <> 'noimage.gif' and
  p.products_image is not null and p.products_image <> ''
  order by p.products_date_added desc limit " .
                                MAX_DISPLAY_NEW_PRODUCTS);
} else {
  $new_products_query = tep_db_query("select distinct
  p.products_id, p.products_image, p.products_tax_class_id,
  if(s.status, s.specials_new_products_price, p.products_price)
```

```
            as products_price from " . TABLE_PRODUCTS . " p left join " .
            TABLE_SPECIALS . " s on p.products_id = s.products_id, " .
            TABLE_PRODUCTS_TO_CATEGORIES .
            " p2c, " . TABLE_CATEGORIES . " c where
            p.products_id = p2c.products_id and p2c.categories_id =
            c.categories_id and c.parent_id = '" .
            (int)$new_products_category_id . "' and
            p.products_status = '1' and
            p.products_image <> 'noimage.gif' and
            p.products_image is not null and p.products_image <> ''
            order by p.products_date_added desc limit " .
                                       MAX_DISPLAY_NEW_PRODUCTS);
    }
```

Your guests will never know! Bon appetit!

34. Set Column Count for New Products

This recipe allows you to modify the default three-column layout within a few seconds. You will now be able to specify how many columns of new products you would like to show.

Presentation

In the following screenshot, the column count was set to 4:

Making a bunch of hors d'oeuvres? It's a cinch!

Ingredients

New:

`database.sql` (to be run in phpMyAdmin)

Modified:

`catalog/includes/modules/new_products.php`

Cooking

1. Run the following SQL statement in your database, creating a new key for the column count used in the New Products box:

```
INSERT INTO configuration (configuration_title,
configuration_key, configuration_value,
configuration_description, configuration_group_id, sort_order,
date_added) VALUES ('New Products To List Per Row',
'MAX_DISPLAY_NEW_PRODUCTS_PER_ROW', '3',
'How many new products to list per row', '3', '14', now());
```

2. Navigate to **Administration | Configuration | Maximum Values** and set the new key **New Products To List Per Row** to the desired column count, in this case **4**.

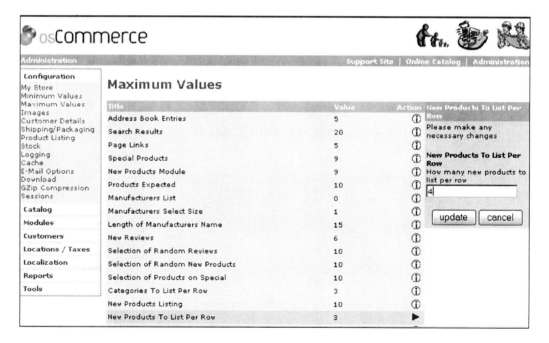

3. Open `catalog/includes/modules/new_products.php` and find this in line 31. Here the new box is being built using three columns in the default layout:

```
$info_box_contents[$row][$col] = array('align' => 'center',
    'params' => 'class="smallText" width="33%" valign="top",
    'text' => '<a href="' . tep_href_link(FILENAME_PRODUCT_INFO,
      'products_id=' . $new_products['products_id']) . '">' .
    tep_image(DIR_WS_IMAGES . $new_products['products_image'],
    $new_products['products_name'],
         SMALL_IMAGE_WIDTH, SMALL_IMAGE_HEIGHT) . '</a><br>
    <a href="' . tep_href_link(FILENAME_PRODUCT_INFO,
      'products_id=' . $new_products['products_id']) . '">' .
    $new_products['products_name'] . '</a><br>' .
    $currencies->display_price($new_products['products_price'],
    tep_get_tax_rate($new_products['products_tax_class_id'])));

$col ++;
if ($col > 2) {
  $col = 0;
  $row ++;
}
```

Replace with this:

```
$info_box_contents[$row][$col] = array('align' => 'center',
    'params' => 'class="smallText"
    width="' . round(100/(MAX_DISPLAY_NEW_PRODUCTS_PER_ROW),
                                                  0). '%"
    valign="top", 'text' => '<a href="' .
    tep_href_link(FILENAME_PRODUCT_INFO,
      'products_id=' . $new_products['products_id']) . '">' .
    tep_image(DIR_WS_IMAGES . $new_products['products_image'],
    $new_products['products_name'], SMALL_IMAGE_WIDTH,
                 SMALL_IMAGE_HEIGHT) . '</a><br>
    <a href="' . tep_href_link(FILENAME_PRODUCT_INFO,
      'products_id=' . $new_products['products_id']) . '">' .
    $new_products['products_name'] . '</a><br>' .
    $currencies->display_price($new_products['products_price'],
    tep_get_tax_rate($new_products['products_tax_class_id'])));

$col ++;
if ($col > (MAX_DISPLAY_NEW_PRODUCTS_PER_ROW - 1)) {
  $col = 0;
  $row ++;
}
```

Save room for the main course! Bon appetit!

Summary

In this chapter you've played with a delicious collection of recipes to modify your product display to your heart's content. Images now obey your gentlest whisk; product-listing colors, styles, sorting, and complete appearance can be cooked up within minutes. You decide whether you prefer to display categories, top categories, or add an entire reviews system to develop a highly distinct look that is pleasing to the senses.

Your Product Detail page can be spiced up with useful anchors for product options, feature interesting add-ons for unique products or offer pop ups for delivery options or charts. You may want to add a **Tell a Friend** or **Ask a Question** button, or implement an elegant way to serve your customers third-party products through your affiliate programs.

For your Also Purchased Products infobox on the Product Detail page, you can now ensure that in all cases your site sports a well filled box to encourage more sales. Your New Products box—by default laid out in a 3 column design—can now be easily modified to display the column count your store really needs, and you will never again have an unsettled stomach from products without images messing with the fabulous look you have implemented for your shop.

Now that you have taken the chef-de-cuisine approach to present your products, we will now move to the chop block to help your customers browse your site with ease, and find those goodies!

5
Dish Up a Better Search

This chapter tackles one of the most important parts of an e-commerce website—the search function. Offering intuitive search options is crucial for a successful online business where customers browse on their own to find the products they need or never even knew existed.

In this chapter, we will talk about how to:

- Add help text to your search-box input field
- Set the search-result value independent of admin listings
- Add an **All Manufacturers** page to the **Manufacturers** infobox
- Customize your product listing with individual boxes for each manufacturer

35. Add Help Text to Your Search-Box Input Field

If your shop maintains a flat categories tree, and doesn't have more than one subcategory level, you can fit a search box into the top navigation bar (even for a screen resolution of 800x600 pixels). This recipe will show you how to move your search box to be visible at first glance, and how to modify code for better search results. Currently, the search box can really be described as hiding near the bottom of the left column; hard to find if you have a few categories, and are displaying new products and the manufacturer box. Additionally, for customers preferring to use an advanced search function, you can add an easy-to-spot link within the **Categories** infobox.

Presentation

This is how your website will look with search added to the navigation bar:

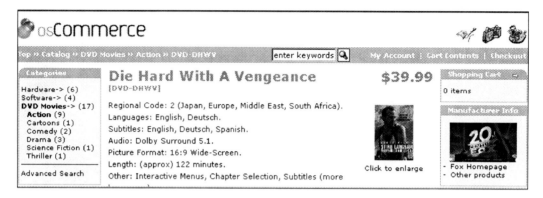

Ready to whet their appetite?

Ingredients

Modified:

```
catalog/includes/languages/english.php
catalog/includes/header.php
catalog/includes/boxes/categories.php
catalog/includes/column_left.php
```

Cooking

1. Add the following `define` statement to `catalog/includes/languages/english.php`:

    ```
    define('TEXT_ENTER_KEYWORDS', 'Enter keywords');
    ```

2. Open `catalog/includes/header.php` and find the following in line 51:

    ```
    if ($messageStack->size('header') > 0) {
      echo $messageStack->output('header');
    }
    ?>
    ```

    Add immediately below it the following function to empty the search-box input field when your customer sets the focus on it:

    ```
    <script language=JavaScript>
    function emptyMe() {
    var form = document.forms["advanced_search"];
    ```

```
form.keywords.value = "";
}
</script>
```

3. Still in `catalog/includes/header.php`, find the line for the navigation bar in line 70:

```
<td class="headerNavigation">  
  <?php echo $breadcrumb->trail(' &raquo; '); ?></td>
<td align="right" class="headerNavigation">
  <?php if (tep_session_is_registered('customer_id')) { ?>
  <a href="<?php echo tep_href_link(FILENAME_LOGOFF,
                                       '', 'SSL'); ?>"
  class="headerNavigation"><?php echo HEADER_TITLE_LOGOFF; ?>
  </a>  | 
  <?php } ?>
  <a href="<?php echo tep_href_link(FILENAME_ACCOUNT,
                                      '', 'SSL'); ?>"
  class=
     "headerNavigation"><?php echo HEADER_TITLE_MY_ACCOUNT; ?>
  </a>  | 
  <a href=
      "<?php echo tep_href_link(FILENAME_SHOPPING_CART); ?>"
    class="headerNavigation">
                  <?php echo HEADER_TITLE_CART_CONTENTS; ?>
  </a>  | 
  <a href="<?php echo tep_href_link(FILENAME_CHECKOUT_SHIPPING,
                                      '', 'SSL');
  ?>"class="headerNavigation">
                        <?php echo HEADER_TITLE_CHECKOUT; ?>
  </a>   
</td>
```

Replace with the following code, which adds a search form that checks subcategories and description in addition to product name for the search field, pre-filled with a short help text:

```
<td class="headerNavigation">  
  <?php echo $breadcrumb->trail(' &raquo; '); ?>
</td>
<td class="headerNavigation" align="right">
  <?php echo tep_draw_form('advanced_search',
  tep_href_link(FILENAME_ADVANCED_SEARCH_RESULT,
                                    '', 'NONSSL', false),
  'get') . tep_draw_hidden_field('inc_subcat','1') .
  tep_draw_hidden_field('search_in_description','1') .
  tep_draw_input_field('keywords', TEXT_ENTER_KEYWORDS ,
             'size="10" maxlength="30" onFocus="emptyMe()"
```

```
          style="width: ' . (BOX_WIDTH-30) . 'px"'); ?>
    </td>
    <td class="headerNavigation" width="10">
      <?php echo tep_hide_session_id() .
      tep_image_submit('button_quick_find.gif', BOX_HEADING_SEARCH,
      'style="border: 1px solid #000000;"') . '</form>';?>
    </td>
    <td align="right" class="headerNavigation" width="35%">
      <?php if (tep_session_is_registered('customer_id')) { ?>
      <a href="<?php echo tep_href_link(FILENAME_LOGOFF, '',
                                                    'SSL'); ?>"
      class="headerNavigation"><?php echo HEADER_TITLE_LOGOFF; ?>
      </a>  | <?php } ?>
      <a href="<?php echo tep_href_link(FILENAME_ACCOUNT,
                                            '', 'SSL'); ?>"
      class="headerNavigation">
                      <?php echo HEADER_TITLE_MY_ACCOUNT; ?>
      </a>  | 
      <a href="<?php echo tep_href_link(FILENAME_SHOPPING_CART); ?>"
      class="headerNavigation">
                      <?php echo HEADER_TITLE_CART_CONTENTS; ?>
      </a>  | 
      <a href="<?php echo tep_href_link(FILENAME_CHECKOUT_SHIPPING,
                                            '', 'SSL'); ?>
      "class="headerNavigation"><?php echo HEADER_TITLE_CHECKOUT; ?>
      </a>   
    </td>
```

A border was added around the search button to make it more intuitive for the user. The help text **enter keywords** is specified as the default value for the search-box input field; the input box clears as soon as the mouse clicks into it.

4. Open `catalog/includes/boxes/categories.php` and find the following in line 132. This is the section where the box content is defined:

```
$info_box_contents[] = array('text' => $categories_string);
```

Add immediately below it the following code to create a link for advanced-search options, which will be added to the category-box content:

```
$info_box_contents[] = array('text' => tep_draw_separator());

$text2 = '';

$text2 .=
'<a href="' . tep_href_link(FILENAME_ADVANCED_SEARCH) . '">' .
BOX_SEARCH_ADVANCED_SEARCH . '</a><br>';

$info_box_contents[] = array('text' => $text2);
```

5. Open `catalog/includes/column_left.php` and find the following in line 51:

```
require(DIR_WS_BOXES . 'search.php');
```

Comment out the search box by adding slashes right before the `require` statement:

```
//require(DIR_WS_BOXES . 'search.php');
```

Didn't that hit the spot? Bon appetit!

36. Set the Search-Result Value Independent of Admin Listings

This recipe will allow you to display as many, or as few, products on your result pages of product listing and **Advanced Search** as you would like, without sacrificing admin usability. We are adding a new key, **Search-Results Catalog**, to be used only for the catalog part of search-result limits while leaving the current value in place, so admin can continue to use it.

Presentation

This is what your product listing will look like when you set the parameter for **Search Results** in **Administration | Configuration | Maximum Values** to list only three products per page:

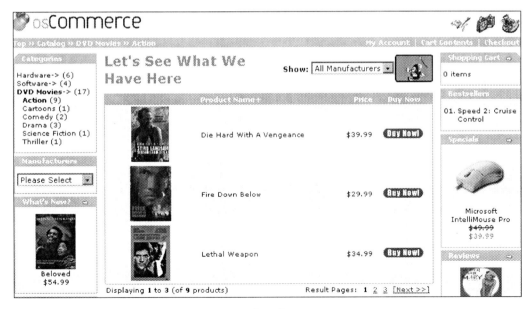

Chef's suggestion:

If you try to modify the value for search results in **Administration | Configuration | Search Results**, you will notice it also influences all listings for admin, resulting in **Countries**, **Catalog**, **Customers**, and **Orders** each displaying lists limited by the modified value. Having an extensive **Countries** list, for example, with display being limited to three per page, makes editing or viewing a tedious process; your listing will look like the one in the following screenshot.

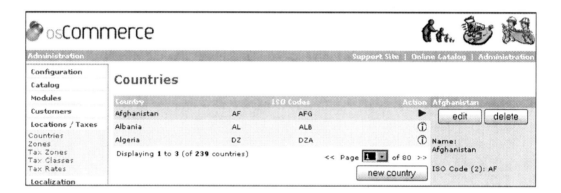

Ready to have your cake and eat it too?

Ingredients

New:

database.sql (to be run in phpMyAdmin)

Modified:

catalog/includes/modules/product_listing.php

Cooking

1. Run the following SQL statement in your database to create the new key MAX_DISPLAY_SEARCH_RESULTS_CATALOG for the **Search Results Catalog**:

```
INSERT INTO configuration (configuration_title,
configuration_key, configuration_value,
configuration_description, configuration_group_id,
sort_order, date_added)
```

```
VALUES ('Search Results Catalog',
    'MAX_DISPLAY_SEARCH_RESULTS_CATALOG', '20',
    'Amount of products to list in catalog', '3', '2', now());
```

Note that while **Amount** is not the perfect choice in wording, it was retained as it was used for the **Search Results** parameter in the original code.

2. Navigate to **Administration | Configuration | Maximum Values**. You will find your new key, **Search Results Catalog**, right above the regular **Search Results** key, with the value preset to **20**, so both are the same to start with. For our example, we have set the value for **Search Results Catalog** to **3**.

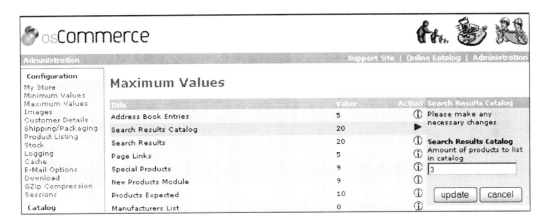

3. Open `catalog/includes/modules/product_listing.php` and find in line 13 the parameter `MAX_DISPLAY_SEARCH_RESULTS`, which does the limiting for paging:

```
$listing_split = new splitPageResults($listing_sql,
    MAX_DISPLAY_SEARCH_RESULTS, 'p.products_id');
```

Change to:

```
$listing_split = new splitPageResults($listing_sql,
    MAX_DISPLAY_SEARCH_RESULTS_CATALOG, 'p.products_id');
```

Wasn't that a piece of cake? Bon appetit!

37. Add an All Manufacturers Page to the Manufacturers Infobox

Many customers prefer to see the logos of all manufacturers instead of just seeing the manufacturers' name in a drop-down list. This module adds a new page that showcases all logos in a neat infobox. The new page can be accessed by a link added at the bottom of the current **Manufacturers** box.

Presentation

Your screen will display all your manufacturers like this:

Let's see what's in Mother Hubard's Cupboards!

Ingredients

> **New:**
>
> catalog/includes/modules/manufacturers.php
>
> **Modified:**
>
> catalog/includes/languages/english.php
> catalog/includes/boxes/manufacturers.php
> catalog/index.php

Cooking

1. Add the following define statement to catalog/includes/languages/english.php:

   ```
   define('TEXT_BOX_ALL_MANUFACTURERS', 'All Manufacturers');
   ```

   Note that the define statement for All Manufacturers already exists for index.php and advanced_search.php, but has to be declared in english.php so that all files can read it. The existing expressions could be converted into this new define and removed; we decided to leave them in so text can be adapted independently.

2. Open catalog/includes/boxes/manufacturers.php and find the array that created the manufacturers drop-down form in line 52:

```
$info_box_contents[] =
                array('form' => tep_draw_form('manufacturers',
    tep_href_link(FILENAME_DEFAULT, '', 'NONSSL', false), 'get'),
        'text' => tep_draw_pull_down_menu('manufacturers_id',
        $manufacturers_array,
                (isset($HTTP_GET_VARS['manufacturers_id']) ?
        $HTTP_GET_VARS['manufacturers_id'] : ''),
        'onChange="this.form.submit();" size="' .
            MAX_MANUFACTURERS_LIST . ' " style="width: 100%"') .
                                    tep_hide_session_id());
```

Add right below it the following code that adds a new link to the
All Manufacturers page:

```
$info_box_contents[] = array('align' => 'center',
    'text' => '<a href="' . tep_href_link(FILENAME_DEFAULT,
    'manufacturers_id=0') . '"><b>' . TEXT_BOX_ALL_MANUFACTURERS .
    '</b></a>');
```

3. Create a new file catalog/includes/modules/manufacturers.php using the following code, which will be included in index.php to show all manufacturers' logos:

```
<?php
/*
  $Id: manufacturers.php,v 1.00 2006/06/24 00:00:00 mm Exp $

  Module written by Monika Mathé
  http://www.monikamathe.com

  Module Copyright (c) 2006 Monika Mathé

  osCommerce, Open Source E-Commerce Solutions
  http://www.oscommerce.com

  Copyright (c) 2003 osCommerce

  Released under the GNU General Public License
*/
?>
<!-- manufacturers //-->
<?php
```

```
$info_box_contents = array();
$info_box_contents[] = array('text' =>
                                TEXT_BOX_ALL_MANUFACTURERS);

new contentBoxHeading($info_box_contents);
$manufacturers_query =
            tep_db_query("select distinct m.manufacturers_id,
m.manufacturers_name, m.manufacturers_image from " .
      TABLE_MANUFACTURERS . " m where manufacturers_name <>
                            '' order by manufacturers_name");

$row = 0;
$col = 0;
$info_box_contents = array();
while ($manufacturers =
                tep_db_fetch_array($manufacturers_query)) {

  $info_box_contents[$row][$col] = array('align' => 'center',
      'params' => 'class="smallText" width="33%"
      valign="middle"', 'text' => '<a href="' .
      tep_href_link(FILENAME_DEFAULT, 'manufacturers_id=' .
      $manufacturers['manufacturers_id']) . '">' .
      tep_image(DIR_WS_IMAGES .
      $manufacturers['manufacturers_image'],
  $manufacturers['manufacturers_name'], SMALL_IMAGE_WIDTH,
  SMALL_IMAGE_HEIGHT) .'</a>');

  $col ++;
  if ($col > 2) {
    $col = 0;
    $row ++;
  }
}

new contentBox($info_box_contents);
?>
<!-- manufacturers_eof //-->
```

4. The **All Manufacturers** page does not require a filter, so we will introduce a conditional statement before the product-list filter in catalog/index.php. Open the file and nest the product-list filter starting on line 234 within a conditional statement as seen below:

```
// optional Product List Filter
if (!isset($HTTP_GET_VARS['manufacturers_id']) ||
(isset($HTTP_GET_VARS['manufacturers_id']) &&
$HTTP_GET_VARS['manufacturers_id'] > 0)) {
```

```
if (PRODUCT_LIST_FILTER > 0) {
  if (isset($HTTP_GET_VARS['manufacturers_id'])) {
    $filterlist_sql = "select distinct c.categories_id as id,
    cd.categories_name as name from " .
                                      TABLE_PRODUCTS . " p, " .
    TABLE_PRODUCTS_TO_CATEGORIES . " p2c, " .
    TABLE_CATEGORIES . " c, " . TABLE_CATEGORIES_DESCRIPTION .
    " cd where p.products_status = '1' and p.products_id =
    p2c.products_id and p2c.categories_id = c.categories_id
    and p2c.categories_id = cd.categories_id
    and cd.language_id = '" . (int)$languages_id . "'
    and p.manufacturers_id = '" .
    (int)$HTTP_GET_VARS['manufacturers_id'] .
    "' order by cd.categories_name";
  } else {
    $filterlist_sql=
                  "select distinct m.manufacturers_id as id,
    m.manufacturers_name as name from " .
    TABLE_PRODUCTS . " p, " . TABLE_PRODUCTS_TO_CATEGORIES .
    " p2c, " . TABLE_MANUFACTURERS . " m
    where p.products_status = '1'
    and p.manufacturers_id = m.manufacturers_id
    and p.products_id = p2c.products_id
    and p2c.categories_id = '" . (int)$current_category_id .
    "' order by m.manufacturers_name";
  }
  $filterlist_query = tep_db_query($filterlist_sql);
  if (tep_db_num_rows($filterlist_query) > 1) {
   echo '            <td align="center" class="main">' .
   tep_draw_form('filter', FILENAME_DEFAULT, 'get') .
   TEXT_SHOW . ' ';
   if (isset($HTTP_GET_VARS['manufacturers_id'])) {
     echo tep_draw_hidden_field('manufacturers_id',
     $HTTP_GET_VARS['manufacturers_id']);
     $options = array(array('id' => '',
                         'text' => TEXT_ALL_CATEGORIES));
   } else {
     echo tep_draw_hidden_field('cPath', $cPath);
     $options = array(array('id' => '',
     'text' => TEXT_ALL_MANUFACTURERS));
   }
   echo tep_draw_hidden_field('sort',
                               $HTTP_GET_VARS['sort']);
   while ($filterlist =
                 tep_db_fetch_array($filterlist_query)) {
     $options[] = array('id' => $filterlist['id'],
```

```
                  'text' => $filterlist['name']);
              }
              echo tep_draw_pull_down_menu('filter_id', $options,
              (isset($HTTP_GET_VARS['filter_id']) ?
              $HTTP_GET_VARS['filter_id'] : ''),
              'onchange="this.form.submit()"');
              echo '</form></td>' . "\n";
            }
          }
        }
```

5. Find in line 279 the call for the product-listing module:

```
<tr>
   <td><?php include(DIR_WS_MODULES .
                          FILENAME_PRODUCT_LISTING); ?></td>
</tr>
```

Replace with the following code, again adding a conditional statement to decide which file to include:

```
<?php
  if (isset($HTTP_GET_VARS['manufacturers_id']) &&
  $HTTP_GET_VARS['manufacturers_id'] > 0) {
?>
 <tr>
  <td><?php include(DIR_WS_MODULES . FILENAME_PRODUCT_LISTING);
                                               ?></td>
 </tr>
<?php
  } else {
?>
 <tr>
    <td><?php include(DIR_WS_MODULES . 'manufacturers.php');
                                               ?></td>
 </tr>
<?php
     }
?>
```

This ensures that the product-listing module will be replaced by the new manufacturers module if the **All Manufacturers** link is used.

That lined up like peas in a pod! Bon appetit!

38. Customize Your Product Listing with Individual Boxes for Each Manufacturer

This recipe will be of great assistance to you when you have many manufacturers and prefer to display each manufacturer's products in a separate product-listing box. This feature replaces the manufacturers drop-down filter and allows you to show all manufacturers at one glance, easily recognizable by the manufacturer's name at the top of the box. For this module to work, all your products must be assigned to a manufacturer.

Chef's suggestion:

You can create a new manufacturer called **Other** or **Uncategorized**, and add that via SQL statement in phpMyAdmin to all products that do not have a manufacturer assigned. For multilingual shops, the **Store Name** may be the best option as manufacturer name is not a language-dependent database entry. This method is explained in the Cooking section.

Presentation

Your product listing will look like this screenshot with all of the manufacturers in the search-result set having a box with navigation of their own:

Chef's suggestion:

For search-result limits set at less than 10, I suggest to also prepare the recipe **Set the Search Result Value Independent of Admin Listings**, discussed in this chapter; the search-result value set in default osCommerce influences all admin listings.

This recipe requires a bit more than shake and bake. Get ready to test your culinary skills!

Ingredients

> **New:**
> catalog/includes/modules/pl_sorting.php
> database.sql (to be run in phpMyAdmin for **Chef's suggestion,** assigning **Other** as the default manufacturer)
>
> **Modified:**
> catalog/index.php

Cooking

1. Open catalog/index.php and find this in line 191:

```
if ( (!isset($HTTP_GET_VARS['sort'])) || (!ereg('[1-8][ad]',
$HTTP_GET_VARS['sort'])) || (substr($HTTP_GET_VARS['sort'],
                                                      0, 1) >
sizeof($column_list)) ) {
  for ($i=0, $n=sizeof($column_list); $i<$n; $i++) {
  case 'PRODUCT_LIST_PRICE':
    $listing_sql .= "final_price " . ($sort_order == 'd' ?
                            'desc' : '') . ", pd.products_name";
    break;
  }
}
```

   Remove this code from index.php; sorting will now be included further down the code from a new, separate modules file as we will need it for each manufacturer of the listing result loop.

2. After you have removed that part from index.php, create the new file catalog/includes/modules/pl_sorting.php using the following code:

```
<?php
/*
    $Id: pl_sorting.php,v 1.00 2006/06/24 00:00:00 mm Exp $

    Module written by Monika Mathé
    http://www.monikamathe.com

    Module Copyright (c) 2006 Monika Mathé
```

```php
   osCommerce, Open Source E-Commerce Solutions
   http://www.oscommerce.com

   Copyright (c) 2003 osCommerce

   Released under the GNU General Public License
*/
?>
<?php
 $order_sql = '';

 if ( (!isset($HTTP_GET_VARS['sort'])) || (!ereg('[1-8][ad]',
 $HTTP_GET_VARS['sort'])) || (substr($HTTP_GET_VARS['sort'],
                                                 0, 1) >
 sizeof($column_list)) ) {
  for ($i=0, $n=sizeof($column_list); $i<$n; $i++) {
   if ($column_list[$i] == 'PRODUCT_LIST_NAME') {
    $HTTP_GET_VARS['sort'] = $i+1 . 'a';
    $order_sql .= " order by pd.products_name";
    break;
   }
  }
 } else {
  $sort_col = substr($HTTP_GET_VARS['sort'], 0 , 1);
  $sort_order = substr($HTTP_GET_VARS['sort'], 1);
  $order_sql .= ' order by ';
  switch ($column_list[$sort_col-1]) {
   case 'PRODUCT_LIST_MODEL':
    $order_sql .= "p.products_model " . ($sort_order == 'd' ?
                          'desc' : '') . ", pd.products_name";
    break;
   case 'PRODUCT_LIST_NAME':
    $order_sql .= "pd.products_name " . ($sort_order == 'd' ?
                                                'desc' : '');
    break;
   case 'PRODUCT_LIST_MANUFACTURER':
    $order_sql .= "m.manufacturers_name " .
    ($sort_order == 'd' ? 'desc' : '') . ", pd.products_name";
    break;
   case 'PRODUCT_LIST_QUANTITY':
    $order_sql .= "p.products_quantity " . ($sort_order == 'd'
                          ? 'desc' : '') . ", pd.products_name";
    break;
   case 'PRODUCT_LIST_IMAGE':
    $order_sql .= "pd.products_name";
```

```
      break;
    case 'PRODUCT_LIST_WEIGHT':
      $order_sql .= "p.products_weight " . ($sort_order == 'd' ?
      'desc' : '') . ", pd.products_name";
      break;
    case 'PRODUCT_LIST_PRICE':
      $order_sql .= "final_price " . ($sort_order == 'd' ?
                          'desc' : '') . ", pd.products_name";
      break;
    }
  }
?>
```

3. Go back to `catalog/index.php` and find this in line 191 where the listing queries are assembled and sorting is currently performed:

```
// show the products of a specified manufacturer
    if (isset($HTTP_GET_VARS['manufacturers_id'])) {
      if (isset($HTTP_GET_VARS['filter_id']) &&
tep_not_null($HTTP_GET_VARS['filter_id'])) {
// We are asked to show only a specific category
        $listing_sql = "select " . $select_column_list .
                                    " p.products_id,
    ...
    ...
    ...
    </table></td>
<?php
  } else { // default page
?>
```

Replace with the following code block, which removes the manufacturer filter, checks for categories, and separates into single manufacturer's boxes:

```
// show the products of a specified manufacturer
  if (isset($HTTP_GET_VARS['manufacturers_id'])) {
    if (isset($HTTP_GET_VARS['filter_id']) &&
    tep_not_null($HTTP_GET_VARS['filter_id'])) {
// We are asked to show only a specific category
      $listing_base_sql = "select " . $select_column_list .
      " p.products_id, p.manufacturers_id, p.products_price,
      p.products_tax_class_id, IF(s.status,
      s.specials_new_products_price,
      NULL) as specials_new_products_price,
      IF(s.status, s.specials_new_products_price,
      p.products_price) as final_price from " .
      TABLE_PRODUCTS . " p left join " . TABLE_SPECIALS .
```

```
                        " s on p.products_id = s.products_id, " .
                        TABLE_PRODUCTS_DESCRIPTION . " pd,
                        " . TABLE_MANUFACTURERS . " m, " .
                        TABLE_PRODUCTS_TO_CATEGORIES . "
                        p2c where p.products_status = '1'
                        and p.manufacturers_id = m.manufacturers_id
                        and m.manufacturers_id = '" .
                        (int)$HTTP_GET_VARS['manufacturers_id'] . "'
                        and p.products_id = p2c.products_id
                        and pd.products_id = p2c.products_id
                        and pd.language_id = '" .
                        (int)$languages_id . "' and p2c.categories_id = '" .
                        (int)$HTTP_GET_VARS['filter_id'] . "'";
                    } else {
        // We show them all
                        $listing_base_sql = "select " .
                        $select_column_list . " p.products_id,
                        p.manufacturers_id, p.products_price,
                        p.products_tax_class_id,
                        IF(s.status, s.specials_new_products_price, NULL) as
                        specials_new_products_price,
                        IF(s.status, s.specials_new_products_price,
                        p.products_price) as final_price from " .
                        TABLE_PRODUCTS . "
                        p left join " . TABLE_SPECIALS . " s on
                        p.products_id = s.products_id,
                        " . TABLE_PRODUCTS_DESCRIPTION . " pd,
                        " . TABLE_MANUFACTURERS . "
                        m where p.products_status = '1'
                        and pd.products_id = p.products_id
                        and pd.language_id = '" . (int)$languages_id . "'
                        and p.manufacturers_id = m.manufacturers_id
                        and m.manufacturers_id = '" .
                        (int)$HTTP_GET_VARS['manufacturers_id'] . "'";
                    }
            } else {
        // show the products in a given categorie
                if (isset($HTTP_GET_VARS['filter_id']) &&
                tep_not_null($HTTP_GET_VARS['filter_id'])) {
        // We are asked to show only specific category
                    $listing_base_sql = "select " . $select_column_list . "
                        p.products_id,
                        p.manufacturers_id, p.products_price,
                        p.products_tax_class_id,
                        IF(s.status, s.specials_new_products_price, NULL) as
```

```
        specials_new_products_price,
        IF(s.status, s.specials_new_products_price,
        p.products_price) as
        final_price from " . TABLE_PRODUCTS . "
        p left join " . TABLE_SPECIALS . "
        s on p.products_id = s.products_id,
        " . TABLE_PRODUCTS_DESCRIPTION . " pd,
        " . TABLE_MANUFACTURERS . " m,
        " . TABLE_PRODUCTS_TO_CATEGORIES . "
        p2c where p.products_status = '1'
        and p.manufacturers_id = m.manufacturers_id
        and m.manufacturers_id = '" .
        (int)$HTTP_GET_VARS['filter_id'] . "'
        and p.products_id = p2c.products_id
        and pd.products_id = p2c.products_id
        and pd.language_id = '" . (int)$languages_id . "'
        and p2c.categories_id = '" .
        (int)$current_category_id . "'";
      } else {
// We show them all
        $listing_base_sql = "select " .
        $select_column_list . "
        p.products_id, p.manufacturers_id, p.products_price,
        p.products_tax_class_id, IF(s.status,
        s.specials_new_products_price, NULL) as
        specials_new_products_price,
        IF(s.status, s.specials_new_products_price,
        p.products_price)
        as final_price from " . TABLE_PRODUCTS_DESCRIPTION . "
        pd, " . TABLE_PRODUCTS . " p left join " .
        TABLE_MANUFACTURERS . "
        m on p.manufacturers_id = m.manufacturers_id left join
        " . TABLE_SPECIALS . " s on p.products_id =
        s.products_id, " . TABLE_PRODUCTS_TO_CATEGORIES . "
        p2c where p.products_status = '1'
        and p.products_id = p2c.products_id
        and pd.products_id = p2c.products_id
        and pd.language_id = '" . (int)$languages_id . "'
        and p2c.categories_id = '" .
        (int)$current_category_id . "'";
        }
      }
    ?>
      <td width="100%" valign="top"><table border="0"
      width="100%" cellspacing="0" cellpadding="0">
        <tr>
```

```
        <td><table border=
        "0" width="100%" cellspacing="0" cellpadding="0">
          <tr>
            <td class=
              "pageHeading"><?php echo HEADING_TITLE; ?></td>
<?php
// optional Product List Filter
  if (PRODUCT_LIST_FILTER > 0) {
    if (!isset($HTTP_GET_VARS['manufacturers_id'])) {
      $filterlist_sql =
                  "select distinct c.categories_id as id,
      cd.categories_name as name from " .
      TABLE_PRODUCTS . " p, " .
      TABLE_PRODUCTS_TO_CATEGORIES . " p2c, " .
      TABLE_CATEGORIES . " c, " .
      TABLE_CATEGORIES_DESCRIPTION .
      " cd where p.products_status = '1'
      and p.products_id = p2c.products_id
      and p2c.categories_id = c.categories_id
      and p2c.categories_id = cd.categories_id
      and cd.language_id = '" . (int)$languages_id . "'
      and p.manufacturers_id = '" .
      (int)$HTTP_GET_VARS['manufacturers_id'] . "'
        order by cd.categories_name";
      $filterlist_query = tep_db_query($filterlist_sql);
      if (tep_db_num_rows($filterlist_query) > 1) {
        echo '             <td align="center" class="main">' .
        tep_draw_form('filter', FILENAME_DEFAULT, 'get') .
        TEXT_SHOW . ' ';
       if (isset($HTTP_GET_VARS['manufacturers_id'])) {
         echo tep_draw_hidden_field('manufacturers_id',
         $HTTP_GET_VARS['manufacturers_id']);
         $options = array(array('id' => '',
         'text' => TEXT_ALL_CATEGORIES));
       } else {
         echo tep_draw_hidden_field('cPath', $cPath);
         $options = array(array('id' => '',
         'text' => TEXT_ALL_MANUFACTURERS));
       }
      echo tep_draw_hidden_field('sort',
      $HTTP_GET_VARS['sort']);
      while ($filterlist =
                  tep_db_fetch_array($filterlist_query)) {
      $options[] = array('id' => $filterlist['id'],
      'text' => $filterlist['name']);
```

```
      }
      echo tep_draw_pull_down_menu('filter_id', $options,
      (isset($HTTP_GET_VARS['filter_id']) ?
      $HTTP_GET_VARS['filter_id'] : ''),
      'onchange="this.form.submit()"');
      echo '</form></td>' . "\n";
    }
  }
}

// Get the right image for the top-right
  $image = DIR_WS_IMAGES . 'table_background_list.gif';
  if (isset($HTTP_GET_VARS['manufacturers_id'])) {
    $image =
        tep_db_query("select manufacturers_image from " .
    TABLE_MANUFACTURERS . " where manufacturers_id = '" .
    (int)$HTTP_GET_VARS['manufacturers_id'] . "'");
    $image = tep_db_fetch_array($image);
    $image = $image['manufacturers_image'];
  } elseif ($current_category_id) {
    $image = tep_db_query("select categories_image from
    " . TABLE_CATEGORIES . " where
    categories_id = '" . (int)$current_category_id . "'");
    $image = tep_db_fetch_array($image);
    $image = $image['categories_image'];
  }
?>
            <td align="right"><?php echo tep_image(
                DIR_WS_IMAGES . $image, HEADING_TITLE,
                HEADING_IMAGE_WIDTH, HEADING_IMAGE_HEIGHT);
          ?></td>
          </tr>
        </table></td>
      </tr>
      <tr>
          <td><?php echo tep_draw_separator('pixel_trans.
                                        gif', '100%', '10');
          ?></td>
      </tr>

<?php
    if (isset($HTTP_GET_VARS['manufacturers_id'])) {

    include(DIR_WS_MODULES . 'pl_sorting.php');
```

```php
      $listing_sql = $listing_base_sql . $order_sql;
?>
        <tr>
          <td><?php include(DIR_WS_MODULES .
          FILENAME_PRODUCT_LISTING); ?></td>
        </tr>
<?php
   } else {
    $manufacturers_query =
          tep_db_query("select distinct m.manufacturers_id,
    m.manufacturers_name from " . TABLE_PRODUCTS . " p, " .
    TABLE_PRODUCTS_TO_CATEGORIES . " p2c, " .
    TABLE_MANUFACTURERS . " m where p.products_status = '1'
    and p.manufacturers_id = m.manufacturers_id
    and p.products_id = p2c.products_id
    and p2c.categories_id = '" .
    (int)$current_category_id . "'
    order by m.manufacturers_name");
    while ($manufacturers =
                 tep_db_fetch_array($manufacturers_query)) {
    $listing_manu_sql = " and m.manufacturers_id = '" .
    $manufacturers['manufacturers_id'] . "'";
    include(DIR_WS_MODULES . 'pl_sorting.php');

    $listing_sql =
          $listing_base_sql . $listing_manu_sql . $order_sql;
?>
    <tr>
      <td class="main"><?php echo '<b>' .
      $manufacturers['manufacturers_name']
      .'</b>'; ?></td>
    </tr>
    <tr>
      <td><?php include(DIR_WS_MODULES .
                            FILENAME_PRODUCT_LISTING); ?></td>
    </tr>
    <tr>
      <td><?php echo tep_draw_separator('pixel_trans.gif',
                                        '100%', '10');
    ?></td>
    </tr>
<?php
   }
  }
?>

    </table></td>
<?php
```

```
    } else { // default page
?>
```

4. If you do not have manufacturers assigned to all products yet, follow the **Chef's suggestion** and create a new manufacturer called **Other**, **Uncategorized**, or your **Store Name** for multilingual stores. Copy its `manufacturers_id` from the URL in admin. (You can see something similar to `http://localhost/catalog/admin/manufacturers.php?page=1&mID=5`, when you click on the manufacturer; the `manufacturers_id` here would be 5.) Run the following SQL statement in your database, replacing the highlighted part with the id that you copied from admin:

```
UPDATE PRODUCTS set manufacturers_id =
                                '5' where manufacturers_id = '0'
or manufacturers_id is NULL;
```

Chef's suggestion:

If you replace line 388, `$manufacturers_array = array(array('id' => '', 'text' => TEXT_NONE));`, in `catalog/admin/categories.php` with the plain array definition, `$manufacturers_array = array();`, you will no longer have the option to create products that have no manufacturer assigned. You can even set your default manufacturer as the default in the drop down by amending line 494, adding a condition to use the default manufacturer if empty.

Excellent work chopping and sifting! Bon appetit!

Summary

With the recipes in this chapter added to your weekly menu list, you can now offer a visually appealing, and in many ways optimized, search function for your customers. Visitors will now immediately find your intuitive search box. They can choose to view all manufacturers' logos with a single click. You can now neatly separate manufacturers in product listing into individual display boxes without having your admin area suffer from these changes!

Now that those perfect products have been found by your customers, it's time to get them added to their carts for checkout! After all, that is what online shopping is about! Let's now take a closer look at how to make this process a most enjoyable treat for your customers.

6

Grill that Checkout Process

Your customer has filled his plate high with the most inviting products of your buffet table, and you are certainly eager to provide him with an intuitive and pleasing experience during the checkout process. Let us take a hearty bite into your **Shopping Cart** page, **Shipping** page, **Payment** page, and your **Order Confirmation** email, which can all be seasoned to suit your customers' tastes.

In this chapter, you will learn how to:

- Make removing products from the cart more intuitive
- Remove Delivery Address modification from your Shipping page
- Modify Shipping Method display for the Confirmation page
- Add a sophisticated gift wrapping option to the Shipping page
- Add the option to donate during checkout
- Personalize your Order Confirmation email
- Add your customers' email addresses and phone numbers to your Order Confirmation email
- Add your customers' fax numbers to your Order Confirmation email
- Add the products' manufacturers to your Order Confirmation email
- Add the products' category tree to your Order Confirmation email

39. Make Removing Products from the Cart more Intuitive

The default version of osCommerce offers checkboxes for the customers to mark products they would like to remove from their cart. While that is a great approach if your customers would like to remove many products at once (which we do not encourage), it requires clicking the **Update** button for the delete process to occur; that means two steps rather than a more intuitive one-step approach. This recipe offers the single-click removal of a product from the cart.

Presentation

Your screen will look like this with the addition of delete buttons for each product:

Is it time to clean up your charcoal grill? Let's get the grate off, and brush it out!

Ingredients

New:

```
catalog/images/icons/delete.gif
```

Modified:

```
catalog/includes/application_top.php
catalog/stylesheet.css
catalog/shopping_cart.php
```

Cooking

1. Open `catalog/includes/application_top.php` and find this in line 329:

```
switch ($HTTP_GET_VARS['action']) {
// customer wants to update the product quantity in
// their shopping cart
```

   Add the following code directly below it to allow a single product to be deleted from the cart:

```
// customer wants to delete a single product from his
// shopping cart
case 'delete_product' :
                    if (isset($HTTP_GET_VARS['products_id'])) {
$cart->remove($HTTP_GET_VARS['products_id']);
}
tep_redirect(tep_href_link($goto,
                        tep_get_all_get_params($parameters)));
break;
```

2. Open `catalog/stylesheet.css` and add the following new class for the column on the left, which has a yellow background color:

```
TD.productListing-data-color {
  font-family: Verdana, Arial, sans-serif;
  font-size: 10px;
  background: #ffcc66;
}
```

3. Add the new image `delete.gif` to your `catalog/images/icons` folder.

4. Open `catalog/shopping_cart.php` and find this in line 60 where the headings for the cart table are created:

```
$info_box_contents[0][] = array('align' => 'center',
  'params' => 'class="productListing-heading"',
  'text' => TABLE_HEADING_REMOVE);
```

   Replace it with the following code to remove the text heading for the delete column, which will now take up much less space:

```
$info_box_contents[0][] = array('align' => 'center',
  'params' => 'class="productListing-heading"',
  'text' => ' ');
```

5. Further down in the same file, find this in line 111:

```
$info_box_contents[$cur_row][] = array('align' => 'center',
  'params' => 'class="productListing-data" valign="top"',
```

```
'text' => tep_draw_checkbox_field('cart_delete[]',
$products[$i]['id']));
```

Replace it with the following code, which creates a delete link for each product and uses the new class for the background color of these cells. The default method we are replacing verified all checkboxes and quantities in the form and changed the cart.

```
$info_box_contents[$cur_row][] = array('align' => 'center',
    'params' => 'class="productListing-data-color"',
    'text' => '<a href="' . tep_href_link(basename($PHP_SELF),
    tep_get_all_get_params(array('action')) .
    'action=delete_product&products_id=' .
    $products[$i]['id']) . '">' . tep_image(DIR_WS_ICONS .
    'delete.gif', IMAGE_BUTTON_DELETE) . '</a>');
```

Fire her up, and get those steaks on the barbie! Bon appetit!

40. Remove Delivery Address Modification from Your Shipping Page

If you want to prohibit customers from specifying a shipping address that differs from their account registration address, then this recipe is for you. It removes the link to the **Checkout Shipping Address** page from your **Shipping** and **Confirmation** pages, and additionally, does not allow manual hacking in the URL.

Chef's suggestion:

This is a decision you should make very carefully, considering all implications such as the fact that sending a gift directly to the recipient is no longer possible or that you cannot have customers order with their home address as the billing address have sent their items to their office. It is often an option for very expensive items though, where you need to make sure that all addresses match to protect yourself from fraud.

Presentation

Your screen will look like this for your Checkout Shipping page:

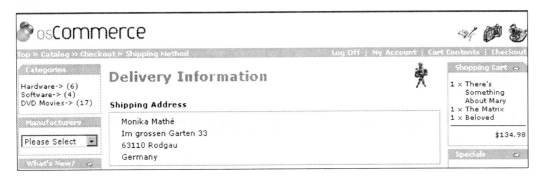

Your Checkout Confirmation page will look like this:

Ready to grill the bird without the stuffing?

Ingredients

> **Modified:**
>
> ```
> catalog/checkout_shipping.php
> catalog/checkout_shipping_address.php
> catalog/checkout_confirmation.php
> ```

Cooking

1. Open `catalog/checkout_shipping.php` and find this in line 229, the spot where the button for shipping address modification is defined:

    ```
    <tr>
      <td><?php echo tep_draw_separator('pixel_trans.gif',
                                          '10', '1'); ?>
    ```

```
        </td>
        <td class="main" width="50%" valign="top">
        <?php echo TEXT_CHOOSE_SHIPPING_DESTINATION . '<br>
        <br><a href="' . tep_href_link(FILENAME_CHECKOUT_SHIPPING_
        ADDRESS, '', 'SSL') . '">' . tep_image_button('button_change_
        address.gif', IMAGE_BUTTON_CHANGE_ADDRESS) . '</a>'; ?>
        </td>
        <td align="right" width="50%" valign="top">
        <table border="0" cellspacing="0" cellpadding="2">
        <tr>
        <td class="main" align="center" valign="top">
        <?php echo '<b>' . TITLE_SHIPPING_ADDRESS . '</b><br>' .
        tep_image(DIR_WS_IMAGES . 'arrow_south_east.gif'); ?>
        </td>
        <td><?php echo tep_draw_separator('pixel_trans.gif',
                                                 '10', '1'); ?>
        </td>
        <td class="main" valign="top">
        <?php echo tep_address_label($customer_id, $sendto, true,
        ' ', '<br>'); ?>
        </td>
        <td><?php echo tep_draw_separator('pixel_trans.gif',
                                                 '10', '1'); ?>
        </td>
        </tr>
        </table></td>
        </tr>
```

Replace it with this:

```
    <tr>
      <td width="10"><?php echo tep_draw_separator('pixel_trans.
                                      gif', '10', '1'); ?>
      </td>
      <td class="main" valign="top">
      <?php echo tep_address_label($customer_id,
      $sendto, true, ' ', '<br>'); ?>
      </td>
      <td><?php echo tep_draw_separator('pixel_trans.gif',
                                      '10', '1'); ?>
      </td>
    </tr>
```

2. Open `catalog/checkout_shipping_address.php` and find this in line 13:

    ```
    require('includes/application_top.php');
    ```

Add the following code below it, redirecting all customers who are trying to call this page by typing in the URL manually:

```
tep_redirect(tep_href_link(FILENAME_CHECKOUT_SHIPPING,
                                        '', 'SSL'));
```

3. Open `catalog/checkout_confirmation.php` and find this in line 130 where you can edit the shipping address on the confirmation page:

```
<tr>
 <td class="main"><?php echo '<b>' . HEADING_DELIVERY_ADDRESS .
                                        '</b>
 <a href="' . tep_href_link(FILENAME_CHECKOUT_SHIPPING_ADDRESS,
  '', 'SSL') . '"><span class="orderEdit">(' . TEXT_EDIT .
                                        ')</span>
 </a>'; ?>
 </td>
</tr>
```

Replace it with the following code, removing the link for editing the shipping address:

```
<tr>
  <td class="main"><?php echo '<b>' . HEADING_DELIVERY_ADDRESS
                                    . '</b>'; ?>
  </td>
</tr>
```

That was better than the Thanksgiving Dinner! Bon appetit!

41. Modify Shipping Method Display for the Confirmation Page

If you have long expressions for your shipping methods, with delivery-date information added for example, you may prefer to display the **Shipping Method** in two lines rather than one on your Checkout Confirmation page. This recipe shows you how to pinpoint where formatting is done, and how to modify the look to suit your needs.

Presentation

Your screen will display your **Shipping Method,** here **Flat Rate (Best way),** as in the following screenshot:

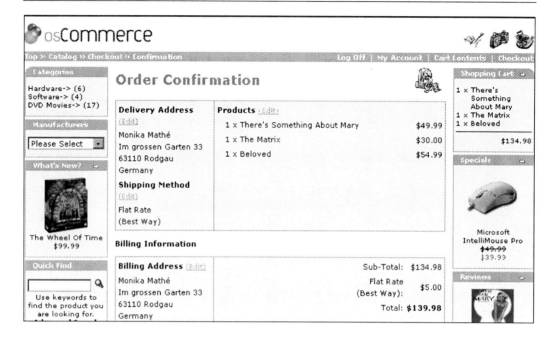

Let's add new flavor to your Marinade!

Ingredients

> **Modified:**
>
> `catalog/checkout_shipping.php`

Cooking

1. The relevant code hides in `catalog/checkout_shipping.php`. As surprising as this may be, that is the spot where the session information for shipping is filled, which includes formatting information. Therefore, find in line 120 the following code:

    ```
    $shipping = array('id' => $shipping,
       'title' => (($free_shipping == true) ? $quote[0]['methods']
       [0]['title'] : $quote[0]['module'] . ' (' . $quote[0]
       ['methods'][0]['title'] . ')'),
       'cost' => $quote[0]['methods'][0]['cost']);
    ```

Replace it with this code snippet, adding in a break to separate two lines:

```
$shipping = array('id' => $shipping,
  'title' => (($free_shipping == true) ?  $quote[0]['methods']
[0]['title'] : $quote[0]['module'] .
'<br>(' . $quote[0]['methods'][0]['title'] . ')'),
  'cost' => $quote[0]['methods'][0]['cost']);
```

A little goes a long way! Bon appetit!

42. Add a Sophisticated Gift Wrapping Option to the Shipping Page

For many shops, adding a gift-wrapping option is critical, as the majority of products purchased are sent as gifts and require that special royal treatment in presentation to their final recipient. This recipe shows you how to specify different gift wrapping options for a set fee, enable taxing if applicable, and offers the option to add a gift card with a personal message too. This module is coded in such a way that you are also able to offer different gift-wrapping papers to customers viewing your site in different languages; this means that you have the flexibility to offer wrapping paper with text in specific languages to specific customer groups.

Chef's suggestion:

This module is written to send all the items in a specific order gift wrapped. If you prefer to offer a gift-wrapping selection to each product instead, use the attribute options feature offered by default osCommerce. Create a new option group called `Gift Wrapping`, create option values for the gift wrapping paper choices, and assign them to each product.

Presentation

Your Checkout Shipping page will look like this:

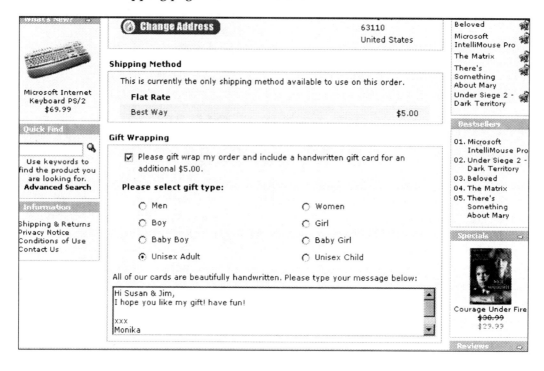

And your Checkout Confirmation page will look like this:

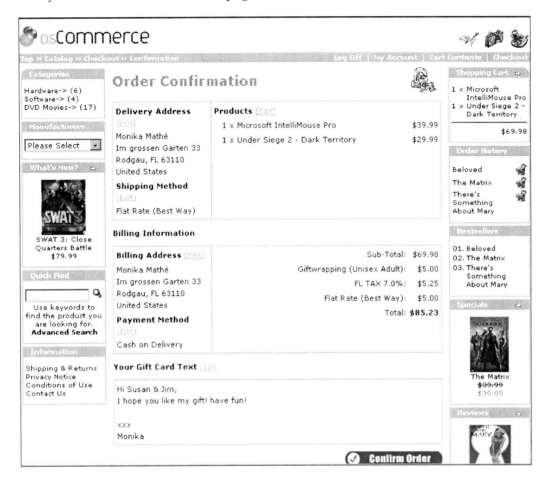

The **Gift Wrapping** option, if chosen for an order, will show on the Order History page with the gift-card text in the comment section.

Grape leaves, banana leaves, phyllo, or rice paper?

Ingredients

New:

catalog/includes/modules/order_total/ot_giftwrapping.php
catalog/includes/languages/english/modules/order_total/
                                    ot_giftwrapping.php
catalog/includes/modules/giftwrapping.php

Modified:

catalog/includes/functions/general.php
catalog/includes/classes/order.php
catalog/checkout_shipping.php
catalog/checkout_confirmation.php
catalog/checkout_process.php

Cooking

1. Open `catalog/includes/functions/general.php` and add the following
   new function directly above the closing `?>` PHP tag to get the cost for gift
   wrapping:

```
function tep_get_giftwrapping_cost() {
global $order, $currencies;

$giftwrapping_cost = MODULE_ORDER_TOTAL_GIFTWRAPPING_COST;
if (MODULE_ORDER_TOTAL_GIFTWRAPPING_TAX_CLASS > 0) {
 $giftwrapping_tax =
   tep_get_tax_rate(MODULE_ORDER_TOTAL_GIFTWRAPPING_TAX_CLASS,
   $order->delivery['country']['id'],
                            $order->delivery['zone_id']);

if (DISPLAY_PRICE_WITH_TAX == 'true') {
  $giftwrapping_cost += tep_calculate_tax($giftwrapping_cost,
  $giftwrapping_tax);
 }
}
return $giftwrapping_cost;
}
```

2. Create the new module file `catalog/includes/modules/order_total/`
   `ot_giftwrapping.php` using the following code:

```
<?php
/*
```

```
$Id: ot_giftwrapping.php,v 1.00 2006/07/04 00:00:00 mm Exp $

Module written by Monika Mathé
http://www.monikamathe.com

Module Copyright (c) 2006 Monika Mathé

osCommerce, Open Source E-Commerce Solutions
http://www.oscommerce.com

Copyright (c) 2003 osCommerce

Released under the GNU General Public License
*/

class ot_giftwrapping {
  var $title, $output;

  function ot_giftwrapping() {
    $this->code = 'ot_giftwrapping';
    $this->title = MODULE_ORDER_TOTAL_GIFTWRAPPING_TITLE;
    $this->description =
                MODULE_ORDER_TOTAL_GIFTWRAPPING_DESCRIPTION;
    $this->enabled =
        ((MODULE_ORDER_TOTAL_GIFTWRAPPING_STATUS == 'true') ?
                                        true : false);
    $this->tax_class =
                MODULE_ORDER_TOTAL_GIFTWRAPPING_TAX_CLASS;
    $this->sort_order =
                MODULE_ORDER_TOTAL_GIFTWRAPPING_SORT_ORDER;

    $this->output = array();

    if ($this->enabled == true) {
      global $giftwrapping_method;
      if ($giftwrapping_method == '') {
        $this->enabled = false;
      }
    }
  }

  function process() {
    global $order, $currencies;

    $giftwrapping_cost = tep_get_giftwrapping_cost();

    if (tep_not_null($order->info['giftwrapping_method'])) {
```

```
                     $order->info['total'] += $giftwrapping_cost;

            if ($this->tax_class > 0) {
              $giftwrapping_tax_description =
              tep_get_tax_description($this->tax_class,
              $order->delivery['country']['id'],
              $order->delivery['zone_id']);
              $giftwrapping_tax =
          tep_get_tax_rate(MODULE_ORDER_TOTAL_GIFTWRAPPING_TAX_CLASS,
$order->delivery['country']['id'], $order->delivery['zone_id']);

              $order->info['tax'] +=
tep_calculate_tax($giftwrapping_cost, $giftwrapping_tax);
$order->info['tax_groups']["$giftwrapping_tax_description"] +=
          tep_calculate_tax($giftwrapping_cost, $giftwrapping_tax);
$order->info['total'] +=
          tep_calculate_tax($giftwrapping_cost, $giftwrapping_tax);
            }

          }
$this->output[] = array(
          'title' => $order->info['giftwrapping_method'] . ':',
          'text' => $currencies->format($giftwrapping_cost, true,
$order->info['currency'], $order->info['currency_value']),
          'value' => $giftwrapping_cost);
        }

    function check() {
          if (!isset($this->_check)) {
$check_query = tep_db_query("select configuration_value from " .
      TABLE_CONFIGURATION . " where configuration_key =
                    'MODULE_ORDER_TOTAL_GIFTWRAPPING_STATUS'");
$this->_check = tep_db_num_rows($check_query);
          }

      return $this->_check;
      }

    function keys() {
      return array('MODULE_ORDER_TOTAL_GIFTWRAPPING_STATUS',
                'MODULE_ORDER_TOTAL_GIFTWRAPPING_SORT_ORDER',
                'MODULE_ORDER_TOTAL_GIFTWRAPPING_COST',
                'MODULE_ORDER_TOTAL_GIFTWRAPPING_TAX_CLASS');
      }
```

```
function install() {
    tep_db_query("insert into " . TABLE_CONFIGURATION .
    " (configuration_title, configuration_key,
        configuration_value, configuration_description,
        configuration_group_id, sort_order,
        set_function, date_added)
    values ('Display Giftwrapping',
    'MODULE_ORDER_TOTAL_GIFTWRAPPING_STATUS', 'true',
    'Do you want to display the order giftwrapping cost?',
    '6', '1','tep_cfg_select_option(array(\'true\',
                                \'false\'), ', now())");
    tep_db_query("insert into " . TABLE_CONFIGURATION .
    " (configuration_title, configuration_key,
        configuration_value, configuration_description,
        configuration_group_id, sort_order, date_added)
    values ('Sort Order',
    'MODULE_ORDER_TOTAL_GIFTWRAPPING_SORT_ORDER',
    '2', 'Sort order of display.', '6', '2', now())");
    tep_db_query("insert into " . TABLE_CONFIGURATION .
    " (configuration_title, configuration_key,
        configuration_value, configuration_description,
        configuration_group_id, sort_order, use_function,
        date_added)
     values ('Giftwrapping surcharge',
     'MODULE_ORDER_TOTAL_GIFTWRAPPING_COST', '5',
     'Surcharge for giftwrapping.', '6', '4',
     'currencies->format', now())");
    tep_db_query("insert into " . TABLE_CONFIGURATION .
    " (configuration_title, configuration_key,
        configuration_value, configuration_description,
        configuration_group_id, sort_order, use_function,
        set_function, date_added)
     values ('Tax Class',
     'MODULE_ORDER_TOTAL_GIFTWRAPPING_TAX_CLASS', '0',
     'Use the following tax class on the giftwrapping fee.',
     '6', '5', 'tep_get_tax_class_title',
     'tep_cfg_pull_down_tax_classes(', now())");
    }

function remove() {
    tep_db_query("delete from " . TABLE_CONFIGURATION .
    " where configuration_key in ('" . implode("', '",
                                $this->keys()) . "')");
    }
}
?>
```

3. Create the matching new language file `catalog/includes/languages/ english/modules/order_total/ot_giftwrapping.php` **with the following define statements:**

```php
<?php
/*
  $Id: ot_giftwrapping.php,v 1.00 2006/07/04 00:00:00 mm Exp $

  Module written by Monika Mathé
  http://www.monikamathe.com

  Module Copyright (c) 2006 Monika Mathé

  osCommerce, Open Source E-Commerce Solutions
  http://www.oscommerce.com

  Copyright (c) 2003 osCommerce

  Released under the GNU General Public License
*/

define('MODULE_ORDER_TOTAL_GIFTWRAPPING_TITLE',
                                        'Giftwrapping');
define('MODULE_ORDER_TOTAL_GIFTWRAPPING_DESCRIPTION',
                                'Order giftwrapping cost');

//attention: commas must only be used for separating different
//papers, if used in a single paper things get messed up! use
//dashes instead!!!
define('MODULE_GIFTWRAPPING_PAPER', 'Men,Women,Boy,Girl,
Baby Boy,Baby Girl,Unisex Adult,Unisex Child');

define('TABLE_HEADING_GIFTWRAPPING', 'Gift Wrapping');
define('TEXT_WANT_GIFTWRAP', 'Please gift wrap my order and
  include a handwritten gift card for an additional %s.');
define('TEXT_CHOOSE_GIFTCARD_METHOD', 'Please select gift
                                        type:');
define('TEXT_CARD_GIFTWRAPPING', 'All of our cards are
  beautifully handwritten. Please type your message below:');
define('TEXT_CARD', 'Gift Card Text: ');
define('HEADING_ORDER_GIFTCARD', 'Your Gift Card Text');
?>
```

As you can see, papers for gift wrapping are specified on a language basis, so you can have the same papers for all languages on your website, or completely different ones for each language.

Chef's suggestion:

You can hack this code and also add images for your gift wrapping choices. You will need another parameter in each key inside MODULE_GIFTWRAPPING_PAPER to match the paper choice, and be careful to display the paper image with the radio button while using the text string for the database. You could create double value keys similar to the Table Rate shipping cost key.

4. Open `catalog/includes/classes/order.php` and find the following code for the shipping query in line 47:

```
$shipping_method_query = tep_db_query("select title from " .
TABLE_ORDERS_TOTAL . " where orders_id = '" .
                (int)$order_id . "' and class = 'ot_shipping'");
$shipping_method = tep_db_fetch_array($shipping_method_query);
```

Add directly below it the following two lines for giftwrapping:

```
$giftwrapping_method_query = tep_db_query("select title from " .
TABLE_ORDERS_TOTAL . " where orders_id = '" . (int)$order_id . "'
                        and class = 'ot_giftwrapping'");
$giftwrapping_method =
                tep_db_fetch_array($giftwrapping_method_query);
```

5. Further down in line 67, find the following code where shipping information is added to the order array:

```
'shipping_method' => ((substr($shipping_method['title'],
-1) == ':') ? substr(strip_tags($shipping_method['title']),
        0, -1) : strip_tags($shipping_method['title']))));
```

Replace it with the following, adding information about the gift wrapping chosen:

```
'shipping_method' => ((substr($shipping_method['title'],
-1) == ':') ? substr(strip_tags($shipping_method['title']),
0, -1) : strip_tags($shipping_method['title'])),
'giftwrapping_method' =>
((substr($giftwrapping_method['title'], -1) == ':')
? substr(strip_tags($giftwrapping_method['title']), 0, -1) :
strip_tags($giftwrapping_method['title']))));
```

6. In line 167, find this define for comments:

```
'comments' => (isset($GLOBALS['comments']) ?
                        $GLOBALS['comments'] : ''));
```

Replace it with the following code, adding all gift-wrapping information from your session globals:

```
'comments' => (isset($GLOBALS['comments']) ?
$GLOBALS['comments'] : ''),
'giftwrap' => (isset($GLOBALS['giftwrap']) ?
$GLOBALS['giftwrap'] : ''),
'giftwrapping_method' => (isset($GLOBALS['giftwrapping_method']) ?
$GLOBALS['giftwrapping_method'] : ''),
'giftcard' => (isset($GLOBALS['giftcard']) ?
                                     $GLOBALS['giftcard'] : ''));
```

7. Create the new file `catalog/includes/modules/giftwrapping.php`, which will be called from the Checkout Shipping page to be included if the module has been enabled:

```php
<?php
/*
    $Id: giftwrapping.php,v 1.00 2006/07/04 00:00:00 mm Exp $

    Module written by Monika Mathé
    http://www.monikamathe.com

    Module Copyright (c) 2006 Monika Mathé

    osCommerce, Open Source E-Commerce Solutions
    http://www.oscommerce.com

    Copyright (c) 2003 osCommerce

    Released under the GNU General Public License
*/
?>
 <tr>
  <td><table border="0" width="100%" cellspacing=
                                    "0" cellpadding="2">
   <tr>
    <td class="main"><b><?php echo TABLE_HEADING_GIFTWRAPPING;
                                    ?></b></td>
   </tr>
  </table></td>
 </tr>
 <tr>
  <td><table border="0" width="100%" cellspacing=
                                    "1" cellpadding="2"
   class="infoBox">
   <tr class="infoBoxContents">
```

```
      <td><table border="0" width="100%" cellspacing=
                                    "1" cellpadding="2">
    <tr>
     <td><table border="0" width="100%" cellspacing=
                                    "0" cellpadding="2">
      <tr>
       <td width="10"><?php echo tep_draw_separator(
                       'pixel_trans.gif', '10', '1'); ?>
       </td>
       <td width="20" valign="top">
         <?php echo tep_draw_checkbox_field('giftwrap','1',
          ($giftwrap == '1' ? true : false)); ?>
        </td>
       <td class="main">
         <?php echo sprintf(TEXT_WANT_GIFTWRAP,
          $currencies->format(tep_get_giftwrapping_cost())); ?>
        </td>
       </tr>
      </table></td>
     </tr>
     <tr>
      <td><table border="0" width="100%" cellspacing=
                                    "0" cellpadding="2">
       <tr>
        <td width="10"><?php echo tep_draw_separator(
                        'pixel_trans.gif', '10', '1'); ?></td>
        <td class="main" width="50%" valign="top"><b><?php echo
         TEXT_CHOOSE_GIFTCARD_METHOD; ?></b></td>
        <td><?php echo tep_draw_separator(
                                'pixel_trans.gif', '10', '1');
         ?></td>
       </tr>
      </table></td>
     </tr>
     <tr>
      <td><table border="0" width="100%" cellspacing=
                                    "0" cellpadding="2">
       <tr>
<?php
   $paperchoice = split("[,]" , MODULE_GIFTWRAPPING_PAPER);
   $size = sizeof($paperchoice);
   $rows = 0;
   for ($i=0, $n=$size; $i<$n; $i++) {
    $rows++;
```

```
            echo '<td>' . tep_draw_separator('pixel_trans.gif',
                                                '10', '1') . '</td>
        <td width="20" valign="top">' .
        tep_draw_radio_field('giftwrapping_method',
        $paperchoice[$i] , $i==0? true : false) .
        '</td><td valign="top" class="main">' .
        $paperchoice[$i] . '</td>' . "\n";
        if ((($rows / 2) == floor($rows / 2)) && ($rows != $n)) {
        echo '</tr>' . "\n";
        echo '<tr>' . "\n";
        }
      }
    ?>
        </table></td>
      </tr>
      <tr>
        <td><table border="0" width="100%" cellspacing=
                                        "0" cellpadding="2">
          <tr>
            <td class="main"><?php echo TEXT_CARD_GIFTWRAPPING;
                                            ?></td>
          </tr>
          <tr>
            <td><?php echo tep_draw_textarea_field('giftcard',
            'soft', '', '', '','style="width:100%; height:70px;"');
                                            ?></td>
          </tr>
         </table></td>
        </tr>
       </table></td>
      </tr>
     </table></td>
    </tr>
    <tr>
     <td><?php echo tep_draw_separator('pixel_trans.gif',
                                        '100%', '10');
     ?></td>
    </tr>
```

8. Open `catalog/checkout_shipping.php` and find this in line 42:

    ```
    require(DIR_WS_CLASSES . 'order.php');
    $order = new order;
    ```

    Add directly *above* it, the following code snippet:

    ```
    //gift wrap section begin
    ```

```
if (tep_session_is_registered('giftwrap'))
   tep_session_unregister('giftwrap');
if (tep_session_is_registered('giftwrapping_method'))
   tep_session_unregister('giftwrapping_method');
if (tep_session_is_registered('giftcard'))
   tep_session_unregister('giftcard');
   tep_session_register('giftwrap');
   tep_session_register('giftwrapping_method');
   tep_session_register('giftcard');

   require(DIR_WS_CLASSES . 'order_total.php');
   $order_total_modules = new order_total;
//gift wrap section end
```

9. Find this in line 106:

```
// process the selected shipping method
  if ( isset($HTTP_POST_VARS['action']) &&
     ($HTTP_POST_VARS['action']
       == 'process') ) {
```

Add right below it the following code to process your customer's gift-wrapping choices:

```
//gift wrap section begin
if (isset($HTTP_POST_VARS['giftwrap'])) {
$giftwrap = MODULE_ORDER_TOTAL_GIFTWRAPPING_TITLE;
} else {
$giftwrap = '';
}

$giftwrapping_method = '';
if ($giftwrap == MODULE_ORDER_TOTAL_GIFTWRAPPING_TITLE) {
 if (tep_not_null($HTTP_POST_VARS['giftwrapping_method'])) {
 $giftwrapping_method = MODULE_ORDER_TOTAL_GIFTWRAPPING_TITLE . '
 (' . $HTTP_POST_VARS['giftwrapping_method'] . ')';
 }
}

$giftcard = '';
if ($giftwrap == MODULE_ORDER_TOTAL_GIFTWRAPPING_TITLE) {
 if (tep_not_null($HTTP_POST_VARS['giftcard'])) {
 $giftcard = tep_db_prepare_input($HTTP_POST_VARS['giftcard']);
 }
}
 //gift wrap section end
```

10. In line 402 find the comment section:

```
<?php
 }
?>
<tr>
 <td><table border="0" width="100%" cellspacing=
                                  "0" cellpadding="2">
  <tr>
   <td class="main"><b><?php echo TABLE_HEADING_COMMENTS;
                                   ?></b></td>
  </tr>
 </table></td>
</tr>
```

Replace it with this, calling the **Gift Wrapping** module if installed and enabled:

```
<?php
 }

 if (MODULE_ORDER_TOTAL_GIFTWRAPPING_STATUS == 'true') {
  include(DIR_WS_MODULES . 'giftwrapping.php');
 }
?>
   <tr>
    <td><table border="0" width="100%" cellspacing=
                                  "0" cellpadding="2">
     <tr>
      <td class="main"><b><?php echo TABLE_HEADING_COMMENTS;
                                   ?></b></td>
     </tr>
    </table></td>
   </tr>
```

11. Open `catalog/checkout_confirmation.php` and find this in line 46:

```
// load the selected payment module
   require(DIR_WS_CLASSES . 'payment.php');
   $payment_modules = new payment($payment);
```

Add the following code right below it to set up the session globals for gift wrapping:

```
if (!tep_not_null($giftwrap))
                          tep_session_unregister('giftwrap');
if (!tep_not_null($giftwrapping_method))
   tep_session_unregister('giftwrapping_method');
```

```
if (!tep_not_null($giftcard))
                                tep_session_unregister('giftcard');
```

12. Find this in line 285:

```
<?php
 if (tep_not_null($order->info['comments'])) {
?>
```

Replace it with this, adding the new module for gift wrapping above the comment section (highlighted):

```
<?php
 if (tep_not_null($order->info['giftcard'])) {
?>
 <tr>
  <td class="main"><?php echo '<b>' .
                                 HEADING_ORDER_GIFTCARD . '</b>
   <a href="' . tep_href_link(FILENAME_CHECKOUT_SHIPPING,
                                        '', 'SSL') . '">
   <span class="orderEdit">(' . TEXT_EDIT . ')</span></a>';
                                                   ?></td>
 </tr>
 <tr>
  <td><?php echo tep_draw_separator('pixel_trans.gif',
                                    '100%', '10'); ?>
  </td>
 </tr>
 <tr>
  <td><table border="0" width="100%" cellspacing=
                                  "1" cellpadding="2"
   class="infoBox">
 <tr class="infoBoxContents">
   <td><table border="0" width="100%" cellspacing=
                                  "0" cellpadding="2">
     <tr>
      <td class=
           "main"><?php echo nl2br(tep_output_string_protected
  ($order->info['giftcard'])) .
        tep_draw_hidden_field('giftcard',
                                 $order->info['giftcard']); ?>
     </td>
    </tr>
   </table></td>
  </tr>
 </table></td>
 </tr>
```

```
<tr>
 <td><?php echo tep_draw_separator('pixel_trans.gif',
                                    '100%', '10'); ?>
 </td>
 </tr>
<?php
 }
 if (tep_not_null($order->info['comments'])) {
?>
```

13. Open `catalog/checkout_process.php` and find this in line 113:

```
'comments' => $order->info['comments']);
```

Replace it with the following code, adding the gift-card text to your history-table comments column:

```
'comments' => ($order->info['comments'] ?
$order->info['comments'] .
"\n" : '') . ($order->info['giftcard'] ? TEXT_CARD .
"\n" . $order->info['giftcard'] : ''));
```

14. Further down in line 236, find this code snippet:

```
for ($i=0, $n=sizeof($order_totals); $i<$n; $i++) {
 $email_order .= strip_tags($order_totals[$i]['title']) . ' ' .
 strip_tags($order_totals[$i]['text']) . "\n";
 }
```

Add right below it the display for a gift-card text:

```
if ($order->info['giftcard']) {
 $email_order .= "\n" . TEXT_CARD . "\n" .
    EMAIL_SEPARATOR . "\n" .
 tep_db_output($order->info['giftcard']) . "\n\n";
}
```

15. In line 276, find the lines freeing up session information:

```
// unregister session variables used during checkout
  tep_session_unregister('sendto');
  tep_session_unregister('billto');
  tep_session_unregister('shipping');
  tep_session_unregister('payment');
  tep_session_unregister('comments');
```

Add below it the following three lines:

```
//giftwrapping
  tep_session_unregister('giftwrap');
  tep_session_unregister('giftwrapping_method');
  tep_session_unregister('giftcard');
```

16. Navigate to **Administration | Modules | Order Total** and install the new **Giftwrapping** module as shown here:

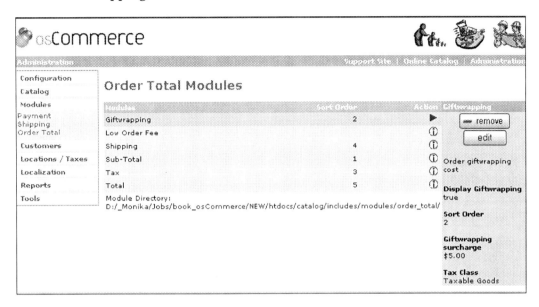

This is where the fun really begins! Now you have to adjust the sort order for your **Order Total** in **Modules** very carefully, depending on your needs. In this case, the setup for the order after the **Sub-Total** is **Giftwrapping**, next **Tax**, then **Shipping** (as seen on the screenshot) determined by the following tax obligations:

- Gift wrapping has to be taxed
- Shipping doesn't require to be taxed

Basically, taxed modules need to be sorted before the **Tax** module.

Chef's suggestion:

Do not use a sorting number twice as you risk the module not displaying at all.

Although what's inside matters most, your guests will relish your detailed presentation! Bon appetit!

43. Add the Option to Donate during Checkout

If your shop is a part of a non-profit organization, such as a church, or if you take donations for any other reason, say for great help in some forums, you will be delighted to find this recipe that allows your customers to add any amount of donation just before choosing a payment gateway.

Presentation

Your Checkout Payment page will look like this with a **Donation** module added above the payment choices:

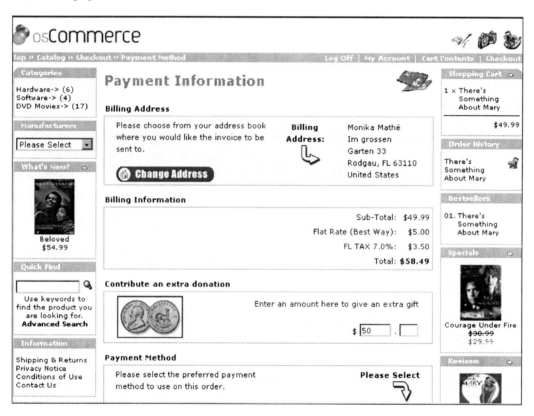

Further, your Checkout Confirmation page will look like this, specifying the donation amount in the totals section as well as in a prominent extra box:

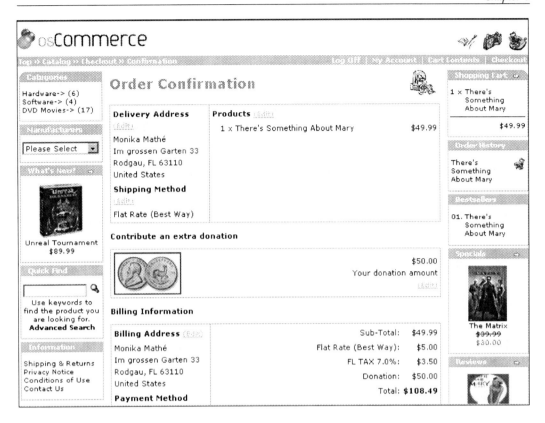

The hostess always deserves recognition!

Ingredients

New:

```
catalog/includes/modules/order_total/ot_donation.php
catalog/includes/languages/english/modules/order_total/
                                    ot_donation.php
catalog/images/icons/donation.gifcatalog/includes/
                                    modules/donation.php
```

Modified:

```
catalog/includes/classes/order_total.php
catalog/checkout_payment.php
catalog/checkout_confirmation.php
catalog/checkout_process.php
```

Cooking

1. Open `catalog/includes/classes/order_total.php` and find the `process()` function in line 34:

```
function process() {
 $order_total_array = array();
```

Add the following new function directly above it:

```
function donation_selection() {
 global $customer_id, $currencies, $language,
 $donation, $messageStack;
$selection_string = '';

//the header of the box
 $selection_string .= '<tr>' . "\n";
 $selection_string .=
        '<td><table border="0" width="100%" cellspacing="0"
cellpadding="2">' . "\n";
 $selection_string .= '<tr>' . "\n";
 $selection_string .= '<td class="main"><b>' .
        TEXT_ENTER_DONATION_HEADER . '</b></td>' . "\n";
 $selection_string .= '</tr>' . "\n";
 $selection_string .= '</table></td>' . "\n";
 $selection_string .= '</tr>' . "\n";
 $selection_string .= '<tr>' . "\n";
 $selection_string .= '<td><table border="0" width="100%"
cellspacing="1" cellpadding="2" class="infoBox">' . "\n";
 $selection_string .= '<tr class="infoBoxContents">' . "\n";
 $selection_string .= '<td><table border="0" width="100%"
cellspacing="0" cellpadding="2">' . "\n";

//the infotext in the box
 $selection_string .= '<tr>' . "\n";
 $selection_string .= '<td colspan="2"
width="100%"><table border="0" width="100%"
cellspacing="0" cellpadding="2">' . "\n";
 $selection_string .= '<tr>' . "\n";
 $selection_string .= '<td width="10">' .
tep_draw_separator('pixel_trans.gif', '10', '1') .
                                        '</td>' . "\n";
 $selection_string .= '<td class="main" align="left">' .
tep_image(DIR_WS_ICONS . 'donation.gif', STORE_NAME) .
                                        '</td>' . "\n";
 $selection_string .= '<td class="main" align="right">'. "\n";
 $selection_string .= TEXT_ENTER_DONATION_INFO . "\n";
```

```
$selection_string .= '<p>$ ' . tep_draw_input_field('dollar',
'', 'size="5" maxlength="10"') . ' . ' .
tep_draw_input_field('cent', '', 'size="2"
                                        maxlength="2"')  . "\n";

$selection_string .= '</td>' . "\n";
$selection_string .= '<td width="10">' .
tep_draw_separator('pixel_trans.gif', '10', '1') .
                                        '</td>' . "\n";
$selection_string .= '</tr>' . "\n";
$selection_string .= '</table></td>' . "\n";
$selection_string .= '</tr>' . "\n";
```

```
//the footer of the box
$selection_string .= '</table></td>' . "\n";
$selection_string .= '</tr>' . "\n";
$selection_string .= '</table></td>' . "\n";
$selection_string .= '</tr>' . "\n";
return $selection_string;
}
```

2. Create the new file `catalog/includes/modules/order_total/`
    `ot_donation.php` using the following code:

```php
<?php
/*
$Id: ot_donation.php,v 1.00 2006/07/05 00:00:00 mm Exp $

Module written by Monika Mathé
http://www.monikamathe.com

Module Copyright (c) 2006 Monika Mathé

osCommerce, Open Source E-Commerce Solutions
http://www.oscommerce.com

Copyright (c) 2003 osCommerce

Released under the GNU General Public License
*/

class ot_donation {
 var $title, $output;

 function ot_donation() {
  $this->code = 'ot_donation';
```

```
$this->title = MODULE_ORDER_TOTAL_DONATION_TITLE;
$this->description =
                  MODULE_ORDER_TOTAL_DONATION_DESCRIPTION;
$this->enabled =
((MODULE_ORDER_TOTAL_DONATION_STATUS == 'true') ?
 true : false);
$this->sort_order = MODULE_ORDER_TOTAL_DONATION_SORT_ORDER;

$this->output = array();

 if ($this->enabled == true) {
  global $donation;
  if ($donation == '') {
   $this->enabled = false;
  }
 }
}


function process() {
 global $order, $currencies, $donation;

 $order->info['total'] += $donation;

 $this->output[] = array('title' => $this->title . ':',
           'text' => $currencies->format($donation, true,
           $order->info['currency'],
           $order->info['currency_value']),
           'value' => $donation);
}

function check() {
 if (!isset($this->_check)) {
  $check_query =
  tep_db_query("select configuration_value from " .
  TABLE_CONFIGURATION . " where configuration_key =
                  'MODULE_ORDER_TOTAL_DONATION_STATUS'");
  $this->_check = tep_db_num_rows($check_query);
 }

 return $this->_check;
}

function keys() {
 return array('MODULE_ORDER_TOTAL_DONATION_STATUS',
```

```
                  'MODULE_ORDER_TOTAL_DONATION_SORT_ORDER');
                }

                function install() {
                 tep_db_query("insert into " . TABLE_CONFIGURATION . "
                 (configuration_title, configuration_key,
                 configuration_value, configuration_description,
                 configuration_group_id, sort_order, set_function,
                 date_added) values ('Display Donation',
                 'MODULE_ORDER_TOTAL_DONATION_STATUS', 'true',
                 'Do you want to display the donation amount?', '6',
                 '1','tep_cfg_select_option(array(\'true\', \'false\'), ',
                                                         now())");
                 tep_db_query("insert into " . TABLE_CONFIGURATION . "
                 (configuration_title, configuration_key,
                  configuration_value, configuration_description,
                  configuration_group_id, sort_order,
                  date_added) values ('Sort Order',
                  'MODULE_ORDER_TOTAL_DONATION_SORT_ORDER', '40',
                  'Sort order of display.', '6', '2', now())");
                }

                function remove() {
                 tep_db_query("delete from " . TABLE_CONFIGURATION . "
                  where configuration_key in ('" . implode("', '",
                                    $this->keys()) . "')");
                }
               }
              ?>
```

3. Create the matching new language file `catalog/includes/languages/english/modules/order_total/ot_donation.php` **with the following define statements:**

```
              <?php
            /*
              $Id: ot_donation.php,v 1.00 2006/07/05 00:00:00 mm Exp $

              Module written by Monika Mathé
              http://www.monikamathe.com

              Module Copyright (c) 2006 Monika Mathé

              osCommerce, Open Source E-Commerce Solutions
              http://www.oscommerce.com
```

```
       Copyright (c) 2003 osCommerce

       Released under the GNU General Public License
  */

       define('MODULE_ORDER_TOTAL_DONATION_TITLE', 'Donation');
       define('MODULE_ORDER_TOTAL_DONATION_DESCRIPTION', 'Donation');

       define('TEXT_ENTER_DONATION_HEADER',
                               'Contribute an extra donation');
       define('TEXT_ENTER_DONATION_INFO',
                   'Enter an amount here to give an extra gift');
       define('TEXT_ENTER_YOUR_DONATION', 'Your donation amount');

       define('TEXT_DONATION_ERROR',
               'Please enter a correct value for your donation.');
  ?>
```

4. Create your own donation image, or use `donation.gif` saved to your `catalog/images/icons` folder.

5. Create the new file, `catalog/includes/modules/donation.php`, which will be called from the Checkout Payment page to be included if the module has been enabled:

```
       <?php
       /*
        $Id: donation.php,v 1.00 2006/07/05 00:00:00 mm Exp $

        Module written by Monika Mathé
        http://www.monikamathe.com

        Module Copyright (c) 2006 Monika Mathé

        osCommerce, Open Source E-Commerce Solutions
        http://www.oscommerce.com

        Copyright (c) 2003 osCommerce

        Released under the GNU General Public License
       */
       ?>
       <tr>
        <td class="main"><b><?php echo TEXT_ENTER_DONATION_HEADER;
                                                    ?></b>
        </td>
```

```
</tr>
<tr>
 <td><?php echo tep_draw_separator('pixel_trans.gif',
                                    '100%', '10'); ?>
 </td>
</tr>
<tr>
 <td><table border="0" width="100%" cellspacing="1"
  cellpadding="2" class="infoBox">
  <tr class="infoBoxContents">
   <td valign="top"><table border="0" width="100%"
    cellspacing="0" cellpadding="2">
    <tr>
    <td class="main"><?php echo tep_image(DIR_WS_ICONS .
                               'donation.gif', STORE_NAME); ?>
     </td>
    <td class="main" align="right">
     <?php echo $currencies->format($donation); ?><br>
     <?php echo TEXT_ENTER_YOUR_DONATION; ?><br>
     <?php echo '<a href="' .
     tep_href_link(FILENAME_CHECKOUT_PAYMENT, '', 'SSL') .
     '"><span class="orderEdit">(' . TEXT_EDIT . ')</span>
     </a>'; ?>
     </td>
    </tr>
   </table></td>
  </tr>
 </table></td>
</tr>
<tr>
 <td><?php echo tep_draw_separator('pixel_trans.gif',
                                   '100%', '10'); ?></td>
</tr>
```

6. Open `catalog/checkout_payment.php` and find this in line 67:

```
if (!tep_session_is_registered('comments'))
tep_session_register('comments');
```

Add right below it the call for the **Order Total** modules so that the billing information can be displayed on this page instead of on Checkout Confirmation only. Calling the **Order Total** modules now allows us to show the new **Donation** module here too. Add the following code:

```
require(DIR_WS_CLASSES . 'order_total.php');
$order_total_modules = new order_total;
```

```
if (tep_session_is_registered('donation'))
 tep_session_unregister('donation');
if (!tep_session_is_registered('donation')) {
 tep_session_register('donation');
  $donation = 0.00;
}
```

7. In line 85, find the call for the language file:

```
require(DIR_WS_LANGUAGES . $language . '/' .
                              FILENAME_CHECKOUT_PAYMENT);
```

Add below it the call for the language file of the Checkout Confirmation page as the display of the billing information uses the defines from that file:

```
require(DIR_WS_LANGUAGES . $language . '/' .
 FILENAME_CHECKOUT_CONFIRMATION);
```

8. In line 214, find the **Payment Method** section:

```
<tr>
 <td><?php echo tep_draw_separator('pixel_trans.gif',
                              '100%', '10'); ?>
 </td>
</tr>
<tr>
 <td><table border="0" width="100%"
                      cellspacing="0" cellpadding="2">
  <tr>
   <td class=
     "main"><b><?php echo TABLE_HEADING_PAYMENT_METHOD; ?></b>
   </td>
  </tr>
 </table></td>
</tr>
```

Add right above it this code snippet, which calls the donation module entry form if installed and enabled:

```
<tr>
 <td><?php echo tep_draw_separator('pixel_trans.gif',
                              '100%', '10'); ?>
 </td>
</tr>
<tr>
 <td><table border="0" width="100%"
                      cellspacing="0" cellpadding="2">
  <tr>
```

```
        <td class=
        "main"><b><?php echo HEADING_BILLING_INFORMATION; ?></b>
        </td>
           </tr>
          </table></td>
        </tr>
    <tr>
     <td><table border="0" width="100%"
              cellspacing="1" cellpadding="2" class="infoBox">
      <tr class="infoBoxContents">
       <td valign="top" align="right"><table
       border="0" cellspacing="0" cellpadding="2">
<?php
 if (MODULE_ORDER_TOTAL_INSTALLED) {
  $order_total_modules->process();
  echo $order_total_modules->output();
 }
?>
        </table></td>
       </tr>
      </table></td>
     </tr>
     <tr>
      <td><?php echo tep_draw_separator('pixel_trans.gif',
                                      '100%', '10'); ?>
      </td>
     </tr>
<?php
 echo $order_total_modules->donation_selection();
?>
```

9. Open `catalog/checkout_confirmation.php` and find this in line 41:

```
if (!tep_session_is_registered('comments'))
 tep_session_register('comments');
if (tep_not_null($HTTP_POST_VARS['comments'])) {
 $comments = tep_db_prepare_input($HTTP_POST_VARS['comments']);
}
```

Add right below it the following code, which checks for correct data entry of the donation amount. If non-numeric values have been added, the donation amount automatically reverts to $0.00.

```
//donation mod begin
  if (tep_not_null($HTTP_POST_VARS['dollar'])) {
   $dollar = tep_db_prepare_input($HTTP_POST_VARS['dollar']);
  }
```

```
     if ($HTTP_POST_VARS['dollar'] == '') {
      $dollar = 0;
     }
     if (tep_not_null($HTTP_POST_VARS['cent'])) {
      $cent = tep_db_prepare_input($HTTP_POST_VARS['cent']);
     }
     if ($HTTP_POST_VARS['cent'] == '') {
      $cent = 0;
     }
      $donation = $dollar . '.' . $cent;
      $donation = round($donation,2);
    //donation mod end
```

10. In the same file, find this in line 221:

```
<tr>
  <td class="main"><b><?php echo HEADING_BILLING_INFORMATION;
                                                        ?></b>
  </td>
</tr>
```

Add above it the call for the total donation display:

```
<?php
 if (MODULE_ORDER_TOTAL_DONATION_STATUS == 'true') {
  include(DIR_WS_MODULES . 'donation.php');
 }
?>
```

11. Open `catalog/checkout_process.php` and find this in line 275, which is the code freeing up session information:

```
// unregister session variables used during checkout
  tep_session_unregister('sendto');
  tep_session_unregister('billto');
  tep_session_unregister('shipping');
  tep_session_unregister('payment');
  tep_session_unregister('comments');
```

Add below it the following line:

```
//donation
  tep_session_unregister('donation');
```

12. Navigate to **Administration | Modules | Order Total** and install the new **Donation** module as here:

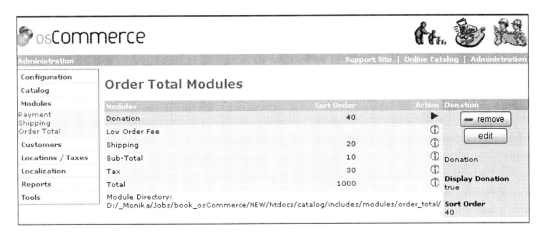

Again, it is very important to set the sort order correctly due to taxation. In this case, the setup for the order after the **Sub-Total** is **Shipping**, next **Tax**, and then **Donation** (as seen on the screenshot), determined by the following tax obligations:

- Shipping must be taxed
- Donation does not require taxation

As a rule of thumb, taxed modules need to be sorted before the **Tax** module. Sorting numbers must be unique, or you risk not displaying the module at all.

Chef's suggestion:

If you are using many new **Order Total** modules within a short time, I suggest using wide spaced sort order numbers as seen in the previous screenshot, clearly marking **Total** as the highest. This will allow you plenty of space to tuck in a new module or two between existing ones without having to shift all numbers.

Enjoy the meal and ensure the leftovers make their way to those in need! Bon appetit!

44. Personalize Your Order Confirmation Email

The Order Confirmation email that osCommerce comes with by default provides no personal greeting to the customer and looks sparse and unfriendly. This recipe adds a nice greeting and some basic information about the order that was processed.

Presentation

Your Order Confirmation email will look like this:

```
Dear Monika,

Thanks for shopping with us online!
Your order has been successfully processed! Your products will arrive at
their destination within 2-5 working days.

osCommerce
-----------------------------------------------------------
Order Number: 1
Detailed Invoice:
http://localhost/catalog/account_history_info.php?order_id=1
Date Ordered: Wednesday 05 July, 2006

Products
-----------------------------------------------------------
1 x There's Something About Mary (DVD-TSAB) = $49.99
-----------------------------------------------------------
Sub-Total: $49.99
FL TAX 7.0%: $3.50
Flat Rate (Best Way): $5.00
Total: $58.49

Delivery Address
-----------------------------------------------------------
```

Rather than the following:

```
osCommerce
-----------------------------------------------------------
Order Number: 1
Detailed Invoice:
http://localhost/catalog/account_history_info.php?order_id=1
Date Ordered: Wednesday 05 July, 2006

Products
-----------------------------------------------------------
1 x There's Something About Mary (DVD-TSAB) = $49.99
-----------------------------------------------------------
Sub-Total: $49.99
FL TAX 7.0%: $3.50
Flat Rate (Best Way): $5.00
Total: $58.49

Delivery Address
-----------------------------------------------------------
```

Pat-a-cake, pat-a-cake, baker's man!! Let's mark it with your customer's initial!

Ingredients

Modified:

```
catalog/includes/languages/english/checkout_process.php
catalog/checkout_process.php
```

Cooking

1. Open `catalog/includes/languages/english/checkout_process.php` and add the following define statement for the greeting:

   ```
   define('TEXT_DEAR', 'Dear ');
   ```

2. Open `catalog/checkout_process.php`. To achieve the same results as in the previous screenshot, look out for this code in line 36:

   ```
   include(DIR_WS_LANGUAGES . $language . '/' .
                                   FILENAME_CHECKOUT_PROCESS);
   ```

   Add right below it the following line:

   ```
   include(DIR_WS_LANGUAGES . $language . '/' .
                                   FILENAME_CHECKOUT_SUCCESS);
   ```

   Chef's suggestion:

   We will be using the same text as the Checkout Success page does, but of course you can add your own defines to the `checkout_process.php` language file and omit the above step.

3. Scroll down to the email generation, which starts in line 224. All email-display text is added here, so if we'd like to add a personal greeting, this is the place to do it. Find this code:

   ```
   // lets start with the email confirmation
     $email_order = STORE_NAME . "\n" .
   ```

   Replace it with the following code, adding the name and some text to personalize the confirmation email:

   ```
   // let's start with the email confirmation
     $email_order = TEXT_DEAR . $order->customer['firstname'] .
   ```

```
       ',' . "\n\n" . TEXT_THANKS_FOR_SHOPPING . "\n" .
                                        TEXT_SUCCESS . "\n\n";

       $email_order .= STORE_NAME . "\n" .
```

Marked with a C for customer and me! Bon appetit!

45. Add Your Customers' Email Addresses and Phone Numbers to Your Order Confirmation Email

If you have subscribed to receive **extra order email** for quick and easy referencing of purchases made, you would have certainly missed the customer's contact info. This recipe adds your customers' email addresses and phone numbers under their billing address. The data used is pulled from the `customers` table where some of the information that your customers enter during registration is saved.

Presentation

Your Order Confirmation email will look like this:

```
Billing Address
----------------------------------------------------
Monika Mathé
Im grossen Garten 33
Rodgau, Hessen    63110
Germany
0178 2038583
codemaster@monikamathe.com
```

Need to add some briquettes to the grill? Let's get going!

Ingredients

```
Modified:

catalog/checkout_process.php
```

Cooking

1. Open `catalog/checkout_process.php` and find this code in line 246 where the billing address is added to the order email:

```
$email_order .= "\n" . EMAIL_TEXT_BILLING_ADDRESS . "\n" .
   EMAIL_SEPARATOR . "\n" .
   tep_address_label($customer_id, $billto, 0,
                                    '', "\n") . "\n\n";
```

Replace it with the following code, adding your customer's phone number and email address:

```
$email_order .= "\n" . EMAIL_TEXT_BILLING_ADDRESS . "\n" .
   EMAIL_SEPARATOR . "\n" .
   tep_address_label($customer_id, $billto, 0, '', "\n") . "\n" .
   $order->customer['telephone'] . "\n" .
   $order->customer['email_address'] . "\n\n";
```

Hotter than ever... well done! Bon appetit!

46. Add Your Customers' Fax Numbers to Your Order Confirmation Email

If you have already successfully added the previous recipe for email address and phone number, you may be wondering why the fax has its own section. Fax number has to be treated separately, as default osCommerce never intended it to be used in any order process section apart from registration and address modification. This means that it was never added to the Order class; so you are not able to automatically pull it.

Presentation

There are basically three methods we could use to make your Order Confirmation email look like this:

```
Delivery Address
------------------------------------------------------
Monika Mathé
Im grossen Garten 33
Rodgau, FL     63110
United States

Billing Address
------------------------------------------------------
Monika Mathé
Im grossen Garten 33
Rodgau, FL     63110
United States
Fax Number: 06106 266 861

Payment Method
------------------------------------------------------
Cash on Delivery
```

We can:

- Add the fax number to the classes so that information can be pulled from them easily, just like for email address and phone number
- Write a function to get the fax number for any `customers_id`
- Simply pull the fax number via a query from the `customers` table right where we plan to use it

For all these cases, you need to consider how often you will be using the pulled result, in this case the fax number. If you want to use it for the order email only, a query is probably the fastest and most obvious method, though as we are connoisseurs in hacking osCommerce code and prefer to create reusable modules, we will be adding the fax number to the Order class and will leave the function for the next recipe!

Ready to add a sauce more potent than Hollandaise?

Ingredients

Modified:

```
catalog/checkout_process.php
catalog/includes/classes/order.php
```

Cooking

1. Open `catalog/checkout_process.php` and look for this code in line 246 with the billing address:

```
$email_order .= "\n" . EMAIL_TEXT_BILLING_ADDRESS . "\n" .
EMAIL_SEPARATOR . "\n" .
tep_address_label($customer_id, $billto, 0,
                                    '', "\n") . "\n\n";
```

Replace that code snippet with this, adding your customer's fax number from the Order class:

```
$email_order .= "\n" . EMAIL_TEXT_BILLING_ADDRESS . "\n" .
EMAIL_SEPARATOR . "\n" .
tep_address_label($customer_id, $billto, 0, '', "\n") . "\n" .
ENTRY_FAX_NUMBER . ' ' . $order->customer['fax'] . "\n\n";
```

2. As your second step, you have to add the fax number to the `cart()` function of `catalog/includes/classes/order.php`, so it can be pulled from the Order class when needed. Find this in line 138 to amend the query:

```
$customer_address_query =
tep_db_query("select c.customers_firstname,
 c.customers_lastname, c.customers_telephone,
 c.customers_email_address,
 ab.entry_company, ab.entry_street_address, ab.entry_suburb,
 ab.entry_postcode, ab.entry_city,
 ab.entry_zone_id, z.zone_name,
 co.countries_id, co.countries_name, co.countries_iso_code_2,
 co.countries_iso_code_3, co.address_format_id,
 ab.entry_state from " . TABLE_CUSTOMERS . " c, " .
TABLE_ADDRESS_BOOK . " ab left join " . TABLE_ZONES .
 " z on (ab.entry_zone_id = z.zone_id)
left join " . TABLE_COUNTRIES .
 " co on (ab.entry_country_id = co.countries_id)
 where c.customers_id = '" .
(int)$customer_id . "' and ab.customers_id =
'" . (int)$customer_id . "'
 and c.customers_default_address_id = ab.address_book_id");
$customer_address =
                tep_db_fetch_array($customer_address_query);
```

Replace with this:

```
$customer_address_query =
tep_db_query("select c.customers_firstname,
 c.customers_lastname, c.customers_telephone, c.customers_fax,
 c.customers_email_address, ab.entry_company,
 ab.entry_street_address, ab.entry_suburb,
 ab.entry_postcode, ab.entry_city, ab.entry_zone_id,
```

```
z.zone_name, co.countries_id, co.countries_name,
co.countries_iso_code_2, co.countries_iso_code_3,
co.address_format_id, ab.entry_state from " .
TABLE_CUSTOMERS . " c, " . TABLE_ADDRESS_BOOK .
" ab left join " . TABLE_ZONES .
" z on (ab.entry_zone_id = z.zone_id) left join " .
TABLE_COUNTRIES . "
co on (ab.entry_country_id = co.countries_id) where
c.customers_id = '" . (int)$customer_id . "' and
ab.customers_id = '" . (int)$customer_id . "' and
c.customers_default_address_id =
ab.address_book_id");
$customer_address =
                tep_db_fetch_array($customer_address_query);
```

3. Next, find this in line 173 to amend the array for displaying:

```
$this->customer = array('firstname' =>
  $customer_address['customers_firstname'],
        'lastname' => $customer_address['customers_lastname'],
        'company' => $customer_address['entry_company'],
        'street_address' =>
                $customer_address['entry_street_address'],
        'suburb' => $customer_address['entry_suburb'],
        'city' => $customer_address['entry_city'],
        'postcode' => $customer_address['entry_postcode'],
        'state' =>
          ((tep_not_null($customer_address['entry_state'])) ?
          $customer_address['entry_state'] :
          $customer_address['zone_name']),
        'zone_id' => $customer_address['entry_zone_id'],
        'country' => array('id' =>
$customer_address['countries_id'],
        'title' => $customer_address['countries_name'],
        'iso_code_2' =>
         $customer_address['countries_iso_code_2'],
        'iso_code_3' =>
$customer_address['countries_iso_code_3']),
        'format_id' => $customer_address['address_format_id'],
        'telephone' => $customer_address['customers_telephone'],
        'email_address' =>
$customer_address['customers_email_address']);
```

Replace it with this, adding the fax number:

```
$this->customer = array('firstname' =>
        $customer_address['customers_firstname'],
        'lastname' => $customer_address['customers_lastname'],
```

```
'company' => $customer_address['entry_company'],
'street_address' =>
 $customer_address['entry_street_address'],
'suburb' => $customer_address['entry_suburb'],
'city' => $customer_address['entry_city'],
'postcode' => $customer_address['entry_postcode'],
'state' =>
((tep_not_null($customer_address['entry_state'])) ?
  $customer_address['entry_state'] :
  $customer_address['zone_name']),
'zone_id' => $customer_address['entry_zone_id'],
'country' =>
array('id' => $customer_address['countries_id'],
'title' => $customer_address['countries_name'],
'iso_code_2' =>
$customer_address['countries_iso_code_2'],
'iso_code_3' =>
$customer_address['countries_iso_code_3']),
'format_id' => $customer_address['address_format_id'],
'telephone' =>
$customer_address['customers_telephone'],
'fax' => $customer_address['customers_fax'],
'email_address' =>
$customer_address['customers_email_address']);
```

Make sure you add a fax number to the customer used for testing!

With or without the raw egg, it's a great condiment! Bon appetit!

47. Add the Products' Manufacturers to Your Order Confirmation Email

It is always a good idea to display manufacturer's names with product names in the order email if a certain product could be associated with several different manufacturers. This recipe shows you how to add the manufacturer's name for each product using a function, just as promised in the previous recipe.

Presentation

Your product listing in the Order Confirmation email will look like the following Screenshot:

```
osCommerce
-----------------------------------------------
Order Number: 7
Detailed Invoice:
http://localhost/catalog/account_history_info.php?order_id=7
Date Ordered: Wednesday 05 July, 2006

Products
-----------------------------------------------
1 x Fox - There's Something About Mary (DVD-TSAB) = $49.99
1 x Warner - Blade Runner - Director's Cut (DVD-BLDRNDC) = $30.00
1 x Microsoft - Microsoft IntelliMouse Explorer (MSIMEXP) = $64.95
         Model PS/2
-----------------------------------------------
Sub-Total: $144.94
FL TAX 7.0%: $10.15
Flat Rate (Best Way): $5.00
Total: $160.09
```

Keen's, Colemans, or Hot Oriental?

Ingredients

> **Modified:**
>
> catalog/includes/functions/general.php
> catalog/checkout_process.php

Cooking

1. Open catalog/includes/functions/general.php and add the following new function before the closing ?> PHP tag to get the manufacturer's name for a given product:

```
function tep_get_manufacturers_name($products_id) {

  $manufacturers_query =
  tep_db_query("select m.manufacturers_name from " .
  TABLE_MANUFACTURERS . " m, " . TABLE_PRODUCTS .
  " p where p.manufacturers_id = m.manufacturers_id and
  p.products_id = '" . $products_id . "'");
  $manufacturers = tep_db_fetch_array($manufacturers_query);

  if ($manufacturers['manufacturers_name'] != '') {
    return $manufacturers['manufacturers_name'] . ' - ';
      } else {
```

```
    return '';
    }
  }
```

2. Next, open `catalog/checkout_process.php` and find this code in line 219 where each product is added as a row to the order email:

```
$products_ordered .= $order->products[$i]['qty'] . ' x ' .
$order->products[$i]['name'] . '
(' . $order->products[$i]['model'] . ') = '
. $currencies->display_price($order->products[$i]
['final_price'], $order->products[$i]['tax'],
$order->products[$i]['qty']) .
$products_ordered_attributes . "\n";
```

Replace that code snippet with this, adding the manufacturer's name to each product:

```
$products_ordered .= $order->products[$i]['qty'] . ' x ' .
tep_get_manufacturers_name($order->products[$i]['id']) .
$order->products[$i]['name'] . '
(' . $order->products[$i]['model'] . ') =
' . $currencies->display_price($order->products[$i]
['final_price'],
$order->products[$i]['tax'], $order->products[$i]['qty']) .
$products_ordered_attributes . "\n";
```

It's not absolutely necessary, but good job adding the bite. Bon appetit!

48. Add the Products' Category Tree to Your Order Confirmation Email

If you need to display the entire path to your products in the Order Confirmation email, like the breadcrumb trail on the product-detail page does, then this recipe is for you. It creates a category name string similar to $cPath, but instead of using category IDs it displays actual category names.

Presentation

This is what your Order Confirmation email will look like when you try this recipe:

```
osCommerce
---------------------------------------------------------
Order Number: 10
Detailed Invoice:
http://localhost/catalog/account_history_info.php?order_id=10
Date Ordered: Thursday 06 July, 2006

Products
---------------------------------------------------------
1 x DVD Movies->Comedy->There's Something About Mary (DVD-TSAB) = $49.99
1 x DVD Movies->Science Fiction->Blade Runner - Director's Cut
(DVD-BLDRNDC) = $30.00
1 x Hardware->Mice->Microsoft IntelliMouse Explorer (MSIMEXP) = $64.95
        Model PS/2
---------------------------------------------------------
Sub-Total: $144.94
FL TAX 7.0%: $10.15
Flat Rate (Best Way): $5.00
Total: $160.09
```

Ready to stack your ribs?

Ingredients

Modified:

```
catalog/checkout_process.php
catalog/includes/functions/general.php
```

Cooking

1. First, open `catalog/checkout_process.php` and find this code in line 219.
   In this snippet, each product is added to the order email.

   ```
   $products_ordered .= $order->products[$i]['qty'] . ' x ' .
   $order->products[$i]['name'] . '
   (' . $order->products[$i]['model'] . ') = '
   . $currencies->display_price($order->products[$i]
   ['final_price'], $order->products[$i]['tax'],
   $order->products[$i]['qty']) .
   $products_ordered_attributes . "\n";
   ```

   Replace that code snippet with this, adding the category tree to each product:

   ```
   $products_ordered .= $order->products[$i]['qty'] . ' x ' .
   tep_get_product_path_names($order->products[$i]['id']) . '->' .
   $order->products[$i]['name'] . '
   (' . $order->products[$i]['model'] . ') = '
   . $currencies->display_price($order->products[$i]
   ['final_price'], $order->products[$i]['tax'],
   $order->products[$i]['qty']) .
   $products_ordered_attributes . "\n";
   ```

2. Open `catalog/includes/functions/general.php` and add the following
new functions before the closing `?>` PHP tag. The first function gets the
category name for a given category and the language used:

```
////
// Return a category's name
 function tep_get_category_name($categories_id,
 $language = '') {
 global $languages_id;

  if (empty($language)) $language = $languages_id;

  $categories_query =
  tep_db_query("select categories_name from " .
  TABLE_CATEGORIES_DESCRIPTION . " where categories_id = '" .
  (int)$categories_id . "' and language_id = '" .
  (int)$language . "'");
  $categories = tep_db_fetch_array($categories_query);

  return $categories['categories_name'];
 }
```

The second function is a variation of the `tep_get_product_path` function
showing category names instead of IDs:

```
////
// Construct a category path to the product in names
 function tep_get_product_path_names($products_id) {
  $cat_namePath = '';

  $category_query =
  tep_db_query("select p2c.categories_id from " .
  TABLE_PRODUCTS . " p, " . TABLE_PRODUCTS_TO_CATEGORIES . "
  p2c where p.products_id = '" . (int)$products_id . "' and
  p.products_status = '1' and
  p.products_id = p2c.products_id limit 1");

  if (tep_db_num_rows($category_query)) {
   $category = tep_db_fetch_array($category_query);

   $categories = array();
   tep_get_parent_categories($categories,
   $category['categories_id']);

   $categories = array_reverse($categories);
```

```
      $cat_namePath =
      tep_get_category_name(implode('_', $categories));

      if (tep_not_null($cat_namePath)) $cat_namePath .= '->';
      $cat_namePath .=
      tep_get_category_name($category['categories_id']);
      }

      return $cat_namePath;
   }
```

So Juicy! Bon appetit!

Summary

In this chapter, you have found many new recipes to quicken your appetite. You can now change your shopping cart design to make it more intuitive when customers need to delete a product from their shopping cart; you can even highlight this function by adding colors and fun icons for a pleasant look.

You are no longer forced to allow customers to choose a shipping address that differs from the address they used at registration. Your display text in **Shipping Method** follows your own ideas as you can henceforth whip the display style of your **Shipping Method** into shape for the Checkout Confirmation page.

In addition to these functions, you have learned about two very exciting new modules, namely, a sophisticated **Gift Wrapping** module that handles proper taxing, added to your Checkout Shipping page, and secondly, a **Donation** module that allows you to collect monetary gifts from your customers on your Checkout Payment page.

The last part of this chapter tackled many small but tasty tweaks that will make your Order Confirmation email special such that it represents your company in the best possible way.

As we have touched the topic of **Shipping** modules in terms of design in this chapter already, let's check out what osCommerce offers already as **Shipping** modules for you to hack as needed in the next chapter. You will quickly see how easy it is to breathe new life into modules that looked like they could not do the trick for you.

7

Whip Up New Shipping Options

osCommerce arrives pre-packaged with a great selection of standard shipping modules, which you will find in **Administration | Modules | Shipping** ready for installation. It is recommended to test each of them and observe their functionality, as this will give you a better understanding of the underlying code. Consider these ready-made modules akin to a selection of base ingredients that will be used to create new modules. While it is convenient to use one of the existing shipping modules, it is highly probable that they will require some spicing up to suit your specific needs. In this chapter, we will use the following osCommerce shipping modules as base ingredients for our recipes:

- Flat Rate Shipping
- Per Item Shipping
- USPS Shipping
- Table Rate Shipping

Chef's suggestion:

Keep the default version of a given shipping module intact and untouched; *always* create a clone of the default shipping module you are basing your new module on before making amendments. The default shipping modules have feature-rich code that you will need to refer to again and again, and will use in new versions. Install only those modules you require, and leave all other modules for future reference.

In this chapter, we will discuss how to:

- Add multiple **Flat Rate** shipping modules
- Add percentage and base price support to **Table Rate**
- Allow **Free Postage** for free items
- Limit **Flat Rate** shipping to a specific top category only
- Hide shipping modules driven by weight
- Create a **Per Item** shipping module with two price levels

Whether you are cloning the **Flat Rate** shipping module (as done in the first recipe of this chapter) or any other shipping module for a new logic, the steps remain the same.

First, using your favorite editor (*Chef* recommends *TextPad*), find and replace all occurrences of the shipping module's name. In the next step, you can edit the text shown for each module's in the edit column after installation. These expressions can be found in each modules file almost at the bottom in the `install()` function.

Repeat these steps for each clone, specifying new names such as `flat2`, `flat3`, etc., for the additional clones.

49. Add Multiple Flat Rate Shipping Modules

This recipe outlines how to clone the **Flat Rate** shipping module for use in several zones and with different rates. While the **Zone Rates** shipping module seems to be a valid alternative for such a scenario, allowing you to set up shipping tables for several different zones, this new set of modules gives you the option to change the business logic for each zone separately. In a separate recipe, you will learn a method to offer free shipping for a catalog, but not for other products; if free shipping is to be valid for one zone only, it would require hard-coding the zone-based shipping module resulting in less freedom for modifications.

Presentation

Your screen in **Administration | Modules | Shipping** will look like this when you have set up three new modules for zone-based **Flat Rate** shipping, specifying zones for **USA**, **Canada**, and the **Rest of the World**:

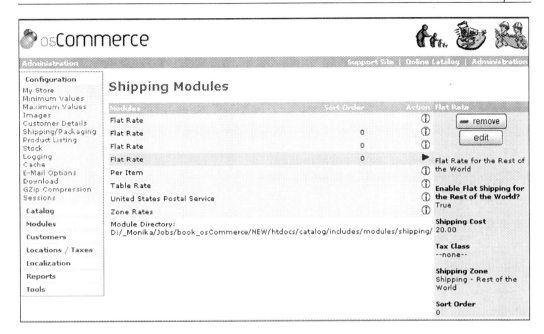

Let's put together a versatile Béchamel!

Ingredients

New:

catalog/includes/modules/shipping/flat1.php
catalog/includes/modules/shipping/flat2.php
catalog/includes/modules/shipping/flat3.php
(these are clones of the catalog/includes/modules/shipping/flat.php file)
catalog/includes/languages/english/modules/shipping/flat1.php
catalog/includes/languages/english/modules/shipping/flat2.php
catalog/includes/languages/english/modules/shipping/flat3.php
(these are clones of the catalog/includes/languages/english/modules/
shipping/flat.php file)

Cooking

1. Open catalog/includes/modules/shipping/flat.php and create a clone,
    then replace all occurrences of the flat expression with flat1, keeping its
    upper or lower case spelling intact. Save this new file as flat1.php, then

repeat for `flat2.php` and `flat3.php`. This is what your `flat1.php` will look like before editing the display text:

```php
<?php
/*
  $Id: flat.php,v 1.40 2003/02/05 22:41:52 hpdl Exp $
  cloned as
  $Id: flat1.php,v 1.00 2006/07/08 00:00:00 mm Exp $

  Modified by Monika Mathé
  http://www.monikamathe.com

  Module Copyright (c) 2006 Monika Mathé
  osCommerce, Open Source E-Commerce Solutions
  http://www.oscommerce.com

  Copyright (c) 2003 osCommerce

  Released under the GNU General Public License
*/

  class flat1 {
    var $code, $title, $description, $icon, $enabled;

// class constructor
    function flat1() {
      global $order;

      $this->code = 'flat1';
      $this->title = MODULE_SHIPPING_FLAT1_TEXT_TITLE;
      $this->description =
                 MODULE_SHIPPING_FLAT1_TEXT_DESCRIPTION;
      $this->sort_order = MODULE_SHIPPING_FLAT1_SORT_ORDER;
      $this->icon = '';
      $this->tax_class = MODULE_SHIPPING_FLAT1_TAX_CLASS;
      $this->enabled = ((MODULE_SHIPPING_FLAT1_STATUS == 'True') ?
      true : false);

      if ( ($this->enabled == true) &&
      ((int)MODULE_SHIPPING_FLAT1_ZONE > 0) ) {
        $check_flag = false;
        $check_query = tep_db_query("select zone_id from " .
        TABLE_ZONES_TO_GEO_ZONES . " where geo_zone_id = '" .
        MODULE_SHIPPING_FLAT1_ZONE . "' and zone_country_id = '" .
        $order->delivery['country']['id'] . "' order by zone_id");
```

```
    while ($check = tep_db_fetch_array($check_query)) {
     if ($check['zone_id'] < 1) {
     $check_flag = true;
      break;
    } elseif ($check['zone_id'] ==
            $order->delivery['zone_id']) {
     $check_flag = true;
      break;
     }
    }

    if ($check_flag == false) {
     $this->enabled = false;
    }
   }
  }

// class methods
  function quote($method = '') {
   global $order;

   $this->quotes = array('id' => $this->code,
            'module' => MODULE_SHIPPING_FLAT1_TEXT_TITLE,
            'methods' => array(array('id' => $this->code,
                'title' => MODULE_SHIPPING_FLAT1_TEXT_WAY,
                'cost' => MODULE_SHIPPING_FLAT1_COST)));

   if ($this->tax_class > 0) {
    $this->quotes['tax'] = tep_get_tax_rate($this->tax_class,
    $order->delivery['country']['id'],
    $order->delivery['zone_id']);
   }

   if (tep_not_null($this->icon)) $this->quotes['icon'] =
                    tep_image($this->icon, $this->title);

   return $this->quotes;
  }

  function check() {
   if (!isset($this->_check)) {
    $check_query = tep_db_query("select configuration_value
    from " . TABLE_CONFIGURATION .
    " where configuration_key =
    'MODULE_SHIPPING_FLAT1_STATUS'");
```

```
      $this->_check = tep_db_num_rows($check_query);
    }
  return $this->_check;
  }

function install() {
 tep_db_query("insert into " . TABLE_CONFIGURATION .
  " (configuration_title, configuration_key,
     configuration_value, configuration_description,
     configuration_group_id, sort_order,
     set_function, date_added)
 values ('Enable Flat1 Shipping',
   'MODULE_SHIPPING_FLAT1_STATUS', 'True',
   'Do you want to offer flat1 rate shipping?', '6', '0',
   'tep_cfg_select_option(array(\'True\', \'False\'), ',
   now())");
 tep_db_query("insert into " . TABLE_CONFIGURATION .
  " (configuration_title, configuration_key,
     configuration_value, configuration_description,
     configuration_group_id, sort_order,
     date_added)
   values ('Shipping Cost',
    'MODULE_SHIPPING_FLAT1_COST', '5.00',
    'The shipping cost for all orders using this shipping
     method.', '6', '0', now())");
 tep_db_query("insert into " . TABLE_CONFIGURATION .
  " (configuration_title, configuration_key,
     configuration_value, configuration_description,
     configuration_group_id, sort_order,
     use_function, set_function, date_added)
 values ('Tax Class',
  'MODULE_SHIPPING_FLAT1_TAX_CLASS', '0',
  'Use the following tax class on the shipping fee.',
  '6', '0', 'tep_get_tax_class_title',
  'tep_cfg_pull_down_tax_classes(', now())");
 tep_db_query("insert into " . TABLE_CONFIGURATION .
  " (configuration_title, configuration_key,
     configuration_value, configuration_description,
     configuration_group_id, sort_order,
     use_function, set_function, date_added)
 values ('Shipping Zone', 'MODULE_SHIPPING_FLAT1_ZONE', '0',
  'If a zone is selected, only enable this shipping method
   for that zone.', '6', '0', 'tep_get_zone_class_title',
  'tep_cfg_pull_down_zone_classes(', now())");
 tep_db_query("insert into " . TABLE_CONFIGURATION .
```

```
    " (configuration_title, configuration_key,
      configuration_value, configuration_description,
      configuration_group_id, sort_order, date_added)
   values ('Sort Order',
    'MODULE_SHIPPING_FLAT1_SORT_ORDER', '0',
    'Sort order of display.', '6', '0', now())");
   }

   function remove() {
    tep_db_query("delete from " . TABLE_CONFIGURATION .
    " where configuration_key in ('" . implode("', '",
                         $this->keys()) . "')");
   }

   function keys() {
    return array('MODULE_SHIPPING_FLAT1_STATUS',
    'MODULE_SHIPPING_FLAT1_COST',
    'MODULE_SHIPPING_FLAT1_TAX_CLASS',
    'MODULE_SHIPPING_FLAT1_ZONE',
    'MODULE_SHIPPING_FLAT1_SORT_ORDER');
   }
  }
 ?>
```

2. As we will be using flat1.php for the **USA**, flat2.php for **Canada**, and flat3.php for **Rest of the World**, we will edit the display text (seen when a module is installed and highlighted) to reflect this in the right column of each module in the admin display. Find in line 81, right after the install() function begins, the following code:

```
tep_db_query("insert into " . TABLE_CONFIGURATION .
   " (configuration_title, configuration_key,
     configuration_value, configuration_description,
     configuration_group_id, sort_order, set_function,
     date_added)
 values ('Enable Flat1 Shipping',
   'MODULE_SHIPPING_FLAT1_STATUS', 'True',
   'Do you want to offer flat1 rate shipping?', '6',
   '0', 'tep_cfg_select_option(array(\'True\', \'False\'), ',
   now())");
```

Replace with the following code to reflect the future use of the module:

```
tep_db_query("insert into " . TABLE_CONFIGURATION .
   " (configuration_title, configuration_key,
     configuration_value, configuration_description,
```

```
    configuration_group_id, sort_order, set_function,
    date_added)
values ('Enable Flat Shipping for USA',
 'MODULE_SHIPPING_FLAT1_STATUS',
 'True', 'Do you want to offer flat rate shipping for USA?
 Remember to edit the zone correctly!', '6', '0',
 'tep_cfg_select_option(array(\'True\',
 \'False\'), ', now())");
```

Modify your `flat2.php` and `flat3.php` in the similar manner, specifying `Canada` for `flat2.php` and `Rest of the World` for `flat3.php`

3. Open `catalog/includes/languages/english/modules/shipping/flat.php` and create a clone, then replace all occurrences of the `flat` expression with `flat1`, keeping its upper or lower case spelling intact. Save this new file as `flat1.php`, then repeat for `flat2.php` and `flat3.php`. This is what your `flat1.php` language file will look like with the description (seen when the module is highlighted) edited to reflect the USA zone:

```
<?php
/*
  $Id: flat.php,v 1.5 2002/11/19 01:48:08 dgw_ Exp $
  cloned as
  $Id: flat1.php,v 1.00 2006/07/08 00:00:00 mm Exp $

  Modified by Monika Mathé
  http://www.monikamathe.com

  Module Copyright (c) 2006 Monika Mathé

  osCommerce, Open Source E-Commerce Solutions
  http://www.oscommerce.com

  Copyright (c) 2002 osCommerce

  Released under the GNU General Public License
*/

define('MODULE_SHIPPING_FLAT1_TEXT_TITLE', 'Flat Rate');
define('MODULE_SHIPPING_FLAT1_TEXT_DESCRIPTION',
       'Flat Rate for USA');
define('MODULE_SHIPPING_FLAT1_TEXT_WAY', 'Best Way');
?>
```

Chef's suggestion:

If you'd prefer the module's name to reflect the module's use in admin as well, you can change the TITLE define also, but remember that this expression will show in the catalog section, when shipping modules are presented for selection.

4. Before you install your new modules, make sure that proper zones have been defined for each shipping zone needed. Navigate to the **Tax Zones** area of your admin, namely **Administration | Locations/Taxes | Tax Zones**, and create three new zones used for shipping. Make sure to fill each zone with the countries it will be used for, by clicking the details button and adding the appropriate countries from the drop-down list. Your **Tax Zones** area will look like this (**Florida** comes with the default osCommerce installation):

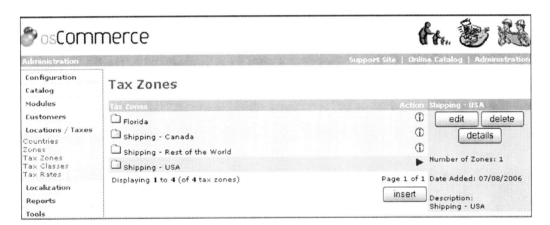

Chef's suggestion:

As there is no separate zone section for tax zones, shipping zones, and payment zones, and as those three areas are often different, it's a good idea to name the zones according to their intended use.

5. You are now ready to install the new shipping modules. Go to **Administration | Modules | Shipping** and uninstall the regular **Flat Rate** shipping module. Highlight each row to see its intended use as you install it. Your **Shipping Modules** area will look like this when installing the flat3.php modules file:

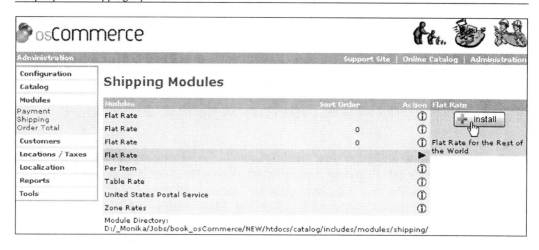

6. After you have installed all modules, open each module in edit mode and assign the correct zone and shipping cost, as here:

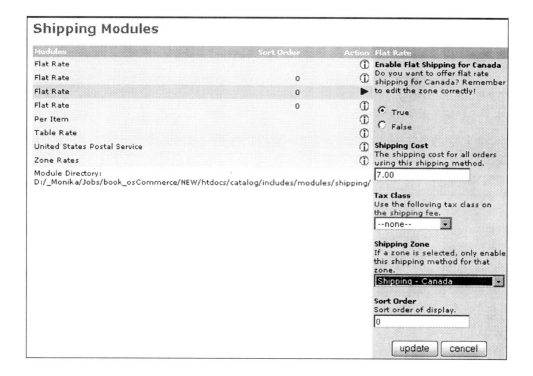

In this example USA is assigned a **Flat Rate** shipping cost of $5.00, Canada $7.00, and the Rest of the World $20.00.

It goes with everything, doesn't it? Bon appetit!

50. Add Percentage and Base Price Support to Table Rate

This recipe will be very useful for you if you'd like to specify a **Table Rate** based on the **Order Total**, but would like to add a percentage to some or all rates in this cost table. It is also possible to use only a percentage of the **Order Total** for a value. An example would be a **Rush Order** module, where all rates are raised by a certain percentage of the **Order Total** compared to regular shipping; that example is explained at the end of the Cooking section.

Here is an example that could be covered by this new flexible module:

Order Total	Shipping Cost
$0.00–25	8.50
$25.01–50	5.50 + 3%
$50.01–10000	3%

Presentation

Your **Shipping Modules** will look like this to follow this shipping plan:

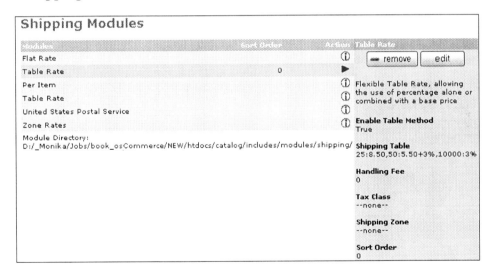

Depending on cart content, the calculated shipping cost will follow our rules. For an **Order Total** equal to or under $25.00, shipping cost will be $8.50. For an **Order Total** over $50.00, shipping cost will be calculated by the formula using only 3% of the **Order Total**. In the case of the following screenshot, the calculation is done like this:

$64.95 * 3 / 100 = $1.9485

As expected, shipping cost is shown as **$1.95**:

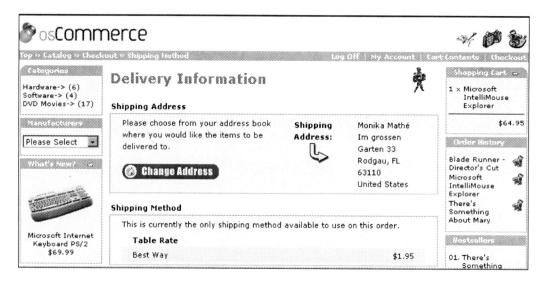

For an **Order Total** between $25.01 and $50.00, shipping cost will be calculated by the formula of using a base price of $5.50 and adding 3% of the **Order Total**. In the case of the following screenshot, the calculation is done like this:

$5.50 + $49.99 * 3 / 100 = $6.9997

Again, shipping cost is shown as **$7.00** just as expected:

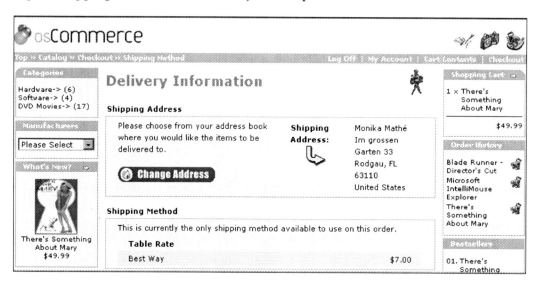

You're ready for a thick Bernaise; let's melt some butter!

Ingredients

New:
```
catalog/includes/modules/shipping/flexible.php
catalog/includes/languages/english/modules/shipping/
                                        flexible.php
```

Modified:
```
catalog/includes/functions/general.php
```

Cooking

1. Open `catalog/includes/functions/general.php` and add the following two trimming functions right before the closing `?>` PHP tag:

```php
//trimming functions, custom made
function after ($this, $inthat){
 if (!is_bool(strpos($inthat, $this)))
 return substr($inthat, strpos($inthat,$this)+strlen($this));
};

function before ($this, $inthat){
 return substr($inthat, 0, strpos($inthat, $this));
};
```

These functions will be used to separate the table rows that have a base price and a percentage added on top.

2. Create the new shipping module `catalog/includes/modules/shipping/flexible.php` using the following code:

```php
<?php
/*
 $Id: flexible.php,v 1.00 2006/07/08 00:00:00 mm Exp $

 Module written by Monika Mathé
 http://www.monikamathe.com

 Module Copyright (c) 2006 Monika Mathé

 osCommerce, Open Source E-Commerce Solutions
 http://www.oscommerce.com

 Copyright (c) 2003 osCommerce
```

```
      Released under the GNU General Public License
*/

class flexible {
 var $code, $title, $description, $icon, $enabled;

// class constructor
  function flexible() {
   global $order;

   $this->code = 'flexible';
   $this->title = MODULE_SHIPPING_FLEXIBLE_TEXT_TITLE;
   $this->description =
               MODULE_SHIPPING_FLEXIBLE_TEXT_DESCRIPTION;
   $this->sort_order = MODULE_SHIPPING_FLEXIBLE_SORT_ORDER;
   $this->icon = '';
   $this->tax_class = MODULE_SHIPPING_FLEXIBLE_TAX_CLASS;
   $this->enabled =
            ((MODULE_SHIPPING_FLEXIBLE_STATUS == 'True') ?
     true : false);

   if ( ($this->enabled == true) &&
      ((int)MODULE_SHIPPING_FLEXIBLE_ZONE > 0) ) {
    $check_flag = false;
    $check_query = tep_db_query("select zone_id from " .
     TABLE_ZONES_TO_GEO_ZONES . " where geo_zone_id = '" .
     MODULE_SHIPPING_FLEXIBLE_ZONE .
     "' and zone_country_id = '" .
     $order->delivery['country']['id'] .
     "' order by zone_id");
    while ($check = tep_db_fetch_array($check_query)) {
     if ($check['zone_id'] < 1) {
      $check_flag = true;
      break;
     } elseif ($check['zone_id'] ==
               $order->delivery['zone_id']) {
      $check_flag = true;
      break;
     }
    }

    if ($check_flag == false) {
     $this->enabled = false;
    }
   }
```

```
    }

// class methods
  function quote($method = '') {
   global $order, $cart;

   $order_total = $cart->show_total();

   $table_cost = split("[:,]" ,
   MODULE_SHIPPING_FLEXIBLE_COST);
   $size = sizeof($table_cost);
   for ($i=0, $n=$size; $i<$n; $i+=2) {
  if ($order_total <= $table_cost[$i]) {

   if ((strpos($table_cost[$i+1],'%')) &&
       (strpos($table_cost[$i+1],'+'))) {
   $shipping = before('+',$table_cost[$i+1]) + $order_total *
(after('+',$table_cost[$i+1])/100);
   } elseif (strpos($table_cost[$i+1],'%')) {
   $shipping = $order_total * ($table_cost[$i+1]/100);
   } else {
   $shipping = $table_cost[$i+1];
   }

   break;
   }
   }

   $this->quotes = array('id' => $this->code,
       'module' => MODULE_SHIPPING_FLEXIBLE_TEXT_TITLE,
       'methods' => array(array('id' => $this->code,
          'title' => MODULE_SHIPPING_FLEXIBLE_TEXT_WAY,
          'cost' => $shipping +
            MODULE_SHIPPING_FLEXIBLE_HANDLING)));

   if ($this->tax_class > 0) {
    $this->quotes['tax'] = tep_get_tax_rate($this->tax_class,
                   $order->delivery['country']['id'],
                   $order->delivery['zone_id']);
   }

   if (tep_not_null($this->icon)) $this->quotes['icon'] =
                        tep_image($this->icon, $this->title);
```

```
        return $this->quotes;
      }

      function check() {
       if (!isset($this->_check)) {
        $check_query =
          tep_db_query("select configuration_value from " .
          TABLE_CONFIGURATION . " where configuration_key =
          'MODULE_SHIPPING_FLEXIBLE_STATUS'");
        $this->_check = tep_db_num_rows($check_query);
       }
       return $this->_check;
      }


      function install() {
       tep_db_query("insert into " . TABLE_CONFIGURATION .
         " (configuration_title, configuration_key,
           configuration_value, configuration_description,
           configuration_group_id, sort_order,
           set_function, date_added)
       VALUES ('Enable Table Method',
         'MODULE_SHIPPING_FLEXIBLE_STATUS',
         'True', 'Do you want to offer flexible rate shipping?',
         '6', '0', 'tep_cfg_select_option(array(\'True\',
           \'False\'), ', now())");
       tep_db_query("insert into " . TABLE_CONFIGURATION .
         " (configuration_title, configuration_key,
           configuration_value, configuration_description,
           configuration_group_id, sort_order, date_added)
       values ('Shipping Table', 'MODULE_SHIPPING_FLEXIBLE_COST',
         '25:8.50,50:5.50,10000:0.00', 'The shipping cost is based
         on the total cost or weight of items.
         Example: 25:8.50,50:5.50,etc..
         Up to 25 charge 8.50, from there to 50 charge 5.50,
         etc', '6', '0', now())");
       tep_db_query("insert into " . TABLE_CONFIGURATION .
         " (configuration_title, configuration_key,
           configuration_value, configuration_description,
           configuration_group_id, sort_order, date_added)
       values ('Handling Fee',
         'MODULE_SHIPPING_FLEXIBLE_HANDLING', '0',
         'Handling fee for this shipping method.', '6',
         '0', now())");
       tep_db_query("insert into " . TABLE_CONFIGURATION .
         " (configuration_title, configuration_key,
           configuration_value, configuration_description,
```

```
        configuration_group_id, sort_order, use_function,
        set_function, date_added)
  values ('Tax Class', 'MODULE_SHIPPING_FLEXIBLE_TAX_CLASS',
    '0', 'Use the following tax class on the shipping fee.',
    '6', '0', 'tep_get_tax_class_title',
    'tep_cfg_pull_down_tax_classes(', now())");
  tep_db_query("insert into " . TABLE_CONFIGURATION .
    " (configuration_title, configuration_key,
        configuration_value, configuration_description,
        configuration_group_id, sort_order, use_function,
        set_function, date_added)
  values ('Shipping Zone', 'MODULE_SHIPPING_FLEXIBLE_ZONE',
    '0', 'If a zone is selected, only enable this shipping
    method for that zone.', '6', '0',
    'tep_get_zone_class_title',
    'tep_cfg_pull_down_zone_classes(', now())");
  tep_db_query("insert into " . TABLE_CONFIGURATION .
    " (configuration_title, configuration_key,
        configuration_value,
        configuration_description, configuration_group_id,
        sort_order, date_added)
  values ('Sort Order',
    'MODULE_SHIPPING_FLEXIBLE_SORT_ORDER',
    '0', 'Sort order of display.', '6', '0', now())");
  }

  function remove() {
   tep_db_query("delete from " . TABLE_CONFIGURATION .
   " where configuration_key in ('" . implode("', '",
                    $this->keys()) . "')");
  }

  function keys() {
   return array('MODULE_SHIPPING_FLEXIBLE_STATUS',
                'MODULE_SHIPPING_FLEXIBLE_COST',
                'MODULE_SHIPPING_FLEXIBLE_HANDLING',
                'MODULE_SHIPPING_FLEXIBLE_TAX_CLASS',
                'MODULE_SHIPPING_FLEXIBLE_ZONE',
                'MODULE_SHIPPING_FLEXIBLE_SORT_ORDER');
  }
 }
?>
```

3. Create matching language file `catalog/includes/languages/english/`
   `modules/shipping/flexible.php` with the following defines:

```
<?php
```

```
/*
   $Id: flexible.php,v 1.00 2006/07/08 00:00:00 mm Exp $

   Module written by Monika Mathé
   http://www.monikamathe.com

   Module Copyright (c) 2006 Monika Mathé

   osCommerce, Open Source E-Commerce Solutions
   http://www.oscommerce.com

   Copyright (c) 2003 osCommerce

   Released under the GNU General Public License
*/

define('MODULE_SHIPPING_FLEXIBLE_TEXT_TITLE', 'Table Rate');
define('MODULE_SHIPPING_FLEXIBLE_TEXT_DESCRIPTION',
       'Flexible Table Rate, allowing the use of percentage
       alone or combined with a base price');
define('MODULE_SHIPPING_FLEXIBLE_TEXT_WAY', 'Best Way');
?>
```

4. Navigate to **Administration | Modules | Shipping** and install your new
    shipping module. Be sure to specify the correct zone if you want to limit
    the display of this module, for example, to your home country. The default
    version uses the plain base prices as seen in the **Table Rate** module that
    comes with osCommerce. With this new module, you have the following
    options for each element (separated by commas, and bundled with :
    as before):

- Use a base price only
- Use a base price and add a percentage of the **Order Total**
- Use a percentage of the **Order Total** only

This module is a perfect choice if you'd like to offer a **Rush Order** shipping module.
In that scenario, add to all pairs 15% of the **Order Total**. Picking up the base setting
osCommerce provides, your Flexible Rate could be the following, with the module
renamed to **Rush Order Shipping** for catalog display:

25:8.50+15%,50:5.50+15%,10000:15%

As expected, the perfect accompaniment! Bon appetit!

51. Allow Free Postage for Free Items

You might have products in your store that are to be given to clients at no cost; these could be catalogues, brochures, or product samples. You might not want to charge for their shipping either. The **Table Rate** shipping module covers this scenario well, using amount-based calculation and setting zero cost for an **Order Total** of $0.00, or using weight-based calculation and setting the weight of the free items to 0. However, you might be using a different system such as USPS (United States Postal Service), and might prefer to hide that information for this type of customer, showing only the following **Free Postage** module.

Presentation

Adding this new recipe will give you the following screen for your **Shipping Modules**, assuming you are using USPS as your primary shipping module:

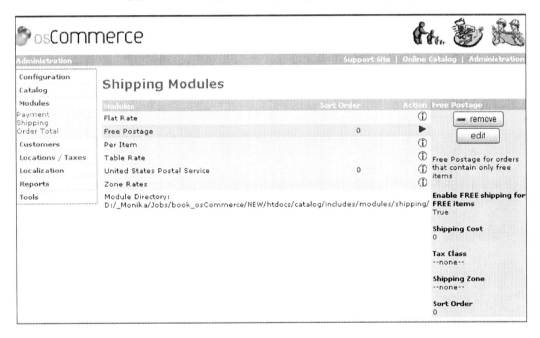

When adding only free items to the cart and checking out, the regular shipping module is hidden and instead the **Free Postage** module is visible:

Let's arrange a sampler tray!

Ingredients

New:

`catalog/includes/modules/shipping/flat1.php`
(this is a clone of the `catalog/includes/modules/shipping/flat.php` file)

`catalog/includes/languages/english/modules/shipping/flat1.php`
(this is a clone of the `catalog/includes/languages/english/modules/shipping/flat.php` file)

Modified:

`catalog/includes/languages/english/modules/shipping/usps.php`

Cooking

1. Open `catalog/includes/modules/shipping/flat.php` and create a clone, then replace all occurrences of the `flat` expression with `flat1`, keeping its upper or lower case spelling intact. Save this new file as `flat1.php`. This is what your `flat1.php` will look like before editing the display text:

   ```
   <?php
   /*
   $Id: flat.php,v 1.40 2003/02/05 22:41:52 hpdl Exp $
   cloned as
   ```

```
$Id: flat1.php,v 1.00 2006/07/08 00:00:00 mm Exp $

Modified by Monika Mathé
http://www.monikamathe.com

Module Copyright (c) 2006 Monika Mathé
osCommerce, Open Source E-Commerce Solutions
http://www.oscommerce.com

Copyright (c) 2003 osCommerce

Released under the GNU General Public License
*/

class flat1 {
 var $code, $title, $description, $icon, $enabled;

// class constructor
  function flat1() {
   global $order;

   $this->code = 'flat1';
   $this->title = MODULE_SHIPPING_FLAT1_TEXT_TITLE;
   $this->description =
              MODULE_SHIPPING_FLAT1_TEXT_DESCRIPTION;
   $this->sort_order = MODULE_SHIPPING_FLAT1_SORT_ORDER;
   $this->icon = '';
   $this->tax_class = MODULE_SHIPPING_FLAT1_TAX_CLASS;
   $this->enabled = ((MODULE_SHIPPING_FLAT1_STATUS == 'True') ?
     true : false);

   if ( ($this->enabled == true) &&
       ((int)MODULE_SHIPPING_FLAT1_ZONE > 0) ) {
    $check_flag = false;
    $check_query = tep_db_query("select zone_id from " .
     TABLE_ZONES_TO_GEO_ZONES . " where geo_zone_id = '" .
     MODULE_SHIPPING_FLAT1_ZONE . "' and zone_country_id = '" .
     $order->delivery['country']['id'] . "' order by zone_id");
    while ($check = tep_db_fetch_array($check_query)) {
     if ($check['zone_id'] < 1) {
      $check_flag = true;
      break;
     } elseif ($check['zone_id'] ==
             $order->delivery['zone_id']) {
```

```
          $check_flag = true;
          break;
        }
      }

      if ($check_flag == false) {
       $this->enabled = false;
      }
     }
    }

  // class methods
    function quote($method = '') {
     global $order;

     $this->quotes = array('id' => $this->code,
               'module' => MODULE_SHIPPING_FLAT1_TEXT_TITLE,
               'methods' => array(array('id' => $this->code,
                   'title' => MODULE_SHIPPING_FLAT1_TEXT_WAY,
                   'cost' => MODULE_SHIPPING_FLAT1_COST)));

     if ($this->tax_class > 0) {
 $this->quotes['tax'] = tep_get_tax_rate($this->tax_class,
   $order->delivery['country']['id'],
   $order->delivery['zone_id']);
 }

 if (tep_not_null($this->icon)) $this->quotes['icon'] =
                     tep_image($this->icon, $this->title);

 return $this->quotes;
 }

    function check() {
     if (!isset($this->_check)) {
      $check_query =
         tep_db_query("select configuration_value from " .
          TABLE_CONFIGURATION . " where configuration_key =
          'MODULE_SHIPPING_FLAT1_STATUS'");
      $this->_check = tep_db_num_rows($check_query);
     }
     return $this->_check;
    }
```

```
function install() {
  tep_db_query("insert into " . TABLE_CONFIGURATION .
    " (configuration_title, configuration_key,
      configuration_value, configuration_description,
      configuration_group_id, sort_order,
      set_function, date_added)
 values ('Enable Flat1 Shipping',
   'MODULE_SHIPPING_FLAT1_STATUS',
   'True', 'Do you want to offer flat1 rate shipping?',
   '6', '0', 'tep_cfg_select_option(array(\'True\',
          \'False\'), ', now())");
  tep_db_query("insert into " . TABLE_CONFIGURATION .
    " (configuration_title, configuration_key,
      configuration_value, configuration_description,
      configuration_group_id, sort_order, date_added)
 values ('Shipping Cost', 'MODULE_SHIPPING_FLAT1_COST',
   '5.00', 'The shipping cost for all orders using this
   shipping method.', '6', '0', now())");
  tep_db_query("insert into " . TABLE_CONFIGURATION .
    " (configuration_title, configuration_key,
      configuration_value, configuration_description,
      configuration_group_id, sort_order,
      use_function, set_function, date_added)
 values ('Tax Class', 'MODULE_SHIPPING_FLAT1_TAX_CLASS',
    '0', 'Use the following tax class on the shipping fee.',
    '6', '0', 'tep_get_tax_class_title',
    'tep_cfg_pull_down_tax_classes(', now())");
  tep_db_query("insert into " . TABLE_CONFIGURATION .
    " (configuration_title, configuration_key,
      configuration_value, configuration_description,
      configuration_group_id, sort_order, use_function,
      set_function, date_added)
 values ('Shipping Zone', 'MODULE_SHIPPING_FLAT1_ZONE', '0',
   'If a zone is selected, only enable this shipping
   method for that zone.', '6', '0',
   'tep_get_zone_class_title',
   'tep_cfg_pull_down_zone_classes(', now())");
  tep_db_query("insert into " . TABLE_CONFIGURATION .
    " (configuration_title, configuration_key,
      configuration_value, configuration_description,
      configuration_group_id, sort_order, date_added)
 values ('Sort Order', 'MODULE_SHIPPING_FLAT1_SORT_ORDER',
   '0', 'Sort order of display.', '6', '0', now())");
}

function remove() {
  tep_db_query("delete from " . TABLE_CONFIGURATION .
```

```
                    " where configuration_key in ('" . implode("', '",
                                                 $this->keys()) . "')");
            }

            function keys() {
             return array('MODULE_SHIPPING_FLAT1_STATUS',
                          'MODULE_SHIPPING_FLAT1_COST',
                          'MODULE_SHIPPING_FLAT1_TAX_CLASS',
                          'MODULE_SHIPPING_FLAT1_ZONE',
                          'MODULE_SHIPPING_FLAT1_SORT_ORDER');
            }
          }
        ?>
```

2. As we will be using `flat1.php` for the **Free Postage** module, we will edit the display text (seen when the module is installed and highlighted) to reflect this in the right column of each module in the admin display. Find in line 81, right after the `install()` function begins, the following code:

```
tep_db_query("insert into " . TABLE_CONFIGURATION .
  " (configuration_title, configuration_key,
    configuration_value, configuration_description,
    configuration_group_id, sort_order,
    set_function, date_added)
 values ('Enable Flat1 Shipping',
   'MODULE_SHIPPING_FLAT1_STATUS', 'True',
   'Do you want to offer flat1 rate shipping?', '6', '0',
   'tep_cfg_select_option(array(\'True\', \'False\'), ',
   now())");
```

Replace it with the following to reflect the future use of the module:

```
tep_db_query("insert into " . TABLE_CONFIGURATION .
  " (configuration_title, configuration_key,
    configuration_value, configuration_description,
    configuration_group_id, sort_order, set_function,
    date_added)
 values ('Enable FREE shipping for FREE items,
   'MODULE_SHIPPING_FLAT1_STATUS', 'True',
   'Do you want to offer FREE shipping for FREE items?',
   '6', '0', 'tep_cfg_select_option(array(\'True\',
       \'False\'), ', now())");
```

3. Now add a clause that will hide this module, even if installed, when the **Order Total** is not $0.00. Find this in line 48:

```
if ($check_flag == false) {
 $this->enabled = false;
```

```
      }
    }
  }
```

Replace it with this:

```
if ($check_flag == false) {
  $this->enabled = false;
 }
}

if (is_object($order)) {
// hide this module if cart total > 0
 if ($this->enabled == true) {
  global $cart;
  if ($cart->show_total() > 0.00) {
   $this->enabled = false;
  }
 }
}
}
```

4. Open `catalog/includes/languages/english/modules/shipping/` `flat.php` and create a clone, then replace all occurrences of the `flat` expression with `flat1`, keeping its upper or lower case spelling intact. Save this new file as `flat1.php`. This is what your `flat1.php` language file will look like with the description (seen when the module is highlighted) edited to reflect the **Free Postage**:

```
<?php
/*
   $Id: flat.php,v 1.5 2002/11/19 01:48:08 dgw_ Exp $
   cloned as
   $Id: flat1.php,v 1.00 2006/07/08 00:00:00 mm Exp $

   Modified by Monika Mathé
   http://www.monikamathe.com

   Module Copyright (c) 2006 Monika Mathé

   osCommerce, Open Source E-Commerce Solutions
   http://www.oscommerce.com
   Copyright (c) 2002 osCommerce

   Released under the GNU General Public License
*/
```

```
define('MODULE_SHIPPING_FLAT1_TEXT_TITLE', 'Free Postage');
define('MODULE_SHIPPING_FLAT1_TEXT_DESCRIPTION',
    'Free Postage for orders that contain only free items');
define('MODULE_SHIPPING_FLAT1_TEXT_WAY', '(free items only)');
?>
```

5. Similar to hiding the **Free Postage** module for orders that do not qualify for free shipping, we'll need to hide the shop's regular shipping module, in this case USPS, for orders that qualify for free shipping. Open `catalog/includes/modules/shipping/usps.php` and find this in line 41, where we hide the module in case all flags were set to `true`. If you are using different default shipping modules, find the line with this expression in the upper part of your module:

```
if ($check_flag == false) {
  $this->enabled = false;
}
}
```

Replace with this code that checks if the cart has only free items:

```
if ($check_flag == false) {
  $this->enabled = false;
}
}

if (is_object($order)) {
// hide this module if cart total = 0
if ($this->enabled == true) {
 global $cart;
 if ($cart->show_total() = 0.00) {
 $this->enabled = false;
 }
 }
}
```

6. Navigate to **Administration | Modules | Shipping** and install the new **Free Postage** shipping module. Edit the shipping cost to **0**, select a shipping zone if applicable, and save your changes.

Tastefully displayed! Bon appetit!

52. Limit Flat Rate Shipping to a Specific Top Category Only

This recipe will be very useful for you if you have a setup similar to the demo shop. For this example we are setting a **Flat Rate** for shipping a single movie DVD. When additional items are added to the cart or a singular product in the cart is not a movie DVD, the shop's default shipping module, in this example, **Table Rate**, will be visible while the new **Flat Rate** module will be hidden.

Presentation

Your Checkout Shipping page will look like this with only a movie DVD in the cart:

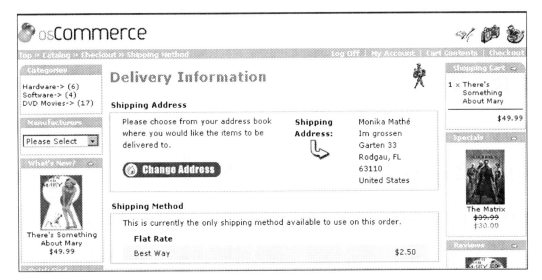

If you add a second DVD or have a product from any other top category in the cart, your shipping calculation will use **Table Rate**:

This is what your **Administration | Modules | Shipping** area will look with the
new **Flat Fee** module added:

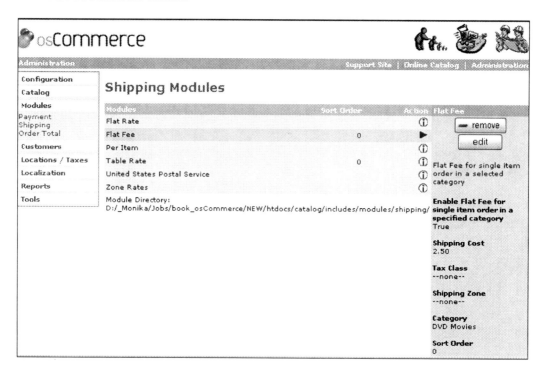

Ready to put out a choice buffet?

Ingredients

New:

catalog/includes/modules/shipping/flat1.php
(this is a clone of the `catalog/includes/modules/shipping/flat.php` file)
catalog/includes/languages/english/modules/shipping/flat1.php
(this is a clone of the `catalog/includes/languages/english/modules/`
`shipping/flat.php` file)

Modified:

catalog/admin/includes/functions/general.php
catalog/includes/languages/english/modules/shipping/table.php

Cooking

1. Open `catalog/admin/includes/functions/general.php` and add the
   following two functions before the closing `?>` PHP tag. The first function
   creates a drop-down list of the top categories, while the second shows the
   category name for a given `categories_id`:

```
function tep_cfg_pull_down_topcategories($categories_id,
                                         $key = '') {
  global $languages_id;

  $name = (($key) ? 'configuration[' . $key . ']' :
        'configuration_value');

  $cat_query = tep_db_query("select c.categories_id,
    cd.categories_name from " . TABLE_CATEGORIES . " c, " .
    TABLE_CATEGORIES_DESCRIPTION . " cd where
    c.categories_id = cd.categories_id and
    c.parent_id = '0' and cd.language_id = '" .
    (int)$languages_id . "' order by categories_name");
  while ($cat = tep_db_fetch_array($cat_query)) {
   $cat_array[] = array('id' => $cat['categories_id'],
                'text' => $cat['categories_name']);
  }

  return tep_draw_pull_down_menu($name, $cat_array,
        $categories_id);
}

function tep_get_categories_title($categories_id,
                                  $language_id = '') {
```

```
global $languages_id;

if (!is_numeric($language_id)) $language_id = $languages_id;

$cat_query = tep_db_query("select categories_name from " .
  TABLE_CATEGORIES_DESCRIPTION . " where categories_id = '" .
  (int)$categories_id . "' and language_id = '" .
  (int)$language_id . "'");
$cat = tep_db_fetch_array($cat_query);

return $cat['categories_name'];
}
```

2. Open `catalog/includes/modules/shipping/flat.php` and create a clone, then replace all occurrences of the `flat` expression with `flat1`, keeping its upper or lower case spelling intact. Save this new file as `flat1.php`. This is what your `flat1.php` will look like before editing the display text:

```php
<?php
/*
$Id: flat.php,v 1.40 2003/02/05 22:41:52 hpdl Exp $
cloned as
$Id: flat1.php,v 1.00 2006/07/08 00:00:00 mm Exp $

Modified by Monika Mathé
http://www.monikamathe.com

Module Copyright (c) 2006 Monika Mathé
osCommerce, Open Source E-Commerce Solutions
http://www.oscommerce.com

Copyright (c) 2003 osCommerce

Released under the GNU General Public License
*/

class flat1 {
 var $code, $title, $description, $icon, $enabled;

// class constructor
  function flat1() {
   global $order;
   $this->code = 'flat1';
   $this->title = MODULE_SHIPPING_FLAT1_TEXT_TITLE;
   $this->description = MODULE_SHIPPING_FLAT1_TEXT_DESCRIPTION;
```

```
    $this->sort_order = MODULE_SHIPPING_FLAT1_SORT_ORDER;
    $this->icon = '';
    $this->tax_class = MODULE_SHIPPING_FLAT1_TAX_CLASS;
    $this->enabled = ((MODULE_SHIPPING_FLAT1_STATUS == 'True') ?
                        true : false);

    if ( ($this->enabled == true) &&
             ((int)MODULE_SHIPPING_FLAT1_ZONE > 0) ) {
     $check_flag = false;
     $check_query = tep_db_query("select zone_id from " .
       TABLE_ZONES_TO_GEO_ZONES . " where geo_zone_id = '" .
       MODULE_SHIPPING_FLAT1_ZONE . "' and zone_country_id = '" .
       $order->delivery['country']['id'] . "' order by zone_id");
     while ($check = tep_db_fetch_array($check_query)) {
      if ($check['zone_id'] < 1) {
       $check_flag = true;
       break;
       } elseif ($check['zone_id'] == $order->delivery['zone_id']) {
       $check_flag = true;
       break;
      }
     }

     if ($check_flag == false) {
      $this->enabled = false;
      }
    }
   }

// class methods
   function quote($method = '') {
    global $order;

    $this->quotes = array('id' => $this->code,
              'module' => MODULE_SHIPPING_FLAT1_TEXT_TITLE,
              'methods' => array(array('id' => $this->code,
                    'title' => MODULE_SHIPPING_FLAT1_TEXT_WAY,
                    'cost' => MODULE_SHIPPING_FLAT1_COST)));

if ($this->tax_class > 0) {
    $this->quotes['tax'] = tep_get_tax_rate($this->tax_class,
    $order->delivery['country']['id'],
    $order->delivery['zone_id']);
    }
```

```
  if (tep_not_null($this->icon)) $this->quotes['icon'] =
      tep_image($this->icon, $this->title);

  return $this->quotes;
}

function check() {
 if (!isset($this->_check)) {
  $check_query =
      tep_db_query("select configuration_value from " .
      TABLE_CONFIGURATION . " where configuration_key =
      'MODULE_SHIPPING_FLAT1_STATUS'");
  $this->_check = tep_db_num_rows($check_query);
 }
 return $this->_check;
}

function install() {
 tep_db_query("insert into " . TABLE_CONFIGURATION .
   " (configuration_title, configuration_key,
     configuration_value, configuration_description,
     configuration_group_id, sort_order,
     set_function, date_added)
  values ('Enable Flat1 Shipping',
   'MODULE_SHIPPING_FLAT1_STATUS', 'True',
   'Do you want to offer flat1 rate shipping?', '6', '0',
   'tep_cfg_select_option(array(\'True\', \'False\'), ',
   now())");
 tep_db_query("insert into " . TABLE_CONFIGURATION .
   " (configuration_title, configuration_key,
     configuration_value, configuration_description,
     configuration_group_id, sort_order, date_added)
  values ('Shipping Cost', 'MODULE_SHIPPING_FLAT1_COST', '5.00',
   'The shipping cost for all orders using this shipping
   method.', '6', '0', now())");
 tep_db_query("insert into " . TABLE_CONFIGURATION .
   " (configuration_title, configuration_key,
     configuration_value, configuration_description,
     configuration_group_id, sort_order,
     use_function, set_function, date_added)
  values ('Tax Class', 'MODULE_SHIPPING_FLAT1_TAX_CLASS', '0',
   'Use the following tax class on the shipping fee.', '6',
   '0', 'tep_get_tax_class_title',
   'tep_cfg_pull_down_tax_classes(', now())");
 tep_db_query("insert into " . TABLE_CONFIGURATION .
   " (configuration_title, configuration_key,
```

```
                configuration_value, configuration_description,
                configuration_group_id, sort_order,
                use_function, set_function, date_added)
        values ('Shipping Zone', 'MODULE_SHIPPING_FLAT1_ZONE', '0',
          'If a zone is selected, only enable this shipping method for
          that zone.', '6', '0', 'tep_get_zone_class_title',
          'tep_cfg_pull_down_zone_classes(', now())");
        tep_db_query("insert into " . TABLE_CONFIGURATION .
          " (configuration_title, configuration_key,
                configuration_value, configuration_description,
                configuration_group_id, sort_order, date_added)
        values ('Sort Order', 'MODULE_SHIPPING_FLAT1_SORT_ORDER', '0',
          'Sort order of display.', '6', '0', now())");
      }

      function remove() {
        tep_db_query("delete from " . TABLE_CONFIGURATION . "
          where configuration_key in ('" . implode("', '",
          $this->keys()) . "')");
      }

      function keys() {
        return array('MODULE_SHIPPING_FLAT1_STATUS',
                     'MODULE_SHIPPING_FLAT1_COST',
                     'MODULE_SHIPPING_FLAT1_TAX_CLASS',
                     'MODULE_SHIPPING_FLAT1_ZONE',
                     'MODULE_SHIPPING_FLAT1_SORT_ORDER');
      }
    }
    ?>
```

3. As we will be using `flat1.php` for the **Flat Fee** for single item order in a specified top-category module, we will edit the display text (seen when the module is installed and highlighted) to reflect this in the right column of each module in the admin display. Find in line 81, right after the `install()` function begins, the following code:

```
    tep_db_query("insert into " . TABLE_CONFIGURATION .
      " (configuration_title, configuration_key,
            configuration_value, configuration_description,
            configuration_group_id, sort_order,
        set_function, date_added)
    values ('Enable Flat1 Shipping',
      'MODULE_SHIPPING_FLAT1_STATUS', 'True',
      'Do you want to offer flat1 rate shipping?', '6', '0',
      'tep_cfg_select_option(array(\'True\', \'False\'), ',
      now())");
```

Replace it with the following code to reflect the future use of the module:

```
tep_db_query("insert into " . TABLE_CONFIGURATION .
   " (configuration_title, configuration_key,
      configuration_value, configuration_description,
      configuration_group_id, sort_order,
      set_function, date_added)
   values ('Enable Flat Fee for single item order in a specified
      category', 'MODULE_SHIPPING_FLAT1_STATUS', 'True',
      'Do you want to offer Flat Fee for single item order in a
      specified category?', '6', '0',
      'tep_cfg_select_option(array(\'True\', \'False\'), ',
         now())");
```

4. Add a new key to the `install()` function of your module. Find this in line 79:

```
tep_db_query("insert into " . TABLE_CONFIGURATION .
   " (configuration_title, configuration_key,
      configuration_value, configuration_description,
      configuration_group_id, sort_order, date_added)
   values ('Sort Order', 'MODULE_SHIPPING_FLAT_SORT_ORDER', '0',
      'Sort order of display.', '6', '0', now())");
```

Add right above it the following line that uses your new functions to pull the top categories of your store:

```
tep_db_query("insert into " . TABLE_CONFIGURATION .
   " (configuration_title, configuration_key,
      configuration_value, configuration_description,
      configuration_group_id, sort_order,
      use_function, set_function, date_added)
   values ('Category', 'MODULE_SHIPPING_FLAT1_CAT_LIMIT', '0',
      'This module is limited to products in this category.', '6',
      '0', 'tep_get_categories_title',
      'tep_cfg_pull_down_topcategories(', now())");
```

5. Add the call of the new key to the `keys()` function of your new module. Find this in line 88:

```
return array('MODULE_SHIPPING_FLAT_STATUS',
            'MODULE_SHIPPING_FLAT_COST',
            'MODULE_SHIPPING_FLAT_TAX_CLASS',
            'MODULE_SHIPPING_FLAT_ZONE',
            'MODULE_SHIPPING_FLAT_SORT_ORDER');
```

And replace with this:

```
return array('MODULE_SHIPPING_FLAT1_STATUS',
            'MODULE_SHIPPING_FLAT1_COST',
```

```
'MODULE_SHIPPING_FLAT1_TAX_CLASS',
'MODULE_SHIPPING_FLAT1_ZONE',
'MODULE_SHIPPING_FLAT1_CAT_LIMIT',
'MODULE_SHIPPING_FLAT1_SORT_ORDER');
```

6. Now add a clause that will hide this module, even if installed, when there is more than one item in the cart, or when there is one item only, but not from the specified category. Find this in line 48:

```
if ($check_flag == false) {
 $this->enabled = false;
 }
 }
}
```

Replace with this:

```
if ($check_flag == false) {
   $this->enabled = false;
   }
  }

if (is_object($order)) {
// hide the module if the order contains more than one item,
// or is not from the specified category
 if ($this->enabled == true) {
  global $cart;
  if ($cart->count_contents() == 1) {

    $products_id = $cart->get_product_id_list();

    //check if the item belongs to the cat specified for flat
    //fee shipping
    $item_path =
          tep_get_product_path(tep_get_prid($products_id));
    $item_cat = explode('_' , $item_path);

    if ($item_cat[0] != MODULE_SHIPPING_FLAT1_CAT_LIMIT) {
     $this->enabled = false;
     }
   } else {
    $this->enabled = false;
    }
   }
  }
 }
```

7. Open `catalog/includes/languages/english/modules/shipping/flat.php` and create a clone, then replace all occurrences of the `flat` expression with `flat1`, keeping its upper or lower case spelling intact. Save this new file as `flat1.php`. This is what your `flat1.php` language file will look like with the description (seen when the module is highlighted) edited to reflect the **Flat Fee** for a single item module:

```php
<?php
/*
  $Id: flat.php,v 1.5 2002/11/19 01:48:08 dgw_ Exp $
  cloned as
  $Id: flat1.php,v 1.00 2006/07/08 00:00:00 mm Exp $

  Modified by Monika Mathé
  http://www.monikamathe.com

  Module Copyright (c) 2006 Monika Mathé

  osCommerce, Open Source E-Commerce Solutions
  http://www.oscommerce.com

  Copyright (c) 2002 osCommerce

  Released under the GNU General Public License
*/

define('MODULE_SHIPPING_FLAT1_TEXT_TITLE', 'Flat Fee');
define('MODULE_SHIPPING_FLAT1_TEXT_DESCRIPTION',
    'Flat Fee for single item order in a selected category');
define('MODULE_SHIPPING_FLAT1_TEXT_WAY', 'Best Way');
?>
```

8. Similar to hiding the **Flat Fee** module for orders that have either more than one item in the cart or not from the correct category, we'll need to hide the shop's regular shipping module, here **Table Rate**, for orders that qualify for **Flat Fee** shipping. Open `catalog/includes/modules/shipping/table.php` and find this in line 41:

```php
if ($check_flag == false) {
  $this->enabled = false;
  }
 }
}
```

Replace it with this:

```php
if ($check_flag == false) {
  $this->enabled = false;
```

```
        }
      }

if (is_object($order) &&
    MODULE_SHIPPING_FLAT1_CAT_LIMIT != '') {
// hide the module if the order contains only one item and is
// from the specified category for flat fee shipping
 if ($this->enabled == true) {
  global $cart;
  if ($cart->count_contents() == 1) {

   $products_id = $cart->get_product_id_list();

   //check if the item belongs to the cat specified for flat
   //fee shipping
   $item_path =
        tep_get_product_path(tep_get_prid($products_id));
   $item_cat = explode('_' , $item_path);

   if ($item_cat[0] == MODULE_SHIPPING_FLAT1_CAT_LIMIT) {
    $this->enabled = false;
   }
  }
 }
}
}
```

9.   Navigate to **Administration | Modules | Shipping** and install the new **Flat Fee** shipping module. Edit the **Shipping Cost** to the flat cost you want to offer, like **$2.50** as in our example, and select a **Shipping Zone** if applicable, and save your changes.

All you can eat! Bon appetit!

53. Hide Shipping Modules Driven by Weight

This recipe is perfect for you if you'd like to hide shipping modules for package weight over a certain limit, say 10lb. A reason for this could be that the shipping partner you use for this module doesn't deliver packages over a certain weight limit or that its prices get too steep after a certain weight limit is reached. In that case, you might just prefer not to show those outrageous prices, but instead a different module. This module will calculate cart weight and compare it to a key value as specified during module installation.

Chef's suggestion:

If you have set a **Package Tare Weight** in **Administration | Configuration | Shipping Packaging**, this number will be added to your cart weight.

Presentation

Your Checkout Shipping page will show two shipping modules when your cart content weighs equal to or less than 10lb for our example (DVD weight is 7lb, and Tare Weight is 3lb), but if your cart weight is more than the specified value of 10lb, your shipping calculation will only use **Table Rate**, the alternative shipping module offered on this site (Software weight is 8lb, and Tare Weight is 3lb).

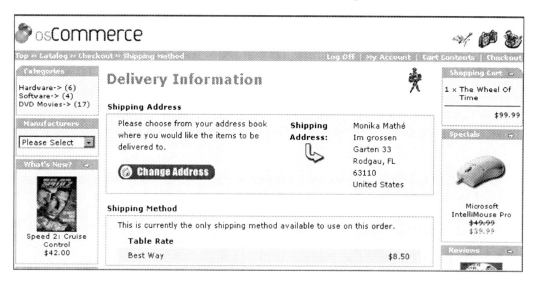

This is what your **Administration | Modules | Shipping** area will look with the modified **USPS** module and **Table Rate** installed (specify your own USPS User ID and Password):

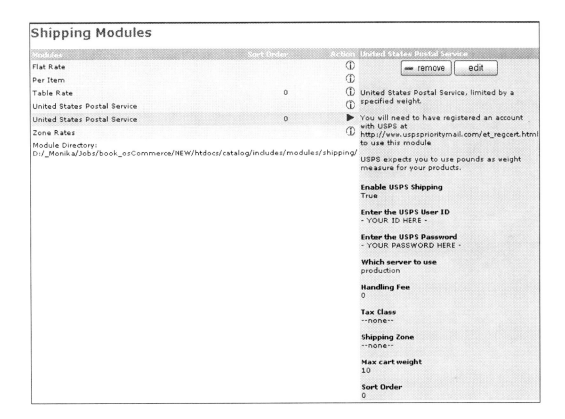

Let's scale up your sauce offerings!

Ingredients

> **New:**
>
> `catalog/includes/modules/shipping/usps1.php`
> (this is a clone of the `catalog/includes/modules/shipping/usps.php` file)
> `catalog/includes/languages/english/modules/shipping/usps1.php`
> (this is a clone of the `catalog/includes/languages/english/modules/`
> `shipping/usps.php` file)

Cooking

1. Open `catalog/includes/modules/shipping/usps.php` and create a clone, then replace all occurrences of the `usps` expression in the keys or module name with `usps1`, keeping its upper or lower case spelling intact. Save this new file as `usps1.php`.

Chef's suggestion:

As this module has the `usps` expression hidden in other parameters, you have to be very careful when doing the search and replace. There are three expressions that have to be left as is throughout the text: USPS in the `install()` function descriptions, `$usps_server`, `$uspsQuote`, and don't change the name of the `shipping_usps.gif` image file.

This is what your `usps1.php` will look like before making further edits to the file:

```php
<?php
/*
$Id: usps.php,v 1.47 2003/04/08 23:23:42 dgw_ Exp $
cloned as
$Id: usps1.php,v 1.00 2006/07/09 00:00:00 mm Exp $

Modified by Monika Mathé
http://www.monikamathe.com

Module Copyright (c) 2006 Monika Mathé

osCommerce, Open Source E-Commerce Solutions
http://www.oscommerce.com

Copyright (c) 2003 osCommerce

Released under the GNU General Public License
*/

class usps1 {
  var $code, $title, $description, $icon,
  $enabled, $countries;

// class constructor
```

```
function usps1() {
 global $order;

 $this->code = 'usps1';
 $this->title = MODULE_SHIPPING_USPS1_TEXT_TITLE;
 $this->description =
             MODULE_SHIPPING_USPS1_TEXT_DESCRIPTION;
 $this->sort_order = MODULE_SHIPPING_USPS1_SORT_ORDER;
 $this->icon = DIR_WS_ICONS . 'shipping_usps.gif';
 $this->tax_class = MODULE_SHIPPING_USPS1_TAX_CLASS;
 $this->enabled = ((MODULE_SHIPPING_USPS1_STATUS == 'True') ?
                  true : false);

 if ( ($this->enabled == true) &&
    ((int)MODULE_SHIPPING_USPS1_ZONE > 0) ) {
  $check_flag = false;
  $check_query = tep_db_query("select zone_id from " .
    TABLE_ZONES_TO_GEO_ZONES . " where geo_zone_id = '" .
    MODULE_SHIPPING_USPS1_ZONE .
    "' and zone_country_id = '" .
    $order->delivery['country']['id'] .
    "' order by zone_id");
  while ($check = tep_db_fetch_array($check_query)) {
   if ($check['zone_id'] < 1) {

    $check_flag = true;
    break;
   } elseif ($check['zone_id'] ==
            $order->delivery['zone_id']) {
    $check_flag = true;
    break;
   }
  }

  if ($check_flag == false) {
   $this->enabled = false;
  }
 }

 $this->types = array('Express' => 'Express Mail',
           'First Class' => 'First-Class Mail',
           'Priority' => 'Priority Mail',
           'Parcel' => 'Parcel Post');
```

```
      $this->intl_types = array('GXG Document' =>
            'Global Express Guaranteed Document Service',
         'GXG Non-Document' => 'Global Express Guaranteed
           Non-Document Service',
         'Express' => 'Global Express Mail (EMS)',
         'Priority Lg' =>
           'Global Priority Mail - Flat-rate Envelope (large)',
         'Priority Sm' =>
           'Global Priority Mail - Flat-rate Envelope (small)',
         'Priority Var' =>
           'Global Priority Mail - Variable Weight
                Envelope (single)',
         'Airmail Letter' => 'Airmail Letter Post',
         'Airmail Parcel' => 'Airmail Parcel Post',
         'Surface Letter' => 'Economy (Surface) Letter Post',
         'Surface Post' => 'Economy (Surface) Parcel Post');

    $this->countries = $this->country_list();
  }

// class methods
  function quote($method = '') {
    global $order, $shipping_weight, $shipping_num_boxes;

    if ( tep_not_null($method) &&
       (isset($this->types[$method]) || in_array($method,
                                  $this->intl_types)) ) {
     $this->_setService($method);
    }

    $this->_setMachinable('False');
    $this->_setContainer('None');
    $this->_setSize('REGULAR');

// usps doesnt accept zero weight
    $shipping_weight =
    ($shipping_weight < 0.1 ? 0.1 : $shipping_weight);
    $shipping_pounds = floor ($shipping_weight);
    $shipping_ounces = round(16 *
        ($shipping_weight - floor($shipping_weight)));
    $this->_setWeight($shipping_pounds, $shipping_ounces);

    $uspsQuote = $this->_getQuote();
```

```
if (is_array($uspsQuote)) {
 if (isset($uspsQuote['error'])) {
  $this->quotes = array('module' => $this->title,
    'error' => $uspsQuote['error']);
 } else {
  $this->quotes = array('id' => $this->code,
    'module' => $this->title . ' (' . $shipping_num_boxes .
         ' x ' . $shipping_weight . 'lbs)');

  $methods = array();
  $size = sizeof($uspsQuote);
  for ($i=0; $i<$size; $i++) {
   list($type, $cost) = each($uspsQuote[$i]);

   $methods[] = array('id' => $type,
      'title' => ((isset($this->types[$type])) ?
           $this->types[$type] : $type),
      'cost' => ($cost + MODULE_SHIPPING_USPS1_HANDLING) *
           $shipping_num_boxes);
  }

  $this->quotes['methods'] = $methods;

  if ($this->tax_class > 0) {
   $this->quotes['tax'] =
   tep_get_tax_rate($this->tax_class,
   $order->delivery['country']['id'],
   $order->delivery['zone_id']);
  }
 }
} else {
 $this->quotes = array('module' => $this->title,
         'error' => MODULE_SHIPPING_USPS1_TEXT_ERROR);
}

if (tep_not_null($this->icon)) $this->quotes['icon'] =
    tep_image($this->icon, $this->title);

return $this->quotes;
}

function check() {
 if (!isset($this->_check)) {
  $check_query =
      tep_db_query("select configuration_value from " .
```

```
                  TABLE_CONFIGURATION . " where configuration_key =
                                      'MODULE_SHIPPING_USPS1_STATUS'");
    $this->_check = tep_db_num_rows($check_query);
   }
   return $this->_check;
  }


  function install() {
   tep_db_query("insert into " . TABLE_CONFIGURATION .
     " (configuration_title, configuration_key,
        configuration_value, configuration_description,
        configuration_group_id, sort_order,
        set_function, date_added)
   values ('Enable USPS Shipping',
     'MODULE_SHIPPING_USPS1_STATUS', 'True',
     'Do you want to offer USPS1 shipping?', '6', '0',
     'tep_cfg_select_option(array(\'True\', \'False\'), ',
        now())");
   tep_db_query("insert into " . TABLE_CONFIGURATION .
     " (configuration_title, configuration_key,
        configuration_value, configuration_description,
        configuration_group_id, sort_order, date_added)
   values ('Enter the USPS User ID',
     'MODULE_SHIPPING_USPS1_USERID',
     'NONE', 'Enter the USPS USERID assigned to you.', '6',
     '0', now())");
   tep_db_query("insert into " . TABLE_CONFIGURATION .
     " (configuration_title, configuration_key,
        configuration_value, configuration_description,
        configuration_group_id, sort_order, date_added)
   values ('Enter the USPS Password',
     'MODULE_SHIPPING_USPS1_PASSWORD',
     'NONE', 'See USERID, above.', '6', '0', now())");
   tep_db_query("insert into " . TABLE_CONFIGURATION .
     " (configuration_title, configuration_key,
        configuration_value, configuration_description,
        configuration_group_id, sort_order,
        set_function, date_added)
   values ('Which server to use',
     'MODULE_SHIPPING_USPS1_SERVER',
     'production', 'An account at USPS is needed to use the
      Production server', '6', '0',
     'tep_cfg_select_option(array(\'test\', \'production\'),
     ', now())");
   tep_db_query("insert into " . TABLE_CONFIGURATION .
     " (configuration_title, configuration_key,
```

```
            configuration_value, configuration_description,
            configuration_group_id, sort_order, date_added)
  values ('Handling Fee', 'MODULE_SHIPPING_USPS1_HANDLING',
    '0', 'Handling fee for this shipping method.', '6', '0',
    now())");
  tep_db_query("insert into " . TABLE_CONFIGURATION .
    " (configuration_title, configuration_key,
        configuration_value, configuration_description,
        configuration_group_id, sort_order,
   use_function, set_function, date_added)

  values ('Tax Class', 'MODULE_SHIPPING_USPS1_TAX_CLASS',
    '0','Use the following tax class on the shipping fee.',
    '6', '0', 'tep_get_tax_class_title',
    'tep_cfg_pull_down_tax_classes(', now())");
  tep_db_query("insert into " . TABLE_CONFIGURATION .
    " (configuration_title, configuration_key,
        configuration_value, configuration_description,
        configuration_group_id, sort_order, use_function,
        set_function, date_added)
  values ('Shipping Zone', 'MODULE_SHIPPING_USPS1_ZONE', '0',
    'If a zone is selected, only enable this shipping method
     for that zone.', '6', '0', 'tep_get_zone_class_title',
    'tep_cfg_pull_down_zone_classes(', now())");
  tep_db_query("insert into " . TABLE_CONFIGURATION .
    " (configuration_title, configuration_key,
        configuration_value, configuration_description,
        configuration_group_id, sort_order, date_added)
  values ('Sort Order', 'MODULE_SHIPPING_USPS1_SORT_ORDER',
    '0', 'Sort order of display.', '6', '0', now())");
  }

  function remove() {
   tep_db_query("delete from " . TABLE_CONFIGURATION .
 " where configuration_key in ('" . implode("', '",
 $this->keys()) . "')");
  }

  function keys() {
   return array('MODULE_SHIPPING_USPS1_STATUS',
               'MODULE_SHIPPING_USPS1_USERID',
               'MODULE_SHIPPING_USPS1_PASSWORD',
               'MODULE_SHIPPING_USPS1_SERVER',
               'MODULE_SHIPPING_USPS1_HANDLING',
               'MODULE_SHIPPING_USPS1_TAX_CLASS',
               'MODULE_SHIPPING_USPS1_ZONE',
               'MODULE_SHIPPING_USPS1_SORT_ORDER');
```

```
}

function _setService($service) {
 $this->service = $service;
}

function _setWeight($pounds, $ounces=0) {
 $this->pounds = $pounds;
 $this->ounces = $ounces;
}

function _setContainer($container) {
 $this->container = $container;
}

function _setSize($size) {
 $this->size = $size;
}

function _setMachinable($machinable) {
 $this->machinable = $machinable;
}

function _getQuote() {
 global $order;

 if ($order->delivery['country']['id'] ==
                             SHIPPING_ORIGIN_COUNTRY) {
  $request = '<RateRequest USERID="' .
      MODULE_SHIPPING_USPS1_USERID .
  '" PASSWORD="' . MODULE_SHIPPING_USPS1_PASSWORD . '">';
  $services_count = 0;

  if (isset($this->service)) {
   $this->types = array($this->service =>
                     $this->types[$this->service]);
  }

  $dest_zip = str_replace(' ', '',
                     $order->delivery['postcode']);
  if ($order->delivery['country']['iso_code_2'] == 'US')
   $dest_zip = substr($dest_zip, 0, 5);

  reset($this->types);
  while (list($key, $value) = each($this->types)) {
```

```
    $request .= '<Package ID="' . $services_count . '">' .
        '<Service>' . $key . '</Service>' .
        '<ZipOrigination>' . SHIPPING_ORIGIN_ZIP .
        '</ZipOrigination>' .
        '<ZipDestination>' . $dest_zip .
        '</ZipDestination>' .
        '<Pounds>' . $this->pounds . '</Pounds>' .
        '<Ounces>' . $this->ounces . '</Ounces>' .
        '<Container>' . $this->container . '</Container>' .
        '<Size>' . $this->size . '</Size>' .
        '<Machinable>' . $this->machinable .
        '</Machinable>' .
        '</Package>';
  $services_count++;
  }
  $request .= '</RateRequest>';

  $request = 'API=Rate&XML=' . urlencode($request);
} else {
  $request = '<IntlRateRequest USERID="' .
      MODULE_SHIPPING_USPS1_USERID .
  '" PASSWORD="' . MODULE_SHIPPING_USPS1_PASSWORD . '">' .
        '<Package ID="0">' .
        '<Pounds>' . $this->pounds . '</Pounds>' .
        '<Ounces>' . $this->ounces . '</Ounces>' .
        '<MailType>Package</MailType>' .
        '<Country>' . $this->countries[
                    $order->delivery['country']
            ['iso_code_2']] . '</Country>' .
        '</Package>' .
        '</IntlRateRequest>';

  $request = 'API=IntlRate&XML=' . urlencode($request);
}

switch (MODULE_SHIPPING_USPS1_SERVER) {
 case 'production': $usps_server =
                            'production.shippingapis.com';
        $api_dll = 'shippingapi.dll';
        break;
 case 'test':
 default: $usps_server = 'testing.shippingapis.com';
        $api_dll = 'ShippingAPITest.dll';
        break;
}
```

```
$body = '';

$http = new httpClient();
if ($http->Connect($usps_server, 80)) {
 $http->addHeader('Host', $usps_server);
 $http->addHeader('User-Agent', 'osCommerce');
 $http->addHeader('Connection', 'Close');

 if ($http->Get('/' . $api_dll . '?' . $request)) $body =
                                    $http->getBody();

 $http->Disconnect();
} else {
 return false;
}

$response = array();
while (true) {
 if ($start = strpos($body, '<Package ID=')) {
  $body = substr($body, $start);
  $end = strpos($body, '</Package>');
  $response[] = substr($body, 0, $end+10);
  $body = substr($body, $end+9);
 } else {
  break;
 }
}

$rates = array();
if ($order->delivery['country']['id'] ==
                            SHIPPING_ORIGIN_COUNTRY) {
 if (sizeof($response) == '1') {
  if (ereg('<Error>', $response[0])) {
   $number = ereg('<Number>(.*)</Number>',
   $response[0], $regs);
   $number = $regs[1];
   $description = ereg('<Description>(.*)</Description>',
       $response[0], $regs);
   $description = $regs[1];

   return array('error' => $number . ' - ' . $description);
  }
 }
```

```php
$n = sizeof($response);
for ($i=0; $i<$n; $i++) {
 if (strpos($response[$i], '<Postage>')) {
  $service = ereg('<Service>(.*)</Service>',
  $response[$i], $regs);
  $service = $regs[1];
  $postage = ereg('<Postage>(.*)</Postage>',
  $response[$i], $regs);
  $postage = $regs[1];

  $rates[] = array($service => $postage);
 }
}
} else {
 if (ereg('<Error>', $response[0])) {
 $number = ereg('<Number>(.*)</Number>',
 $response[0], $regs);
 $number = $regs[1];
 $description = ereg('<Description>(.*)</Description>',
      $response[0], $regs);
 $description = $regs[1];

 return array('error' => $number . ' - ' . $description);
 } else {
 $body = $response[0];
 $services = array();
 while (true) {
  if ($start = strpos($body, '<Service ID=')) {
   $body = substr($body, $start);
   $end = strpos($body, '</Service>');
   $services[] = substr($body, 0, $end+10);
   $body = substr($body, $end+9);
  } else {
   break;
  }
 }

 $size = sizeof($services);
 for ($i=0, $n=$size; $i<$n; $i++) {
  if (strpos($services[$i], '<Postage>')) {
   $service = ereg('<SvcDescription>(.*)
   </SvcDescription>',
      $services[$i], $regs);
   $service = $regs[1];
   $postage = ereg('<Postage>(.*)</Postage>',
```

```
              $services[$i], $regs);
              $postage = $regs[1];

              if (isset($this->service) &&
                    ($service != $this->service) ) {
                continue;
              }

              $rates[] = array($service => $postage);
            }
          }
        }
      }

      return ((sizeof($rates) > 0) ? $rates : false);
    }

    function country_list() {
      $list = array('AF' => 'Afghanistan',
            'AL' => 'Albania',
            'ZM' => 'Zambia',
            'ZW' => 'Zimbabwe');

      return $list;
    }
  }
?>
```

2. As we will be using `usps1.php` only for carts with a limited weight, we will
   edit the display text (seen when the module is installed and highlighted) to
   reflect this in the right column of each module in the admin display. Find in
   line 135, right after the `install()` function begins, the following code:

```
tep_db_query("insert into " . TABLE_CONFIGURATION .
    " (configuration_title, configuration_key,
      configuration_value, configuration_description,
      configuration_group_id, sort_order,
      set_function, date_added)
  values ('Enable USPS Shipping',
   'MODULE_SHIPPING_USPS1_STATUS', 'True',
    'Do you want to offer USPS1 shipping?', '6', '0',
    'tep_cfg_select_option(array(\'True\', \'False\'), ',
      now())");
```

Replace it with the following to reflect the future use of the module:

```
tep_db_query("insert into " . TABLE_CONFIGURATION .
  " (configuration_title, configuration_key,
    configuration_value, configuration_description,
    configuration_group_id, sort_order,
    set_function, date_added)
  values ('Enable USPS Shipping with limited weight',
   'MODULE_SHIPPING_USPS1_STATUS', 'True',
   'Do you want to offer USPS
   shipping with limited weight?', '6', '0', '
   tep_cfg_select_option(array(\'True\', \'False\'), ',
   now())");
```

3. Add a new key to the `install()` function of your module. Find this in line 79:

```
tep_db_query("insert into " . TABLE_CONFIGURATION .
  " (configuration_title, configuration_key,
    configuration_value, configuration_description,
    configuration_group_id, sort_order, date_added)
  values ('Sort Order', 'MODULE_SHIPPING_USPS1_SORT_ORDER',
   '0', 'Sort order of display.', '6', '0', now())");
```

3. Add right above it the following line, allowing you to enter a weight limit:

```
tep_db_query("insert into " . TABLE_CONFIGURATION .
  " (configuration_title, configuration_key,
    configuration_value,
    configuration_description, configuration_group_id,
    sort_order, date_added)
  values ('Max cart weight',
   'MODULE_SHIPPING_USPS1_WEIGHT_LIMIT',
   '0', 'This module is limited to carts with the maximum
   weight specified here.', '6', '0', now())");
```

4. Add the call of the new key to the `keys()` function of your new module. Find this in line 151:

```
return array('MODULE_SHIPPING_USPS1_STATUS',
             'MODULE_SHIPPING_USPS1_USERID',
             'MODULE_SHIPPING_USPS1_PASSWORD',
             'MODULE_SHIPPING_USPS1_SERVER',
             'MODULE_SHIPPING_USPS1_HANDLING',
             'MODULE_SHIPPING_USPS1_TAX_CLASS',
             'MODULE_SHIPPING_USPS1_ZONE',
             'MODULE_SHIPPING_USPS1_SORT_ORDER');
```

Replace it with this:

```
return array('MODULE_SHIPPING_USPS1_STATUS',
             'MODULE_SHIPPING_USPS1_USERID',
             'MODULE_SHIPPING_USPS1_PASSWORD',
             'MODULE_SHIPPING_USPS1_SERVER',
             'MODULE_SHIPPING_USPS1_HANDLING',
             'MODULE_SHIPPING_USPS1_TAX_CLASS',
             'MODULE_SHIPPING_USPS1_ZONE',
             'MODULE_SHIPPING_USPS1_WEIGHT_LIMIT',
             'MODULE_SHIPPING_USPS1_SORT_ORDER');
```

5. Now add a clause that will hide this module, even if installed, when cart weight is more than the specified weight limit. Find this in line 48:

```
if ($check_flag == false) {
  $this->enabled = false;
 }
}
```

Replace with this:

```
if ($check_flag == false) {
  $this->enabled = false;
 }
}

if (is_object($order)) {
 // disable the module if the order weighs more than the
 // specified max weight
 if ($this->enabled == true) {
  global $cart;
  if ($cart->show_weight() >
      (MODULE_SHIPPING_USPS1_WEIGHT_LIMIT -
          SHIPPING_BOX_WEIGHT)) {
   $this->enabled = false;
  }
 }
}
```

6. Open `catalog/includes/languages/english/modules/shipping/usps.php` and create a clone, then replace all occurrences of the `usps` expression with `usps1`, keeping its upper or lower case spelling intact. Save this new file as `usps1.php`. This is what your `usps1.php` language file will look like with the description (seen when the module is highlighted) edited to reflect the **Flat Fee** for a single item module:

```
<?php
```

```
/*
  $Id: usps.php,v 1.8 2003/02/14 12:54:37 dgw_ Exp $
  cloned as
  $Id: usps1.php,v 1.00 2006/07/09 00:00:00 mm Exp $

  Modified by Monika Mathé
  http://www.monikamathe.com

  Module Copyright (c) 2006 Monika Mathé

  osCommerce, Open Source E-Commerce Solutions
  http://www.oscommerce.com

  Copyright (c) 2002 osCommerce

  Released under the GNU General Public License
*/

define('MODULE_SHIPPING_USPS1_TEXT_TITLE',
       'United States Postal Service');
define('MODULE_SHIPPING_USPS1_TEXT_DESCRIPTION',
    'United States Postal Service,
    limited by a specified weight.<br>
    <br>You will need to have registered an account with USPS at
    http://www.uspsprioritymail.com/et_regcert.html to use this
    module<br><br>USPS expects you to use pounds as weight
    measure for your products.');
define('MODULE_SHIPPING_USPS1_TEXT_OPT_PP', 'Parcel Post');
define('MODULE_SHIPPING_USPS1_TEXT_OPT_PM', 'Priority Mail');
define('MODULE_SHIPPING_USPS1_TEXT_OPT_EX', 'Express Mail');
define('MODULE_SHIPPING_USPS1_TEXT_ERROR', 'An error occured
    with the USPS shipping calculations.<br>If you prefer to use
    USPS as your shipping method, please contact the store
    owner.');
?>
```

7. Navigate to **Administration | Modules | Shipping** and install the new **USPS** shipping module limited by weight. Edit the **Max Cart Weight** parameter to limit weight to **10**lb in our example, select a **Shipping Zone** if applicable, and save your changes.

Topped off for every taste! Bon appetit!

54. Create a Per Item Shipping Module with Two Price Levels

You'll be thrilled about this recipe if you would like to offer a **Per Item** shipping module, but need two price levels as some of the items you sell can be shipped very cheaply and some are rather costly to send. This recipe also allows you to define a few selected items that have free shipping while all other items use the **Per Item** calculation as the default module.

Presentation

The following situations will be covered by this module:

	Shipping cost per item	
	Standard Group	**Exception Group**
Example 1	$1.00	$20.00
Example 2	$1.50	free

As you can see from Example 1, this is the perfect setup when you have products of about equal costs for shipping (Standard Group), but a few bulky shipping items (Exception Group) that require a different shipping method and will be sent separately.

Example 2 outlines a situation where you have a small group of differently priced products that you would like to offer free shipping for. This is also perfect for promotional offers as you can very quickly assign products to the exception group.

Chef's suggestion:

This module can be added very quickly and is of great value if your exception group is fairly small. There is no need to create an additional column for your products table and go through each product in your catalogue (a nightmare for large shops). The only information you must specify is the two cost levels and a list of the product IDs from the exception group.

Your **Shipping Modules** will look like this to follow this shipping plan (`products_id` of **27** for a printer, **25** for a keyboard, and both marked as bulky items):

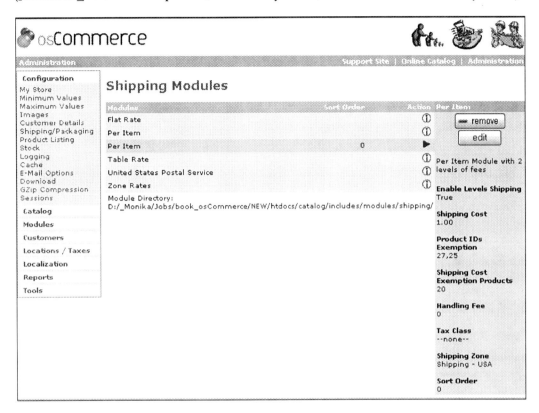

For a cart holding the below contents, calculation is done like this if we are following Example 1:

3 * $1.00 + 1*$20.00 = $23.00

As expected, shipping is shown as **$23.00**:

For Example 2, the DVD Movie "There's Something About Mary" has a promotional offer of free shipping. Calculation is done like this:

3 * $1.50 + 1*$0.00 = $4.50

Again, shipping is shown as **$4.50** just as expected:

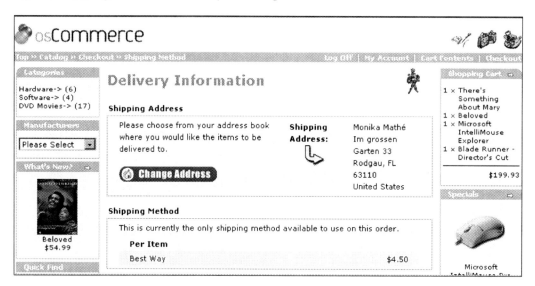

A line about the shipping rate being different for this item is automatically added to your Product Detail page; marking **FREE Shipping**, as an exception if the shipping cost is set at $0.00.

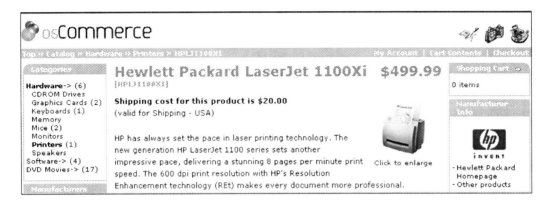

Ready to smooth out the gravy?

Ingredients

New:

`catalog/includes/modules/shipping/levels.php`
(this is a clone of the `catalog/includes/modules/shipping/item.php` file)
`catalog/includes/languages/english/modules/shipping/levels.php`
(this is a clone of the `catalog/includes/languages/english/modules/`
                                                    `shipping/item.php` file)

Modified:

`catalog/product_info.php`
`catalog/includes/languages/english/product_info.php`

Cooking

1. Open `catalog/includes/modules/shipping/item.php` and create a clone, then replace all occurrences of the `item` expression in the keys or module name with `levels`, keeping its upper or lower case spelling intact. Save this new file as `levels.php`. This is what your `levels.php` will look like before making further edits to the file:

    ```
    <?php
    /*
    $Id: levels.php,v 1.00 2006/07/09 00:00:00 mm Exp $

    Module written by Monika Mathé
    http://www.monikamathe.com
    ```

```
     Module Copyright (c) 2006 Monika Mathé

     osCommerce, Open Source E-Commerce Solutions
     http://www.oscommerce.com

     Copyright (c) 2003 osCommerce

     Released under the GNU General Public License
  */

  class levels {
   var $code, $title, $description, $icon, $enabled;

// class constructor
   function levels() {
    global $order;

    $this->code = 'levels';
    $this->title = MODULE_SHIPPING_LEVELS_TEXT_TITLE;
    $this->description =
               MODULE_SHIPPING_LEVELS_TEXT_DESCRIPTION;
    $this->sort_order = MODULE_SHIPPING_LEVELS_SORT_ORDER;
    $this->icon = '';
    $this->tax_class = MODULE_SHIPPING_LEVELS_TAX_CLASS;
    $this->enabled =
               ((MODULE_SHIPPING_LEVELS_STATUS == 'True') ?
               true : false);

    if ( ($this->enabled == true) &&
       ((int)MODULE_SHIPPING_LEVELS_ZONE > 0) ) {
     $check_flag = false;
     $check_query = tep_db_query("select zone_id from " .
       TABLE_ZONES_TO_GEO_ZONES . " where geo_zone_id = '" .
       MODULE_SHIPPING_LEVELS_ZONE .
       "' and zone_country_id = '" .
       $order->delivery['country']['id'] .
       "' order by zone_id");
     while ($check = tep_db_fetch_array($check_query)) {
      if ($check['zone_id'] < 1) {
       $check_flag = true;
       break;
      } elseif ($check['zone_id'] ==
               $order->delivery['zone_id']) {
       $check_flag = true;
       break;
```

```
        }
      }

    if ($check_flag == false) {
     $this->enabled = false;
    }
   }
  }

// class methods
  function quote($method = '') {
   global $order, $total_count;

   $this->quotes = array('id' => $this->code,
       'module' => MODULE_SHIPPING_LEVELS_TEXT_TITLE,
       'methods' => array(array('id' => $this->code,
           'title' => MODULE_SHIPPING_LEVELS_TEXT_WAY,
           'cost' => (MODULE_SHIPPING_LEVELS_COST *
           $total_count) + MODULE_SHIPPING_LEVELS_HANDLING)));

   if ($this->tax_class > 0) {
    $this->quotes['tax'] = tep_get_tax_rate($this->tax_class,
                     $order->delivery['country']['id'],
                     $order->delivery['zone_id']);
   }

   if (tep_not_null($this->icon)) $this->quotes['icon'] =
           tep_image($this->icon, $this->title);

   return $this->quotes;
  }

  function check() {
   if (!isset($this->_check)) {
    $check_query =
         tep_db_query("select configuration_value from " .
      TABLE_CONFIGURATION . " where configuration_key =
      'MODULE_SHIPPING_LEVELS_STATUS'");
    $this->_check = tep_db_num_rows($check_query);
   }
   return $this->_check;
  }

  function install() {
```

```
tep_db_query("insert into " . TABLE_CONFIGURATION .
  " (configuration_title, configuration_key,
    configuration_value, configuration_description,
    configuration_group_id, sort_order,
    set_function, date_added)
values ('Enable Levels Shipping',
  'MODULE_SHIPPING_LEVELS_    STATUS',
  'True', 'Do you want to offer per levels rate shipping?',
  '6', '0', 'tep_cfg_select_option(array(\'True\',
  \'False\'), ', now())");
tep_db_query("insert into " . TABLE_CONFIGURATION .
  " (configuration_title, configuration_key,
    configuration_value, configuration_description,
    configuration_group_id, sort_order, date_added)
values ('Shipping Cost',
  'MODULE_SHIPPING_LEVELS_COST', '2.50',
  'The shipping cost will be multiplied by the number of
  items in an order that uses this shipping method.', '6',
  '0', now())"); tep_db_query("insert into " .
  TABLE_CONFIGURATION .
  " (configuration_title, configuration_key,
    configuration_value, configuration_description,
    configuration_group_id, sort_order, date_added)
values ('Handling Fee', 'MODULE_SHIPPING_LEVELS_HANDLING',
  '0', 'Handling fee for this shipping method.', '6', '0',
  now())");
tep_db_query("insert into " . TABLE_CONFIGURATION .
  " (configuration_title, configuration_key,
    configuration_value, configuration_description,
    configuration_group_id, sort_order,
    use_function, set_function, date_added)
values ('Tax Class', 'MODULE_SHIPPING_LEVELS_TAX_CLASS',
  '0', 'Use the following tax class on the shipping fee.',
  '6', '0', 'tep_get_tax_class_title',
  'tep_cfg_pull_down_tax_classes(', now())");
tep_db_query("insert into " . TABLE_CONFIGURATION .
  " (configuration_title, configuration_key,
    configuration_value, configuration_description,
    configuration_group_id, sort_order,
    use_function, set_function, date_added)
values ('Shipping Zone', 'MODULE_SHIPPING_LEVELS_ZONE',
  '0', 'If a zone is selected, only enable this shipping
  method for that zone.', '6', '0',
  'tep_get_zone_class_title',
  'tep_cfg_pull_down_zone_classes(', now())");
tep_db_query("insert into " . TABLE_CONFIGURATION .
  " (configuration_title, configuration_key,
```

```
            configuration_value, configuration_description,
            configuration_group_id, sort_order, date_added)
      values ('Sort Order', 'MODULE_SHIPPING_LEVELS_SORT_ORDER',
        '0', 'Sort order of display.', '6', '0', now())");
      }

      function remove() {
       tep_db_query("delete from " . TABLE_CONFIGURATION .
       " where configuration_key in ('" . implode("', '",
              $this->keys()) . "')");
      }

      function keys() {
       return array('MODULE_SHIPPING_LEVELS_STATUS',
                   'MODULE_SHIPPING_LEVELS_COST',
                   'MODULE_SHIPPING_LEVELS_HANDLING',
                   'MODULE_SHIPPING_LEVELS_TAX_CLASS',
                   'MODULE_SHIPPING_LEVELS_ZONE',
                   'MODULE_SHIPPING_LEVELS_SORT_ORDER');
      }
     }
    ?>
```

2. As we will be using `levels.php` as a **Per Item** shipping module with two cost levels, we will edit the display text (seen when the module is installed and highlighted) to reflect this in the right column of each module in the admin display. Find in line 80, right after the `install()` function begins, the following code:

```
     tep_db_query("insert into " . TABLE_CONFIGURATION .
      " (configuration_title, configuration_key,
        configuration_value, configuration_description,
        configuration_group_id, sort_order,
        set_function, date_added)
      values ('Enable Levels Shipping',
        'MODULE_SHIPPING_LEVELS_STATUS',
        'True', 'Do you want to offer per levels rate shipping?',
        '6', '0', 'tep_cfg_select_option(array(\'True\',
        \'False\'), ', now())");
```

Replace it with the following to reflect the future use of the module:

```
     tep_db_query("insert into " . TABLE_CONFIGURATION .
      " (configuration_title, configuration_key,
        configuration_value, configuration_description,
        configuration_group_id, sort_order,
        set_function, date_added)
```

```
values ('Enable Per Item Shipping with 2 Levels',
  'MODULE_SHIPPING_LEVELS_STATUS', 'True',
  'Do you want to offer
  per item shipping with levels?', '6', '0',
  'tep_cfg_select_option(array(\'True\', \'False\'), ',
  now())");
```

3. Add a new key to the `install()` function of your module. Find this in line 81:

```
tep_db_query("insert into " . TABLE_CONFIGURATION .
  " (configuration_title, configuration_key,
    configuration_value, configuration_description,
    configuration_group_id, sort_order, date_added)
  values ('Shipping Cost',
    'MODULE_SHIPPING_LEVELS_COST', '2.50',
    'The shipping cost will be multiplied by the number of
    items in an order that uses this shipping method.', '6',
    '0', now())");
```

Add right below it the following line, allowing you to enter a second cost level for the products belonging to the exception group:

```
tep_db_query("insert into " . TABLE_CONFIGURATION .
  " (configuration_title, configuration_key,
    configuration_value, configuration_description,
    configuration_group_id, sort_order, date_added)
  values ('Product IDs Exception',
    'MODULE_SHIPPING_LEVELS_PRODUCTS', '',
    'Comma separated list of products to use the exception rate
    fee.', '6', '0', now())");
tep_db_query("insert into " . TABLE_CONFIGURATION .
  " (configuration_title, configuration_key,
    configuration_value, configuration_description,
    configuration_group_id, sort_order, date_added)
  values ('Shipping Cost Exception Products',
    'MODULE_SHIPPING_LEVELS_COST2',
    '10', 'The alternative shipping cost for products belonging
    into the exception group will be multiplied by the number
    of items in an order that uses this shipping method.', '6',
    '0', now())");
```

4. Add the call of the new keys to the `keys()` function of your new module. Find this in line 95:

```
return array('MODULE_SHIPPING_LEVELS_STATUS',
             'MODULE_SHIPPING_LEVELS_COST',
             'MODULE_SHIPPING_LEVELS_HANDLING',
             'MODULE_SHIPPING_LEVELS_TAX_CLASS',
```

```
'MODULE_SHIPPING_LEVELS_ZONE',
'MODULE_SHIPPING_LEVELS_SORT_ORDER');
```

Replace it with this:

```
return array('MODULE_SHIPPING_LEVELS_STATUS',
             'MODULE_SHIPPING_LEVELS_COST',
             'MODULE_SHIPPING_LEVELS_PRODUCTS',
             'MODULE_SHIPPING_LEVELS_COST2',
             'MODULE_SHIPPING_LEVELS_HANDLING',
             'MODULE_SHIPPING_LEVELS_TAX_CLASS',
             'MODULE_SHIPPING_LEVELS_ZONE',
             'MODULE_SHIPPING_LEVELS_SORT_ORDER');
```

5. Now add a clause that will calculate shipping cost for this module, separating
    the cart content into the two levels of fees and multiplying by the appropriate
    quantity of items. Find this in line 54:

```
global $order, $total_count;

$this->quotes = array('id' => $this->code,
        'module' => MODULE_SHIPPING_LEVELS_TEXT_TITLE,
        'methods' => array(array('id' => $this->code,
                'title' => MODULE_SHIPPING_LEVELS_TEXT_WAY,
                'cost' => (MODULE_SHIPPING_LEVELS_COST *
        $total_count) + MODULE_SHIPPING_LEVELS_HANDLING)));
```

Replace it with this:

```
global $order, $total_count, $cart;

$cost = 0;
 $count_level1 = 0;
 $count_level2 = 0;

$level2_array =
            explode(',' , MODULE_SHIPPING_LEVELS_PRODUCTS);

$products = $cart->get_products();
for ($i=0, $n=sizeof($products); $i<$n; $i++) {
if (in_array(tep_get_prid($products[$i]['id']),
                        $level2_array)) {
 $count_level2 += $products[$i]['quantity'];
} else {
 $count_level1 += $products[$i]['quantity'];
}
}
```

```
$cost_level1 = MODULE_SHIPPING_LEVELS_COST * $count_level1;
$cost_level2 = MODULE_SHIPPING_LEVELS_COST2 * $count_level2;
$cost = $cost_level1 + $cost_level2;

 $this->quotes = array('id' => $this->code,
            'module' => MODULE_SHIPPING_LEVELS_TEXT_TITLE,
            'methods' => array(array('id' => $this->code,
                  'title' => MODULE_SHIPPING_LEVELS_TEXT_WAY,
                  'cost' => $cost)));
```

6.   Open `catalog/includes/languages/english/modules/shipping/
item.php` and create a clone, then replace all occurrences of the `item`
expression with `levels`, keeping its upper or lower case spelling intact. Save
this new file as `levels.php`. This is what your `levels.php` language file will
look like with the description (seen when the module is highlighted) edited
to reflect the **Per Item** module with two levels:

```
<?php
/*
  $Id: levels.php,v 1.00 2006/07/09 00:00:00 mm Exp $

  Module written by Monika Mathé
  http://www.monikamathe.com

  Module Copyright (c) 2006 Monika Mathé

  osCommerce, Open Source E-Commerce Solutions
  http://www.oscommerce.com

  Copyright (c) 2002 osCommerce

  Released under the GNU General Public License
*/

define('MODULE_SHIPPING_LEVELS_TEXT_TITLE', 'Per Item');
define('MODULE_SHIPPING_LEVELS_TEXT_DESCRIPTION',
    'Per Item Module with 2 levels of fees');
define('MODULE_SHIPPING_LEVELS_TEXT_WAY', 'Best Way');
?>
```

7.   Open `catalog/product_info.php` and find this in line 120:

```
<p><?php echo stripslashes(
            $product_info['products_description']); ?></p>
```

Add right above it the following code to display a line of information if a product belongs to the shipping exception group:

```php
<?php
  if ( MODULE_SHIPPING_LEVELS_STATUS == 'True') {

  $level2_array =
          explode(',' , MODULE_SHIPPING_LEVELS_PRODUCTS);
    if (in_array((int)$HTTP_GET_VARS['products_id'],
          $level2_array)) {
    if (MODULE_SHIPPING_LEVELS_COST2 > 0) {
     echo '<b>' . sprintf(TEXT_EXCEPTION_SHIPPING,
       $currencies->display_price(MODULE_SHIPPING_LEVELS_COST2,
       MODULE_SHIPPING_LEVELS_TAX_CLASS)) . '</b>';
    } else {
     echo '<b>' . TEXT_FREE_SHIPPING . '</b>';
    }

    if ((int)MODULE_SHIPPING_LEVELS_ZONE > 0) {
     $check_query =
          tep_db_query("select geo_zone_description from " .
       TABLE_GEO_ZONES . " where geo_zone_id = '" .
       MODULE_SHIPPING_LEVELS_ZONE . "'");
     $check = tep_db_fetch_array($check_query);
     echo '<br>' . sprintf(TEXT_EXCEPTION_ZONE,
     $check['geo_zone_description']);
    }
   }
  }
  ?>
```

Chef's Suggestion:

As `$check['geo_zone_description']` is pulled from the table `geo_zones`, which stores only one language, you need to keep this expression neutral for multilingual stores, for example by using country codes.

8. Open `catalog/includes/languages/english/product_info.php` and add the following define statements:

```php
define('TEXT_EXCEPTION_SHIPPING',
        'Shipping cost for this product is %s');
define('TEXT_FREE_SHIPPING', 'FREE Shipping!');
define('TEXT_EXCEPTION_ZONE', '(valid for %s)');
```

9. Navigate to **Administration | Modules | Shipping** and install the new **Per Item** with 2 levels shipping module. Edit the second cost parameter and specify your comma-separated list of exception products, select a **Shipping Zone** if applicable, and save your changes.

Nothing goes better with meat and potatoes! Bon appetit!

Summary

This chapter has seen you become an expert at creating a unique buffet of shipping modules. You have learned how to cook your shipping module recipes using the feature-rich default shipping modules offered by osCommerce as ingredients.

By creating clones of existing modules and adding your own flavor, you can offer your customers a smorgasbord of free shipping offers, or flat fees for single items or whole groups based on your criteria, or a selection by category. You can now hide or show modules to meet your wishes, driven by weight or a cluster of modules cloned for different shipping zones.

From now onwards, you will be able to recreate any shipping plan on the substructure of the **Per Item**, **Table Rate**, **Flat Rate**, and **USPS** shipping modules at your convenience, and fulfil the exact business requirements of your company. This knowledge allows you to offer the best value to your customers while ensuring that your costs are safely covered.

Modifying copies of the original shipping modules is an exceptionally rewarding task that finds its mate only in the sophisticated presentation of **Payment Modules**. Let's now enjoy the refreshing taste of a few select and invaluable recipes.

8

Season Your Payment Modules

Payment Modules have to follow your business guidelines in the same way **Shipping Modules** do. The default osCommerce setup unfortunately does not cater to the following three indispensable options:

- Hide **Payment Modules** from public eyes (while you test them in their future home, not a development site)

- Create dependencies between **Shipping Modules** and **Payment Modules**

- Offer customized payment options for selected customers

This chapter provides you with the necessary code snippets to implement all of the above. After trying out the following recipes, you will agree that the **Payment Modules** that used to appear completely static are, in fact highly flexible, and able to react to your shop's profile.

55. Hide Payment Modules from Public Eyes

This recipe allows you to specify your own `customers_id` from your dummy account for safely testing a payment module while keeping it hidden from all other users. While the test is under progress, other users can freely access all other payment modules. This hack is highly adaptable as you will be using the same code for whichever payment module you require hidden. The define for you as a Master Customer is done in the main configuration area, and only a few lines of code need to be added to hide for the time being the modules you would like to test.

Presentation

Your screen in **Administration | Configuration | Hide Payment Modules** will look like the following when you are planning to hide a payment module (this recipe uses **PSiGate**) while you are running your tests.

(PSiGate is a great Credit Card Gateway for testing as it doesn't require you to sign up for a merchant account for testing purposes.)

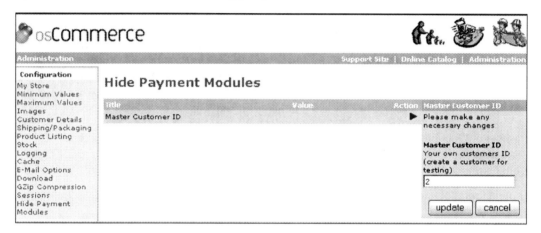

In this scenario, the standard osCommerce **Credit Card** module will be replaced with **PSiGate** once the necessary tests are run. Your Checkout Payment page will show all installed payment modules. The regular **Credit Card** module remains intact and is visible to visitors, while the **PSiGate** module is hidden from everyone except the Master Customer.

It is important that customers will not see the hidden module, as two credit card modules visible at the same time could be sufficiently confusing to lose their confidence in your shop. This is what all other customers will see on the Payment page, with the payment module being tested hidden:

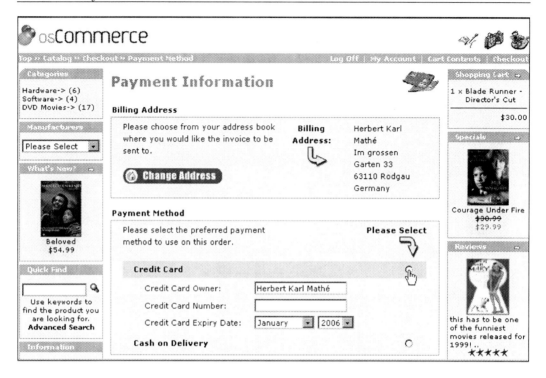

Let's add a few secret ingredients to the mix!

Ingredients

> **New:**
>
> `database.sql` (to be run in phpMyAdmin)
>
> **Modified:**
>
> `catalog/includes/modules/payment/psigate.php`

Cooking

1. Run the SQL statement in phpMyAdmin to create a new configuration group #4321 (ensure that this ID is not already in use), adding an option for you to define your own `customers_id`:

```
INSERT INTO configuration_group
VALUES ('4321', 'Hide Payment Modules',
  'You can hide payment modules from everyone apart yourself by
  specifying your customers_id here', '100', '1');
```

```
INSERT INTO configuration (configuration_title,
  configuration_key, configuration_value,
  configuration_description, configuration_group_id,
  sort_order, date_added)
VALUES ('Master Customer ID', 'MASTER_CUSTOMERS_ID', '',
  'Your own customers ID (create a customer for testing)',
  '4321', '0', now());
```

2. Navigate to your catalog and create a new customer that you will use as the Master Customer for module testing purposes. Open **Administration | Customers**, highlight your new dummy user and get the `customers_id` from the URL; it is presented as `cID`. The customer for this example has the `cID` of 2, as the URL is `http://localhost/catalog/admin/customers.php?selected_box=customers&page=1&cID=2`.

3. Navigate to **Administration | Configuration | Hide Payment Modules** and edit the **Master Customer ID** to reflect your own `customers_id` as seen in the first screenshot.

4. Open `catalog/includes/modules/payment/psigate.php` and find this in line 52, right at the end of the `update_status()` function, where the visibility of a module is determined:

```
if ($check_flag == false) {
  $this->enabled = false;
  }
 }
}
```

Replace it with the following code, which will disable and thus hide the module if a **Master Customer ID** was set:

```
if ($check_flag == false) {
  $this->enabled = false;
  }
 }
}

// disable the module if a valid Master Customer ID has been set
 if ($this->enabled == true) {
  if (MASTER_CUSTOMERS_ID > 0) {
   global $customer_id;
   if (MASTER_CUSTOMERS_ID != $customer_id) { //hide for public
    $this->enabled = false;
   }
  }
 }
}
```

5. Make sure that your **PSiGate Payment Module** is installed and ready to run a test.

Chef's suggestion:

If you need to allow several Master Customer IDs instead of just one as in this recipe, take a look at the last recipe in this chapter for a solution.

Kept as safe as the Colonel's! Bon appetit!

56. Create Dependencies between Shipping and Payment Modules

With this recipe you will be able to define dependencies between your **Shipping Modules** and **Payment Modules**. It is often necessary to limit certain payment methods to specific delivery methods. An example of this would be **Cash on Delivery Payment (COD)** method. You may only want to accept this form of payment with **Spot Delivery** as the shipping method.

Presentation

When choosing **Spot Delivery**, your customer will be able to select the **Cash On Delivery** option as shown here, while it will not be offered for any other shipping method selected:

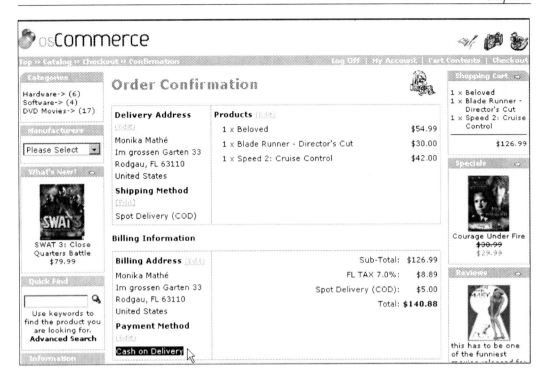

Fine Herbs for Fish, Rosemary for Beef, and Mint for Lamb!

Ingredients

> **Modified:**
>
> catalog/includes/languages/english/modules/shipping/flat.php
> catalog/includes/modules/payment/cod.php

Cooking

1. Open catalog/includes/languages/english/modules/shipping/ flat.php and modify the defines to reflect manual delivery. As we are not changing the underlying module structure, cloning is not necessary here. Just find the following lines:

   ```
   define('MODULE_SHIPPING_FLAT_TEXT_TITLE', 'Flat Rate');
   define('MODULE_SHIPPING_FLAT_TEXT_DESCRIPTION', 'Flat Rate');
   define('MODULE_SHIPPING_FLAT_TEXT_WAY', 'Best Way');
   ```

Replace them with the following lines:

```
define('MODULE_SHIPPING_FLAT_TEXT_TITLE', 'Spot Delivery');
define('MODULE_SHIPPING_FLAT_TEXT_DESCRIPTION', 'Spot Delivery,
  tied to COD payment only');
define('MODULE_SHIPPING_FLAT_TEXT_WAY', 'COD');
```

2. Navigate to **Administration | Modules | Shipping** and highlight **Spot Delivery** shipping, which you intend to tie to the **Cash On Delivery** payment module as the only allowed method. The URL will look like this:
   ```
   http://localhost/catalog/admin/modules.php?set=shipping&
                                              module=flat
   ```

3. Note down the module name, in this case `flat`; it is to be used in the code limiting this payment module.

4. Open `catalog/includes/modules/payment/cod.php` and find this in line 55:
   ```
   // disable the module if the order only contains
   // virtual products
   if ($this->enabled == true) {
    if ($order->content_type == 'virtual') {
     $this->enabled = false;
     }
    }
   ```

   Add right below it the following code:
   ```
   // disable the module if not spot delivery is selected
   if ($this->enabled == true) {
    global $shipping;
    if ($shipping['id'] != 'flat_flat') { //Spot Delivery
     $this->enabled = false;
     }
    }
   ```

Chef's suggestion:

Take special note that in **Shipping Modules** that do not have methods (separate choices for different delivery options like USPS offers), the module name is used twice, concatenated by an underscore. If you plan to exclude several methods, either use an array or add each one to the "if" statement.

5. Ensure that both **Spot Delivery** and **Cash On Delivery** modules are installed before testing, and don't forget to offer an alternative payment method for customers choosing a different shipping module.

Distinct dishes for distinct tastes! Bon appetit!

57. Offer Customized Payment Options for Selected Customers

This is a great recipe if you'd like to offer specific payment options to a small group of trusted customers and not to others. The next time your favorite customer calls and asks for immediate shipment while he or she sends a bank draft, you can make this possible without risking another visitor to your store finding the same option available to them when you installed it specifically for the two minutes needed to enter the special order.

There are contributions such as **Separate Pricing Per Customer**, which besides offering different pricing options, offers the functionality to allow or disallow certain shipping or payment modules to each specific customer. These contributions are time consuming to install and more importantly, they modify your core files to such a degree that adding further modules can become a painstaking task. With this module you need not change any file other than the specific payment module you are offering to this specific group.

Chef's suggestion:

Although there is no reason why you cannot add as many customers to the list of allowed users as will fit in the 255 characters permitted for value defines (column `configuration_value` in table `configuration`), your list may become burdensome to maintain as it uses customer IDs and not names as reference.

Presentation

The following screenshot shows **Administration | Modules | Payment** with the payment module **Check/Money Order** only allowed to be used by a selected group of trusted customers:

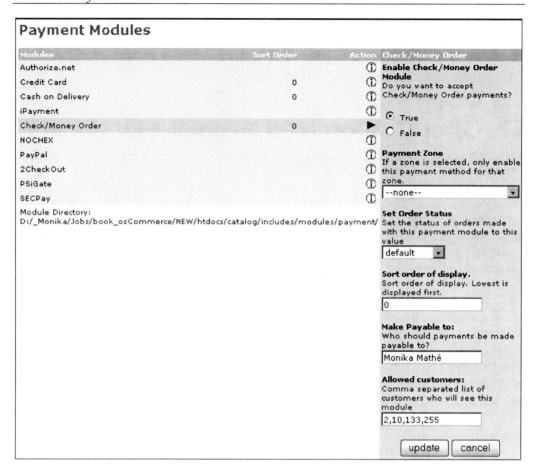

This payment method will only be displayed if the customer logged in is within the defined group; the rest of your customers will see your alternative payment module(s) only. The following screenshot was taken logged in as a trusted customer:

Let's spice it up for the few, and leave it bland for the rest!

Ingredients

Modified:

`catalog/includes/modules/payment/moneyorder.php`

Cooking

1. Open `catalog/includes/modules/payment/moneyorder.php` and find this in line 52:

    ```
    if ($check_flag == false) {
      $this->enabled = false;
    }
    }
    }
    ```

Replace it with the following code, which checks if the customer logged in belongs to the specified customer group that is allowed to see this payment module:

```
if ($check_flag == false) {
  $this->enabled = false;
  }
}


$allowed_array = explode(',' ,
        MODULE_PAYMENT_MONEYORDER_ALLOWED_CUSTOMERS);
global $customer_id;
if (!(in_array($customer_id, $allowed_array))) {
    $this->enabled = false;
  }
}
```

2. Find the following code in line 110 as part of the `install()` function:

```
tep_db_query("insert into " . TABLE_CONFIGURATION .
  " (configuration_title, configuration_key,
    configuration_value,
    configuration_description, configuration_group_id,
    sort_order, set_function, use_function, date_added)
  values ('Set Order Status',
    'MODULE_PAYMENT_MONEYORDER_ORDER_STATUS_ID', '0',
    'Set the status of orders made with this payment module to
    this value', '6', '0',
    'tep_cfg_pull_down_order_statuses(',
                    'tep_get_order_status_name', now())");
```

Add directly below it the new key for the allowed customer group:

```
tep_db_query("insert into " . TABLE_CONFIGURATION .
  " (configuration_title, configuration_key,
    configuration_value,
    configuration_description, configuration_group_id,
    sort_order, date_added)
  values ('Allowed customers:',
    'MODULE_PAYMENT_MONEYORDER_ALLOWED_CUSTOMERS',
    '', 'Comma separated list of customers who will see this
    module', '6', '1', now());");
```

3. A bit further down, find the call for the `keys()` in line 119:

```
return array('MODULE_PAYMENT_MONEYORDER_STATUS',
  'MODULE_PAYMENT_MONEYORDER_ZONE',
  'MODULE_PAYMENT_MONEYORDER_ORDER_STATUS_ID',
```

```
        'MODULE_PAYMENT_MONEYORDER_SORT_ORDER',
    'MODULE_PAYMENT_MONEYORDER_PAYTO');
```

Replace it with this line, adding the new key:

```
return array('MODULE_PAYMENT_MONEYORDER_STATUS',
    'MODULE_PAYMENT_MONEYORDER_ZONE',
    'MODULE_PAYMENT_MONEYORDER_ORDER_STATUS_ID',
    'MODULE_PAYMENT_MONEYORDER_SORT_ORDER',
    'MODULE_PAYMENT_MONEYORDER_PAYTO',
    'MODULE_PAYMENT_MONEYORDER_ALLOWED_CUSTOMERS');
```

4. Install the module and enter the customer IDs for the small group that will be allowed to see this module. If this was a module already in use, be sure to uninstall it first before uploading your new file to install. Offer an alternative payment module for all other customers.

Chef's suggestion:

This is a highly portable module as it modifies code sections that are similar for all payment modules. All you need to do for a different payment module is to add the check function to the visibility verification, as in step 1, and add the new key with correct naming for the module used, as in steps 2 and 3 to the keys() and install() functions.

Seasoned to perfection for all! Bon appetit!

Summary

This chapter provides you with exciting new options that allow you to recreate even the most sophisticated payment plans in osCommerce with minimal work on your default code.

You can now settle back when running final testing on new payment modules in your live environment. You, and you alone, will have permission to view them; they remain hidden to the public eye while you make sure all is properly seasoned before releasing a new payment method.

Careful testing is especially important when you are working on cascading strategies, where a certain shipping method will trigger the payment choices offered. You have studied an example for **Spot Delivery**, which was the only shipping choice that allowed a customer to select **Cash on Delivery** payment in the next step.

In the last part of this trilogy, you had a taste of a highly practical modification that allows you to offer certain payment methods to small select groups of customers—without the overload of an extensive contribution installation or database table structure manipulation.

Your customers will appreciate that you strive to cater to their needs, and that will lead to a higher sales volume for you. On that note, we move on to the next chapter where we'll dish out ideas for increasing sales with the help of strategically placed banners, directing customers to external sites or internal pages.

9

Cook Up a Multiple Banner System

Banners are an important marketing tool on websites in general, and can generate extra income for your business. You might already be selling advertising space or working with affiliate membership systems, but standard osCommerce was configured for defined groups of banners linking your customer to external sites only. As a result, a new browser window will automatically open when you click on a banner. An additional drawback of the default system is that you cannot specify which category is linked to which banner; this is critical for target-group-specific advertising.

In this chapter, we will address solutions to the following highly important topics, so you will be able to:

- Set up category-driven banners
- Create rotating banners that link within your own shop

58. Set Up Category-Driven Banners

Advertising via banners can only be effective if you target the specific group of visitors actually interested in viewing further websites about the advertised topic. (You absolutely do not want to advertise barbeques or stoves to a customer who is specifically interested in viewing your range of shoes.) This recipe allows you to define a category-driven banner system, which checks your banner repository according to the following steps:

1. Check for a banner defined for the current category
2. Check for a banner one category level up if a `products_id` is part of the URL
3. Check for a banner for the current category if `cPath` is part of the URL
4. Use a default banner if no banner was found in steps 1–3

Chef's suggestion:

Category-driven banners are especially important if you are working with affiliate banners, which provide direct revenue for each click or purchase on the partner site.

Presentation

Your **Administration | Tools | Banner Manager** will look like the following screenshot with groups of banners defined for categories. (You can define several rotating banners for each group; only one for each group has been added here.)

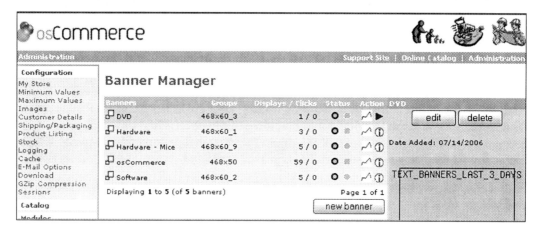

Note how IDs have been attached to the group names, separated by underscores; this allows for a dynamic display of category-specific banners on each page load. In this example, all main categories have been defined for target-group specific banners. In addition to this, a subcategory, in this case **Mice** from the category **Hardware**, has been added to the banners section also, which leads to the following display when clicking on the **Mice** category in the catalog section of the shop:

As no other subcategory was defined for banner display, clicking on **Printers**, which is a child category of **Hardware** just like **Mice** from the above example, displays the main banner for **Hardware**, the parent category, instead.

This new banner system chooses the relevant category information even if it is not on a Product Listing or Product Detail page, as on the following Reviews page:

A defined default banner will be displayed if no category-relevant information can be found as is the case on information pages like Privacy or general product pages like New Products.

Let's smoke the salmon and cream the cheese!

Ingredients

New:

```
catalog/includes/modules/category_driven_banners.php
catalog/images/banners/hardware.jpg
catalog/images/banners/software.jpg
catalog/images/banners/dvd.jpg
catalog/images/banners/mice.jpg
```

Modified:

```
catalog/includes/header.php
```

Cooking

1. Open `catalog/includes/header.php` and find this in line 58, which holds the image icons for the account, cart, and checkout links:

```
<td align="right" valign="bottom">
<?php echo '<a href="' . tep_href_link(FILENAME_ACCOUNT, '',
  'SSL') . '">' .
  tep_image(DIR_WS_IMAGES . 'header_account.gif',
  HEADER_TITLE_MY_ACCOUNT) . '</a>  
<a href="' . tep_href_link(FILENAME_SHOPPING_CART) . '">' .
tep_image(DIR_WS_IMAGES . 'header_cart.gif',
  HEADER_TITLE_CART_CONTENTS) . '</a>  
```

```
<a href="' . tep_href_link(FILENAME_CHECKOUT_SHIPPING,
  '', 'SSL') . '">' .
tep_image(DIR_WS_IMAGES . 'header_checkout.gif',
  HEADER_TITLE_CHECKOUT) . '</a>'; ?>  
</td>
```

Replace with the following line, removing the above links and replacing with the new banner system:

```
<?php include(DIR_WS_MODULES .
              'category_driven_banners.php'); ?>
```

2. Create the new file `catalog/includes/modules/`
    `category_driven_banners.php` using the following code. Note that the
    default banner, provided by osCommerce in the default setup, is a bit smaller
    in height (50 pixels versus 60 pixels) than the regular banners used. As the
    space set up for the banner at the end of the following code holds banner up
    to 70 pixels high, this difference in height will not distort our layout.

```php
<?php
/*
  $Id: category_driven_banners.php,v 1.00 2006/07/14 00:00:00
mm Exp $

  osCommerce, Open Source E-Commerce Solutions
  http://www.oscommerce.com

  Copyright (c) 2003 osCommerce

  Released under the GNU General Public License
*/

$banner_exists = false;
$banner_code = $current_category_id;
$groupname = '468x60_';
$groupname_default = '468x50';

if ($banner = tep_banner_exists('dynamic', $groupname .
      $banner_code)) {
 $banner_exists = true;
} else {
 if (isset($HTTP_GET_VARS['products_id'])) {
  $cPath = tep_get_product_path($HTTP_GET_VARS['products_id']);
 } elseif (isset($HTTP_GET_VARS['cPath'])) {
```

```
        $cPath = substr(tep_get_path($current_category_id), 6);
      }
      $cat_array = array_reverse(explode('_', $cPath));
      $n = sizeof($cat_array);
      for ($i=0; $i<$n; $i++) {
       if ($banner = tep_banner_exists('dynamic',
             $groupname . $cat_array[$i])) {
        $banner_exists = true;
        break;
       }
      }
     }

    if ($banner_exists == false) {
     if ($banner = tep_banner_exists('dynamic',
    $groupname_default)) {
       $banner_exists = true;
      }
     }

    if ($banner_exists == true) {
        echo '<td align="center" height="70">' .
          tep_display_banner('static', $banner) . '</td>';
     }
    ?>
```

3. Navigate to **Administration | Tools | Banner Manager** and set up your new banners using the provided banners or your own. Make sure to use the banner group name (468x60) with the category ID attached after the underscore, or modify the name in the code in `category_driven_banners.php`. Customize the default-banner group name to your needs in the same file.

[

Chef's suggestion:

You can find the correct category ID by highlighting a category in the catalog section of your shop and taking note of the last number in the expression for cPath. The following URL
`http://localhost/catalog/index.php?cPath=1_5`
stands for the category ID 5.

]

As fine as good wine! Bon appetit!

59. Create Rotating Banners that Link within Your Own Shop

This recipe shows you how to define product placement banners used in a box or added to any other part of your website. The placement groups can hold rotating banners of different formats—horizontal, vertical, or square, depending on where you would like to display them.

Presentation

Your **Administration | Tools | Banner Manager** will look like the following screenshot with groups of banners defined for product placement. One of the new groups with the format **120x120** pixels will be used in the right column, while the new horizontal group **468x60** pixels will be used in the footer instead of the default osCommerce banner. As two banners, **HP Printer** and **There's Something About Mary**, have been added to the **120x120** pixels group, the banners in that section will rotate with each page load.

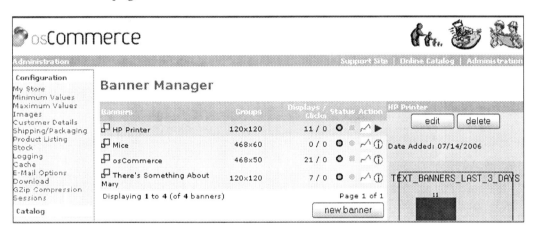

Your catalog section will pull a random advertisement for the box in the right column right from the 120x120 pixels group of banners defined for this recipe. Each banner is linked to a different product that you want to set special focus on.

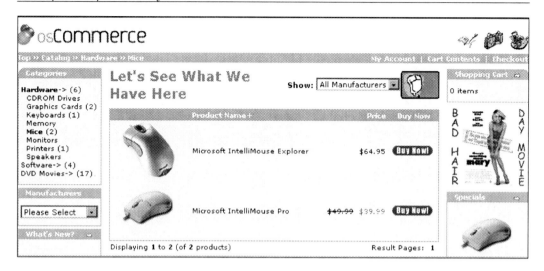

In the following screenshot, you can see the footer of the page where the banner group of 468x60 pixels is displayed. A category search is tied to the banner group specified in the footer banner code. Clicking on it will take your customers to the category **Mice**.

Ready to divvy it up?

Ingredients

New:

```
catalog/images/banners/mary.jpg
catalog/images/banners/mice.jpg
catalog/includes/boxes/product_placement.php
```

Modified:

```
catalog/includes/functions/general.php
catalog/includes/functions/banner.php
catalog/includes/column_right.php
catalog/includes/footer.php
```

Cooking

1. Navigate to **Administration | Tools | Banner Manager** and create a new banner using your own images, or `mary.jpg` and `mice.jpg` from the file set. To enter the correct URL for the banner, browse your catalog and get the URL from the Product Detail page. It will look similar to `http://localhost/catalog/product_info.php?products_id=19`.

   You may see a session ID attached like `&osCsid=3o9g5t9s54ahu5hg2qu9438t80`. It is absolutely critical that you remove this part, or your customers will be kicked out of their session. You only need to use the filename part (`product_info.php?products_id=19`) for the form entry, as the link is to your own site.

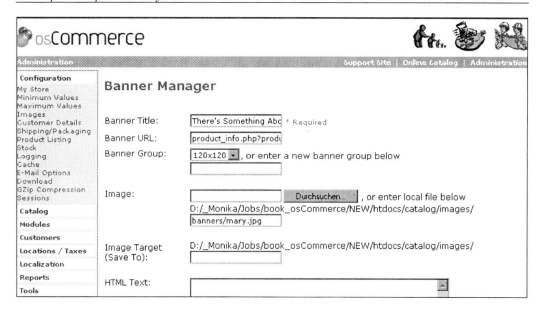

2. For adding a banner that links to a keyword search, a whole category, or a subcategory, use the URL after either clicking on that category or performing the search. For a search, enter your relevant keywords in your advanced search form and perform the search, then save the URL generated to be used in the banner manager. For the horizontal banner in the footer, clicking the category **Mice** from the categories box in catalog displays the URL `http://localhost/catalog/index.php?cPath=1_9`. Use the part after the catalog folder — `index.php?cPath=1_9`, so only the relative path is used, again with the session ID removed if one is attached.

3. Open `catalog/includes/functions/general.php` and add the following two functions right before the closing `?>` PHP tag to allow for separating the banner URL into the filename and parameters:

```
function after ($this, $inthat) {
  if (!is_bool(strpos($inthat, $this)))
    return substr($inthat,
         strpos($inthat,$this)+strlen($this));
};
function before ($this, $inthat) {
  return substr($inthat, 0, strpos($inthat, $this));
};
```

4. Open `catalog/includes/functions/banner.php` and find the following function in line 59. Add a third parameter that will determine whether the banner link opens a new window or stays on the same page. The default value is set to `false`.

```
function tep_display_banner($action, $identifier) {
 if ($action == 'dynamic') {
...

} else {
  return '<b>TEP ERROR! (tep_display_banner(' .
    $action . ', ' .
    $identifier . ') ->
        Unknown $action parameter value - it must
        be either \'dynamic\' or \'static\'</b>';
}

 if (tep_not_null($banner['banners_html_text'])) {
  $banner_string = $banner['banners_html_text'];
 } else {
  $banner_string = '<a href="' .
    tep_href_link(FILENAME_REDIRECT,
    'action=banner&goto=' . $banner['banners_id']) . '
    " target="_blank">' . tep_image(DIR_WS_IMAGES .
    $banner['banners_image'], $banner['banners_title']) .
       '</a>';
}

 tep_update_banner_display_count($banner['banners_id']);

 return $banner_string;
}
```

Replace the default function with this new function with the added
parameter:

```
function tep_display_banner($action, $identifier,
  $staypage = false) {
 if ($action == 'dynamic') {
  $banners_query =
  tep_db_query("select count(*) as count from "
  . TABLE_BANNERS . " where status = '1'
  and banners_group = '" .
   $identifier . "'");
  $banners = tep_db_fetch_array($banners_query);
  if ($banners['count'] > 0) {
   $banner = tep_random_select("select banners_id, banners_url,
     banners_title, banners_image, banners_html_text from " .
     TABLE_BANNERS . " where status = '1' and
     banners_group = '" . $identifier . "'");
  } else {
```

```
     return '<b>TEP ERROR!
       (tep_display_banner(' . $action . ', ' .
       $identifier . ') -> No banners with group \'' .
       $identifier . '\' found!</b>';
  }
} elseif ($action == 'static') {
 if (is_array($identifier)) {
  $banner = $identifier;
 } else {
  $banner_query = tep_db_query("select banners_id, banners_url,
  banners_title, banners_image, banners_html_text from " .
  TABLE_BANNERS . " where status = '1' and banners_id = '" .
  (int)$identifier . "'");
   if (tep_db_num_rows($banner_query)) {
    $banner = tep_db_fetch_array($banner_query);
   } else {
    return '<b>TEP ERROR! (tep_display_banner(' .
    $action . ', ' . $identifier . ') -> Banner with ID \'' .
    $identifier . '\' not found, or status inactive</b>';
   }
  }
} else {
 return '<b>TEP ERROR!
 (tep_display_banner(' . $action . ', ' .
 $identifier . ') ->
 Unknown $action parameter value - it must be either
 \'dynamic\' or \'static\'</b>';
}

if (tep_not_null($banner['banners_html_text'])) {
 $banner_string = $banner['banners_html_text'];
} else {
 $staypage_text = '';
 if ($staypage == false) {
 $banner_string = '<a href="' .
   tep_href_link(FILENAME_REDIRECT,
   'action=banner&goto=' . $banner['banners_id']) . '"
   target="_blank">' .
 tep_image(DIR_WS_IMAGES . $banner['banners_image'],
   $banner['banners_title']) . '</a>';
 } else {
  tep_update_banner_click_count($banner['banners_id']);
  $banner_string = '<a href="' . tep_href_link(before
    ('?', $banner['banners_url']), after ('?',
   $banner['banners_url'])) . '">' . tep_image(DIR_WS_IMAGES .
   $banner['banners_image'],
```

```
    $banner['banners_title']) . '</a>';
   }
  }

  tep_update_banner_display_count($banner['banners_id']);

  return $banner_string;
 }
```

5. Below the previous function, find the function that checks if a banner exists, and then generates the array for its identifier:

```
////
// Check to see if a banner exists
function tep_banner_exists($action, $identifier) {
 if ($action == 'dynamic') {
  return tep_random_select("select banners_id, banners_title,
    banners_image, banners_html_text from " . TABLE_BANNERS .
    " where status = '1' and banners_group = '" .
    $identifier . "'");
 } elseif ($action == 'static') {
    $banner_query = tep_db_query("select banners_id,
      banners_title, banners_image,
      banners_html_text from " . TABLE_BANNERS . "
      where status = '1' and banners_id = '" .
      (int)$identifier . "'");
    return tep_db_fetch_array($banner_query);
   } else {
    return false;
    }
 }
```

Replace with the following, adding the call for the URL to the query:

```
////
// Check to see if a banner exists
function tep_banner_exists($action, $identifier) {
 if ($action == 'dynamic') {
  return tep_random_select("select banners_id, banners_url,
    banners_title, banners_image, banners_html_text from " .
    TABLE_BANNERS . " where status = '1'
    and banners_group = '" . $identifier . "'");
 } elseif ($action == 'static') {
    $banner_query = tep_db_query("select banners_id,
    banners_url, banners_title, banners_image,
    banners_html_text from " . TABLE_BANNERS . "
    where status = '1' and banners_id = '" .
```

```
        (int)$identifier . "'");
    return tep_db_fetch_array($banner_query);
      } else {
        return false;
      }
    }
}
```

6. Create a new file `catalog/includes/boxes/product_placement.php` with the following code, using the parameters for your own banner group:

```php
<?php
/*
  $Id: product_placement.php,
      v 1.00 2006/07/14 00:00:00 mm Exp $

  Module written by Monika Mathé
  http://www.monikamathe.com

  Module Copyright (c) 2006 Monika Mathé

  osCommerce, Open Source E-Commerce Solutions
  http://www.oscommerce.com

  Copyright (c) 2003 osCommerce

  Released under the GNU General Public License
*/

$banner_group = '120x120';
  if ($banner = tep_banner_exists('dynamic', $banner_group)) {
?>
<!--product_placement //-->
        <tr>
          <td><?php echo tep_display_banner('static', $banner,
            true);?></td>
        </tr>
<!-- product_placement _eof //-->
<?php
  }
?>
```

7. Open `catalog/includes/column_right.php` and find this code in line 13:

```php
require(DIR_WS_BOXES . 'shopping_cart.php');
```

Immediately below this line, add the call for your banner box:

```
require(DIR_WS_BOXES . 'product_placement.php');
```

8. For a second group, like the horizontal banner group in the footer where
    Mice belongs, open catalog/includes/footer.php and find this code
    in line 27:

```
<?php
  if ($banner = tep_banner_exists('dynamic', '468x50')) {
?>
<br>
<table border="0" width="100%" cellspacing="0" cellpadding="0">
  <tr>
    <td align="center"><?php echo tep_display_banner('static',
    $banner); ?></td>
  </tr>
</table>
<?php
  }
?>
```

Replace it with this, specifying the group you would like to use:

```
<?php
  $banner_group = '468x60';
  if ($banner = tep_banner_exists('dynamic', $banner_group)) {
?>
<br>
<table border="0" width="100%" cellspacing="0" cellpadding="0">
  <tr>
    <td align="center"><?php echo tep_display_banner('static',
    $banner); ?></td>
  </tr>
</table>
<?php
  }
?>
```

Everyone was served what they wanted! Bon appetit!

Summary

This chapter has enhanced the gastronome in you, creating the perfect business chef able to set up sophisticated marketing strategies utilizing the full power of an osCommerce website.

With minor tweaks to the core code, an incredibly sophisticated multiple-layer banner system can be cooked up that can offer links within your own site to set special focus on products, categories, or keyword searches.

In addition to this new function, you have learned how to define category-driven banner groups that reach the specific target group intended, thus opening a completely new potential for advertising sales on your site or earning through affiliate programs.

Before moving to the final chapter, which offers mouth-watering administration tweaks, we will next look at a collection of very special recipes for specific areas of your shop that will indulge your sweet tooth.

10
Throw Together Dessert– Extra Treats for You!

This chapter holds a selection of my favorite sugar-sweet recipes that you will just love to try out. These recipes discuss specific areas of your shopping cart that will make your customer's life and your life easy. With the mouthwatering recipes in this chapter, you will be able to:

- Display a dynamic shipping table for **Table Rate** shipping
- Restructure and customize your file-download module
- Create a dual website combining Shopping Cart and Showroom features

60. Display a Dynamic Shipping Table for Table Rate Shipping

If your shop uses **Table Rate** shipping or even multiple table rates as suggested in Chapter 7, your customers will love to see a structured display of those rates on the Shipping Information page as well as the Shopping Cart page. The following recipe pulls the cost data from your configuration table and displays it in a nicely formatted module you can include on any page as needed.

Presentation

The following screenshot shows the Shopping Cart page with the new Table Rate display added:

Note that if you have set a handling fee, that amount will automatically be added to the shipping cost and displayed as the total value for price transparency towards your customer.

If you are using multiple table rates combined with zones, similar to the first recipe in Chapter 7, you can safely clone this recipe, changing only a few parameter names. The zone name will then automatically be displayed below the table like in this screenshot:

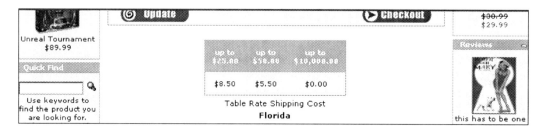

If this is the right cookie for your sweet tooth, bite in!

Ingredients

> **New:**
> catalog/includes/modules/shipping_table.php
>
> **Modified:**
> catalog/includes/languages/english.php
> catalog/shopping_cart.php
> catalog/shipping.php

Cooking

1. Create the new file `catalog/includes/modules/shipping_table.php` using the following code. It will create a nicely formatted table with the name of your module below it, and with a column for each rate/cost pair.

```php
<?php
/*
  $Id: shipping_table.php,v 1.00 2006/07/20 00:00:00 mm Exp $

  Module written by Monika Mathé
  http://www.monikamathe.com

  Module Copyright (c) 2006 Monika Mathé

  osCommerce, Open Source E-Commerce Solutions
  http://www.oscommerce.com

  Copyright (c) 2003 osCommerce

  Released under the GNU General Public License
*/
if (MODULE_SHIPPING_TABLE_STATUS === 'True') {

$prices = tep_db_query("SELECT * FROM " .
  TABLE_CONFIGURATION . " WHERE configuration_key =
  'MODULE_SHIPPING_TABLE_COST'");
$price = tep_db_fetch_array($prices);

$price_text .= '<table border="0" cellspacing="0"
  cellpadding="10">';
$price_text .= '<tr>';
$parameters_price = split("[,]",
  $price['configuration_value']);
```

```
$first_row ='';
$second_row ='';
$last_price=NULL;
for($i=0; isset($parameters_price[$i]); $i++){
 $pair_prices = split("[:]",$parameters_price[$i]);

 if(!isset($pair_prices[0])){
  $price_text .= '<b>Error: </b>: ' .
  $price['configuration_value'];
  break;
 }

 if(NULL == $last_price){
  $first=false;
 }
 $first_row .= '<td class="infoboxHeading" align="center">' .
   TEXT_UP_TO . '<br>' .
 (MODULE_SHIPPING_TABLE_MODE == 'weight' ? $pair_prices[0] .
  'lb' : $currencies->format($pair_prices[0])) .'</td>';

 $last_price = $pair_prices[0];
 if(!isset($pair_prices[1])){
  $price_text .= '<b>Error: no price:</b> ' .
  $price['configuration_value'];
  break;
 }
 $second_row .= '<td class="infoboxContents" align="center"
   height="20">' .
 $currencies->format($pair_prices[1] +
       MODULE_SHIPPING_TABLE_HANDLING) . '</td>';
}
$price_text .=  $first_row . "\n</tr>\n<tr>\n" .
$second_row . "</tr>\n";
$price_text .= "</table>\n";

// load the text defines
 include(DIR_WS_LANGUAGES . $language .
         '/modules/shipping/table.php');

if ((int)MODULE_SHIPPING_TABLE_ZONE > 0) {
 $check_query = tep_db_query("select geo_zone_name from " .
   TABLE_GEO_ZONES . " where geo_zone_id = '" .
   MODULE_SHIPPING_TABLE_ZONE . "'");
 $check = tep_db_fetch_array($check_query);
```

```
    $table_zone = $check['geo_zone_name'];
  }
?>

<tr>
 <td><?php echo tep_draw_separator('pixel_trans.gif',
    '100%', '20'); ?></td>
</tr>
<tr>
 <td><table align="center" border="0" cellspacing="1"
  cellpadding="0" class="infoBox">
  <tr class="infoBoxContents">
   <td><table border="0" width="100%" cellspacing="0"
      cellpadding="0">
    <tr>
     <td><?php echo $price_text; ?></td>
    </tr>
   </table></td>
  </tr>
 </table></td>
</tr>
<tr>
 <td><table border="0" width="100%" cellspacing="0"
   cellpadding="2">
  <tr>
   <td class="main" align="center">
    <?php echo MODULE_SHIPPING_TABLE_TEXT_TITLE .
     TEXT_SHIPPING_TABLE . '<br><b>' . $table_zone . '</b>';
    ?></td>
  </tr>
 </table></td>
</tr>
<?php
 }
?>
```

2. Open `catalog/includes/languages/english.php` and add the following defines needed for your new module file:

```
define('TEXT_SHIPPING_TABLE', ' Shipping Cost');
define('TEXT_UP_TO', 'up to');
```

3. Open `catalog/shopping_cart.php` and add the new module below the code for the buttons of the cart display. Find the following code in line 204:

```
<?php
 } else {
?>
  <tr>
    <td align="center" class="main">
     <?php new infoBox(array(array('text' => TEXT_CART_EMPTY)));
     ?></td>
  </tr>
```

Add directly above it the following code to call the shipping table module:

```
<?php require(DIR_WS_MODULES . 'shipping_table.php'); ?>
```

4. You will also have to add your new shipping table to `catalog/shipping. php`. Find the following code in line 53:

```
<tr>
 <td><table border="0" width="100%" cellspacing="0"
     cellpadding="2">
  <tr>
   <td class="main"><?php echo TEXT_INFORMATION; ?></td>
  </tr>
 </table></td>
</tr>
```

Add the following line just below it:

```
<?php require(DIR_WS_MODULES . 'shipping_table.php'); ?>
```

Chef's suggestion:

Apply this recipe for multiple-zone-based **Table Rate** modules by cloning step 1, using the secondary table rates' naming convention and adding each module call to `shipping.php` and `shopping_cart.php`.

Delicious! Like pudding in the mix! Bon appetit!

61. Restructure and Customize Your File Download Module

This recipe is extremely useful if you want to tie several file options to a product for downloading. Customers may want to mix and match file types, and zipping files is not always an option if your customers don't know how to unzip them. With this recipe, several file downloads can be done directly one after the other; each download opening in a new window, then reloading the parent window to show the correct count for additional downloads.

In standard osCommerce, only the product name, not the file name, is shown for downloading; that can lead to great confusion in multiple-download options. Files that have not been zipped may open in the window of the link itself, giving no option to return easily to the underlying window for subsequent downloads. Customers will not see the updated number of possible downloads either, even when saving and not opening the file. This can be extremely frustrating for clientele not proficient with the Internet and browsers. Offering a comfortable alternative to these confusions is certainly your goal.

Presentation

Your **Administration | Catalog | Products Attributes** will look like this with the new product **Book** added. It has two options, namely, **Screenshot** and **Chapters**. Again, **Screenshot** offers a choice of two different files, **gif Format** and **jpg Format**, while **Chapters** offers **Excel** file and **Text** file.

Products Attributes

1 | 2 | >>

ID	Product Name	Option Name	Option Value	Value Price	Prefix	Action
31	Book	Screenshot	gif Format	0.0000	+	edit
29	Book	Chapters	Excel File	0.0000	+	edit
32	Book	Screenshot	jpg Format	0.0000	+	edit
30	Book	Chapters	Text File	0.0000	+	edit
1	Matrox G200 MMS	Memory	4 mb	0.0000	+	edit

In your catalog section, customers will be offered two choices for each option, so they can choose the correct file format for their needs:

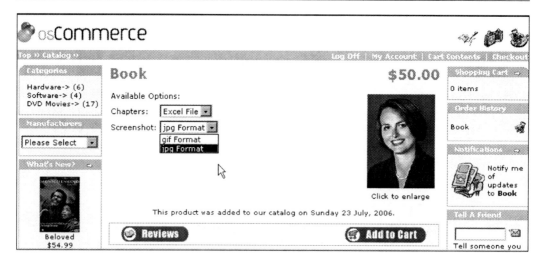

After payment, your customers will see the download table with the appropriate file names in the list. Clicking on a link refreshes the parent window and adjusts the number of remaining downloads:

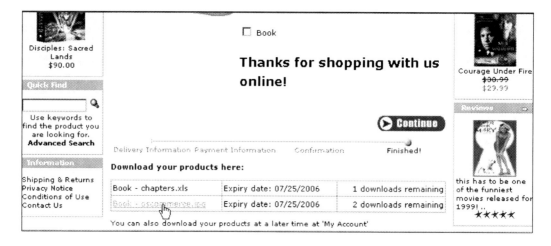

No sweet without sweat, they say—nonsense, this will be easy as a pie!

Ingredients

Modified:
`catalog/includes/modules/downloads.php`

Cooking

1. Navigate to **Administration | Catalog** and create a new product, adding two
    sets of downloadable attributes; here **Chapters** with **Excel File** and **Text File**,
    and **Screenshot** with **jpg Format** and **gif Format** as options.

> **Chef's suggestion:**
>
> For creating downloadable products, **Administration |
> Configuration | Download | Enable download** must be
> set to `true`.

2. Open `catalog/includes/modules/downloads.php` and find this in line 55:

```
if ( ($downloads['download_count'] > 0) &&
    (file_exists(DIR_FS_DOWNLOAD .
    $downloads['orders_products_filename'])) &&
    ( ($downloads['download_maxdays'] == 0) ||
    ($download_timestamp > time())) ) {
  echo '        <td class="main"><a href="' .
    tep_href_link(FILENAME_DOWNLOAD, 'order=' . $last_order .
    '&id=' . $downloads['orders_products_download_id']) . '">' .
    $downloads['products_name'] . '</a></td>' . "\n";
} else {
  echo '        <td class="main">' . $downloads['products_name'] .
  '</td>' . "\n";
  }
```

Replace it with the following code, which calls the downloaded file in a new
window, refreshes the underlying window, and appends the file name to the
product name:

```
if ( ($downloads['download_count'] > 0) &&
    (file_exists(DIR_FS_DOWNLOAD .
    $downloads['orders_products_filename'])) &&
    ( ($downloads['download_maxdays'] == 0) ||
    ($download_timestamp > time())) ) {
  echo '        <td class="main"><a target="_blank"
    onClick="window.location.reload();" href="' .
    tep_href_link(FILENAME_DOWNLOAD, 'order=' . $last_order .
    '&id=' . $downloads['orders_products_download_id']) . '">' .
    $downloads['products_name'] . ' - ' .
    $downloads['orders_products_filename'] . '</a></td>' . "\n";
} else {
  echo '        <td class="main">' . $downloads['products_name'] .
```

```
            ' - ' . $downloads['orders_products_filename'] .
        '</td>' . "\n";
    }
```

3. A few lines further down, find this in line 63:

```
echo '                <td class="main">' .
    TABLE_HEADING_DOWNLOAD_DATE . tep_date_long($download_expiry) .
    '</td>' . "\n" .
```

Change the date format to the short date display, as adding the file name used up space.

```
echo '                <td class="main">' . TABLE_HEADING_DOWNLOAD_DATE
. tep_date_short($download_expiry) . '</td>' . "\n" .
```

Chef's suggestion:

Step 3 is optional for stores that are not centered and have plenty of space to work with.

Your house smells sweet! Everything is in apple-pie order! Bon appetit!

62. Create a Dual Website Combining Shopping Cart and Showroom Features

As an artist or a business offering customized products, you may have a large collection of completed projects that you would like to showcase, but not offer for sale. This recipe shows you how to set up a category that can be used for showcasing product images like an exhibition. All features of osCommerce, like search and display in new products, remain as they were, only your showroom will show no prices and offer no cart button.

Presentation

The following screenshot shows the **Showroom** category set up for this purpose, holding the category **Hardware**. A second category, **For Sale**, was created as top category for **Software** and **DVD Movies**:

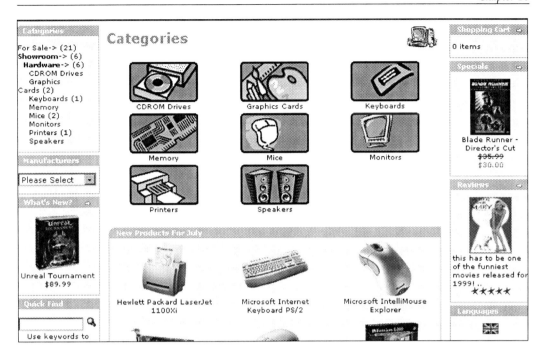

Note how prices show in all areas that feature products from the **For Sale** category, while they are hidden for the **Showroom**.

Chef's suggestion:

When combining a showroom with a shopping cart website, separating the top categories into their own boxes, as discussed in Chapter 2 (*Create Separate Boxes for Each Top Category*), is a layout that will offer intuitive navigation to your customers.

When you click on a subcategory, the columns **Price** and **Buy** are hidden for the **Showroom**, as you can see here:

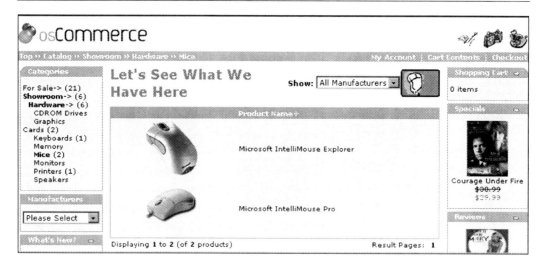

Chef's suggestion:

Here is another great spot to mix in another recipe for added ease of your customers: in this case, *Add Top Category in ProductListing*, discussed in Chapter 4. Also, you can add the name of the top category, here **Showroom**, below the product name in brackets.

On the Product Detail page, prices as well as the button bar are hidden, while you can still offer options, which are important for special order items that customers like to check out online, but will order only after a personal consultation with you:

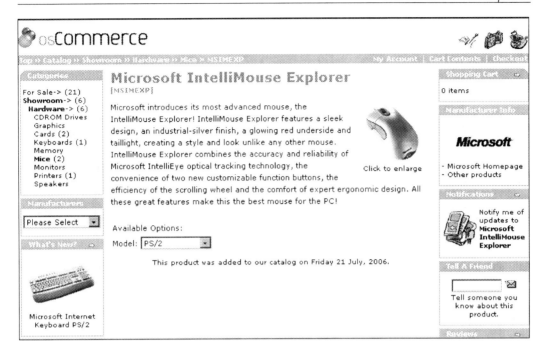

Key Lime, Pumpkin, Rhubarb, Apple, and all the rest... let's get baking!

Ingredients

> **New:**
> database.sql (to be run in phpMyAdmin)
>
> **Modified:**
> catalog/includes/classes/currencies.php
> catalog/includes/functions/general.php
> catalog/includes/modules/product_listing.php
> catalog/index.php
> catalog/product_info.php

Cooking

1. Navigate to **Administration | Catalog | Categories/Products** and restructure your category tree. Create two new categories, with the first being used for the products you sell, and the second to be used for the products on showcase only. Move the categories you already have into your new categories according to their purpose.

2. Navigate to **Administration | Catalog | Specials** and look over the products list in this section. Make sure that no product from your **Showroom** category has been added to the **Specials** section or it will show a price in any case.

3. Run the following SQL statement in phpMyAdmin to create a new row in the section for product listing parameters. It will add an option to define the top-category ID that will hold your new showroom:

```
INSERT INTO configuration (configuration_title,
    configuration_key, configuration_value,
    configuration_description, configuration_group_id,
    sort_order, date_added)
VALUES ('Showroom Top Category ID', 'SHOWROOM_TOPCAT_ID',
    '-1', 'Specify the top category id for your showroom',
    '8', '20', now());
```

4. Navigate to **Administration | Configuration| Product Listing**. Note how the default value for your new key **Showroom Top Category ID** is set to **-1** to disable the showroom module. Edit the parameter, entering the category ID of your **Showroom** category. (To find out how to obtain the correct `categories_id`, refer to the Chef's suggestion in *Set Up Category-Driven Banners*, Chapter 9.)

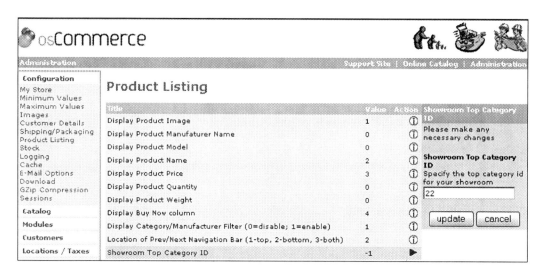

5. Open `catalog/includes/classes/currencies.php` and find this in line 35:

```
function format($number, $calculate_currency_value = true,
    $currency_type = '', $currency_value = '') {
    global $currency;

    if (empty($currency_type)) $currency_type = $currency;
```

```
    if ($calculate_currency_value == true) {
     $rate = (tep_not_null($currency_value)) ?
     $currency_value : $this->currencies[$currency_type]['value'];
     $format_string = $this->currencies[$currency_type]
      ['symbol_left'] . number_format(tep_round($number * $rate,
       $this->currencies[$currency_type]['decimal_places']),
       $this->currencies[$currency_type]['decimal_places'],
       $this->currencies[$currency_type]['decimal_point'],
       $this->currencies[$currency_type]['thousands_point']) .
       $this->currencies[$currency_type]['symbol_right'];
// if the selected currency is in the european euro-conversion
// and the default currency is euro,
// the currency will displayed in the national currency and
// euro currency
if ( (DEFAULT_CURRENCY == 'EUR') && ($currency_type == 'DEM' ||
     $currency_type == 'BEF' || $currency_type == 'LUF' ||
     $currency_type == 'ESP' || $currency_type == 'FRF' ||
     $currency_type == 'IEP' || $currency_type == 'ITL' ||
     $currency_type == 'NLG' || $currency_type == 'ATS' ||
     $currency_type == 'PTE' || $currency_type == 'FIM' ||
     $currency_type == 'GRD') ) {
         $format_string .= ' <small>[' . $this->format($number,
             true, 'EUR') . ']</small>';
  }
 } else {
  $format_string = $this->currencies[$currency_type]
   ['symbol_left'] . number_format(tep_round($number,
     $this->currencies[$currency_type]['decimal_places']),
     $this->currencies[$currency_type]['decimal_places'],
     $this->currencies[$currency_type]['decimal_point'],
     $this->currencies[$currency_type]['thousands_point']) .
     $this->currencies[$currency_type]['symbol_right'];
  }

  return $format_string;
 }
```

This function handles the display of your prices. Add the following code, which will allow you to leave the formatting function and return only an empty string instead of a formatted price of $0.00 if the price to be formatted was indeed $0.00. This will allow you to hide prices very easily. The top part should now look like this:

```
function format($number, $calculate_currency_value = true,
  $currency_type = '', $currency_value = '') {
    global $currency;

    if ($number == 0) return '';

    if (empty($currency_type)) $currency_type = $currency;
```

6. Open `catalog/includes/functions/general.php` and add the following two functions right before the closing `?>` PHP tag:

```
function after ($this, $inthat) {
if (!is_bool(strpos($inthat, $this)))
return substr($inthat, strpos($inthat,$this)+strlen($this));
};


function tep_get_topcategory_id($product_id,
                  $categories_id = '') {


if ($product_id > 0) {
 $topcat_array = explode('_' ,
              tep_get_product_path($product_id));
 $top_cat = $topcat_array[0];
 } else {
 $topcat_array = explode('_' , tep_get_path($categories_id));
 $top_cat = after ('=', $topcat_array[0]);
 }


return $top_cat;
}
```

The first function allows you to cut off strings after a specified character position, which is used in the second function that either gets the top-category ID for a product or for your current category ID.

7. Open `catalog/includes/modules/product_listing.php` and find this in line 131:

```
case 'PRODUCT_LIST_BUY_NOW':
$lc_align = 'center';
$lc_text = '<a href="' . tep_href_link(basename($PHP_SELF),
    tep_get_all_get_params(array('action')) .
 'action=buy_now&products_id=' . $listing['products_id']) . '">'
 . tep_image_button('button_buy_now.gif', IMAGE_BUTTON_BUY_NOW) .
 '</a> ';
break;
```

The **Buy Now** button needs to stay visible for items you sell when the product listing file is called by your search function. It needs to hide though if the product belongs to the **Showroom** category. Therefore replace it with the following code that will check for the top category of the product, and either show or hide the **Buy Now** button:

```
case 'PRODUCT_LIST_BUY_NOW':
$lc_align = 'center';

if (tep_get_topcategory_id($listing['products_id']) !=
    SHOWROOM_TOPCAT_ID) {
  $lc_text = '<a href="' . tep_href_link(basename($PHP_SELF),
    tep_get_all_get_params(array('action')) .
  'action=buy_now&products_id=' . $listing['products_id']) . '">'
  . tep_image_button('button_buy_now.gif', IMAGE_BUTTON_BUY_NOW)
  . '</a> ';
} else {
  $lc_text = ' ';
}
break;
```

8. Open `catalog/index.php` and find this in line 128:

```
$define_list = array('PRODUCT_LIST_MODEL' => PRODUCT_LIST_MODEL,
        'PRODUCT_LIST_NAME' => PRODUCT_LIST_NAME,
        'PRODUCT_LIST_MANUFACTURER' => PRODUCT_LIST_MANUFACTURER,
        'PRODUCT_LIST_PRICE' => PRODUCT_LIST_PRICE,
        'PRODUCT_LIST_QUANTITY' => PRODUCT_LIST_QUANTITY,
        'PRODUCT_LIST_WEIGHT' => PRODUCT_LIST_WEIGHT,
        'PRODUCT_LIST_IMAGE' => PRODUCT_LIST_IMAGE,
        'PRODUCT_LIST_BUY_NOW' => PRODUCT_LIST_BUY_NOW);
```

This is the column list used for displaying your product listing. As you can not set the value for **Price** and **Buy Now** to **0** in your admin area (which would result in no listing, not even search showing those columns), this list has to be modified in `index.php`, which only displays subcategory listings. It is the perfect place to check for the top category of that listing and decide on which columns to exclude. Replace the above code with the following new code snippet:

```
// create column list

if (tep_get_topcategory_id(0, $current_category_id) ==
    SHOWROOM_TOPCAT_ID) {
  $define_list = array('PRODUCT_LIST_MODEL' => PRODUCT_LIST_MODEL,
        'PRODUCT_LIST_NAME' => PRODUCT_LIST_NAME,
        'PRODUCT_LIST_MANUFACTURER' => PRODUCT_LIST_MANUFACTURER,
        'PRODUCT_LIST_QUANTITY' => PRODUCT_LIST_QUANTITY,
```

```
                    'PRODUCT_LIST_WEIGHT' => PRODUCT_LIST_WEIGHT,
                    'PRODUCT_LIST_IMAGE' => PRODUCT_LIST_IMAGE);
        } else {
        $define_list = array('PRODUCT_LIST_MODEL' => PRODUCT_LIST_MODEL,
                    'PRODUCT_LIST_NAME' => PRODUCT_LIST_NAME,
                    'PRODUCT_LIST_MANUFACTURER' => PRODUCT_LIST_MANUFACTURER,
                    'PRODUCT_LIST_PRICE' => PRODUCT_LIST_PRICE,
                    'PRODUCT_LIST_QUANTITY' => PRODUCT_LIST_QUANTITY,
                    'PRODUCT_LIST_WEIGHT' => PRODUCT_LIST_WEIGHT,
                    'PRODUCT_LIST_IMAGE' => PRODUCT_LIST_IMAGE,
                    'PRODUCT_LIST_BUY_NOW' => PRODUCT_LIST_BUY_NOW);
        }
```

9. Open `catalog/product_info.php` and find this in line 206:

```
<tr>
 <td><table border="0" width="100%" cellspacing="1"
  cellpadding="2" class="infoBox">
 <tr class="infoBoxContents">
  <td><table border="0" width="100%" cellspacing="0"
      cellpadding="2">
    <tr>
     <td width="10">
      <?php echo tep_draw_separator('pixel_trans.gif', '10',
      '1'); ?></td>
     <td class="main"><?php echo '<a href="' .
       tep_href_link(FILENAME_PRODUCT_REVIEWS,
         tep_get_all_get_params()) . '">' .
       tep_image_button('button_reviews.gif',
         IMAGE_BUTTON_REVIEWS) . '</a>'; ?></td>
     <td class="main" align="right">
      <?php echo tep_draw_hidden_field('products_id',
          $product_info['products_id']) .
       tep_image_submit('button_in_cart.gif',
          IMAGE_BUTTON_IN_CART); ?></td>
     <td width="10">
       <?php echo tep_draw_separator('pixel_trans.gif', '10',
       '1'); ?></td>
    </tr>
   </table></td>
  </tr>
 </table></td>
</tr>
<tr>
 <td><?php echo tep_draw_separator('pixel_trans.gif', '100%',
```

```
                 '10'); ?></td>
    </tr>
```

To hide this button bar for products of the **Showroom** category, wrap a conditional statement around the whole bar to verify the top category ID:

```php
<?php
 if (tep_get_topcategory_id($product_info['products_id']) !=
     SHOWROOM_TOPCAT_ID) {
?>
 <tr>
  <td><table border="0" width="100%" cellspacing="1"
      cellpadding="2" class="infoBox">
   <tr class="infoBoxContents">
    <td><table border="0" width="100%" cellspacing="0"
      cellpadding="2">
     <tr>
      <td width="10">
        <?php echo tep_draw_separator('pixel_trans.gif', '10',
         '1'); ?></td>
      <td class="main"><?php echo '<a href="' .
        tep_href_link(FILENAME_PRODUCT_REVIEWS,
        tep_get_all_get_params()) . '">' .
        tep_image_button('button_reviews.gif',
        IMAGE_BUTTON_REVIEWS) . '</a>'; ?></td>
      <td class="main" align="right">
        <?php echo tep_draw_hidden_field('products_id',
         $product_info['products_id']) .
         tep_image_submit('button_in_cart.gif',
         IMAGE_BUTTON_IN_CART); ?></td>
      <td width="10">
        <?php echo tep_draw_separator('pixel_trans.gif', '10',
         '1'); ?></td>
     </tr>
    </table></td>
   </tr>
  </table></td>
 </tr>
 <tr>
 <td><?php echo tep_draw_separator('pixel_trans.gif', '100%',
     '10'); ?></td>
 </tr>
<?php
 }
?>
```

For testing, edit all showroom prices to $0.00, "à la mode"! Bon appetit!

Summary

Sugar 'n spice, and everything nice; that's what the recipes in this chapter are made from. You have been allowed to peek into the Chef's secret favorites and learn about honey-sweet functions that allow you to whip up shipping tables for display in a few minutes; you can even clone the recipe for multiple tables and even more fun!

Several different file downloads can be tied to the same product as now the customer interface has been changed to a structured display table with relevant instructions.

For artists and stores that need a window-shopping section showing their counter of showcase products in addition to those offered for purchase, we have discussed a recipe that makes implementing such a display a piece of cake.

You are now ready to taste the last chapter of this book where we offer a turntable of delectable recipes for your administration delight. Enjoy!

11
Beef Up Your Admin

Having discussed all catalog-related parts of osCommerce in the first ten chapters of this cookbook, what now remains is what is hidden from the public eye. We will now take a close look at your **Administration** area, which is your very own kitchen, the place you will spend the most time when your shop is up and running. A few of the recipes in this chapter will affect the customers' shopping experience, without them realizing that it has. Let's view together a collection of recipes that will enhance your job as the Grand Chef.

This chapter will tantalize your taste buds with the following recipes—created for famished administrators, so you can:

- Reset date added for products
- Set an expiry date for products
- Limit Also Purchased Products selection by date
- Display full information for customer, delivery, and billing addresses at a glance
- Highlight orders according to their order status
- Sort your **Administration** menu configuration-box entries
- Allow entering products in an additional currency

Let's stir the pot to get started!

63. Reset Date Added for Products

This recipe is perfect for you if you want to specify which products are showcased in the New Products box of your homepage and category pages. The New Products box uses the value of the `products_date_added` column of the `products` table for sorting, which makes a change in display fairly easy to achieve. You may want to be cheeky and reset items on purpose to get them up on the list, or you may use this feature after updating a product thoroughly, so it is basically a new product indeed. If you use this tool in the cheeky way a lot, consider renaming the box, as New Products will not fit any more.

Presentation

The following screenshot shows **Administration | Catalog | Categories/Products** with the DVD Movie **Speed** highlighted. Here you are about to have it reset as new:

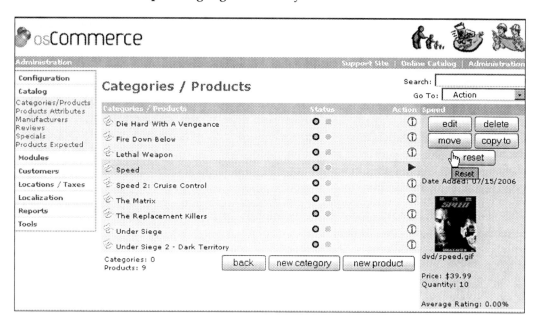

As soon as the **reset** button is clicked, the `products_date_added` and `products_last_modified` columns in the `products` table are modified to hold the current date as shown here:

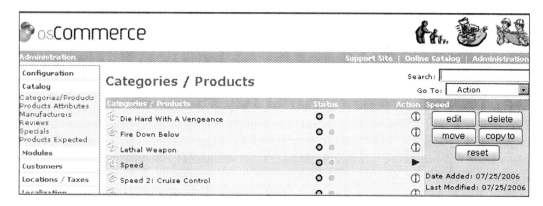

Let's skewer this one!

Ingredients

Modified:

`catalog/admin/categories.php`

Cooking

1. Open `catalog/admin/categories.php` and find this in line 272:

   ```
   break;
   case 'copy_to_confirm':
   ```

   In this upper part of the `categories.php` file, all action commands are checked by a switch statement. Add the new command for resetting the products date between two existing commands. Each command starts with `case` and ends with `break;`. Replace the above code with this:

   ```
   break;
   case 'reset_product':
    tep_db_query("update " . TABLE_PRODUCTS . "
     set products_date_added = now(), products_last_modified = now()
     where products_id = '" . $HTTP_GET_VARS['pID'] . "'");

     tep_redirect(tep_href_link(FILENAME_CATEGORIES,
       'cPath=' . $HTTP_GET_VARS['cPath'] .
       '&pID=' . $HTTP_GET_VARS['pID']));
   break;
   case 'copy_to_confirm':
   ```

2. At the bottom of the same file on line 986 find the following code, which displays the action button. This button is seen in the right column when a product is highlighted:

   ```
   $contents[] = array('align' => 'center',
   'text' => '<a href="' . tep_href_link(FILENAME_CATEGORIES,
   'cPath=' . $cPath . '&pID=' . $pInfo->products_id .
    '&action=new_product') . '">' .
   tep_image_button('button_edit.gif', IMAGE_EDIT) . '</a>
   <a href="' . tep_href_link(FILENAME_CATEGORIES,
   'cPath=' . $cPath . '&pID=' . $pInfo->products_id .
   '&action=delete_product') . '">' .
   ```

```
tep_image_button('button_delete.gif', IMAGE_DELETE) . '</a>
<a href="' . tep_href_link(FILENAME_CATEGORIES,
'cPath=' . $cPath . '&pID=' . $pInfo->products_id .
'&action=move_product') . '">' .
tep_image_button('button_move.gif', IMAGE_MOVE) . '</a>
<a href="' . tep_href_link(FILENAME_CATEGORIES,
'cPath=' . $cPath . '&pID=' . $pInfo->products_id .
'&action=copy_to') . '">' .
tep_image_button('button_copy_to.gif', IMAGE_COPY_TO) . '</a>');
```

Replace with the following line, adding the new reset button to the group:

```
$contents[] = array('align' => 'center',
  'text' => '<a href="' . tep_href_link(FILENAME_CATEGORIES,
  'cPath=' . $cPath . '&pID=' . $pInfo->products_id .
  '&action=new_product') . '">' .
  tep_image_button('button_edit.gif', IMAGE_EDIT) . '</a>
  <a href="' . tep_href_link(FILENAME_CATEGORIES,
  'cPath=' . $cPath . '&pID=' . $pInfo->products_id .
  '&action=delete_product') . '">' .
  tep_image_button('button_delete.gif', IMAGE_DELETE) . '</a>
  <a href="' . tep_href_link(FILENAME_CATEGORIES,
  'cPath=' . $cPath . '&pID=' . $pInfo->products_id .
  '&action=move_product') . '">' .
  tep_image_button('button_move.gif', IMAGE_MOVE) . '</a>
  <a href="' . tep_href_link(FILENAME_CATEGORIES,
  'cPath=' . $cPath . '&pID=' . $pInfo->products_id .
  '&action=copy_to') . '">' .
  tep_image_button('button_copy_to.gif', IMAGE_COPY_TO) . '</a>
  <a href="' . tep_href_link(FILENAME_CATEGORIES,
  'cPath=' . $cPath . '&pID=' . $pInfo->products_id .
  '&action=reset_product') . '">' .
  tep_image_button('button_reset.gif', IMAGE_RESET) . '</a>');
```

As good as Shish Kabobs can get! Bon appetit!

64. Set an Expiry Date for Products

This recipe is perfect for displaying seasonal products or one-day-only offers without the hassle of correcting product status manually. A function set up in your catalog area will automatically check for expiring products and adjust status in a similar way to that in which **Specials** or banners are checked for expiry in the default osCommerce version. This is a wonderful example of how code from one area can be used for a different section of the site with only minor adjustments.

Presentation

Your **Administration | Catalog | Categories/Products** page will look like this with the DVD Movie **Speed** having been on display for four days only (Date Added of July 20, Expiry Date of July 24). On July 24, it was set automatically to inactive.

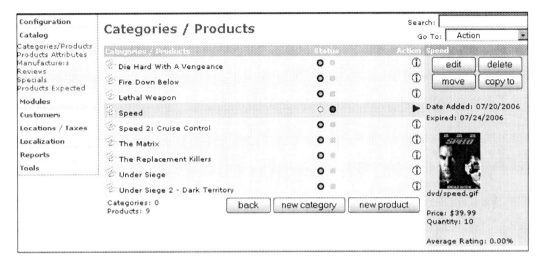

You will be able to see the expiry date set for each product as applicable. Here **Speed 2** will be available till September 30, and then will automatically expire:

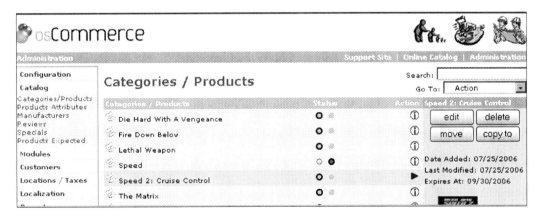

Let's slap on those cold-cuts before their due date!

Ingredients

New:

database.sql (to be run in phpMyAdmin)

catalog/includes/functions/products.php

Modified:

catalog/admin/categories.php
catalog/admin/includes/languages/english/categories.php
catalog/includes/application_top.php

Cooking

1. Run the following SQL statement in phpMyAdmin, which will create two new columns in your products table. They will store information about products that you would like to expire at a specific date.

```
ALTER TABLE products
ADD products_expires_date datetime,
ADD products_date_status_change datetime;
```

2. Open catalog/admin/categories.php and modify the file to add the new columns. Find this in line 215 where the array is created for inserting or updating a product:

```
$sql_data_array = array('products_quantity' =>
  tep_db_prepare_input($HTTP_POST_VARS['products_quantity']),
                      'products_model' =>
  tep_db_prepare_input($HTTP_POST_VARS['products_model']),
                      'products_price' =>
  tep_db_prepare_input($HTTP_POST_VARS['products_price']),
                      'products_date_available' =>
  $products_date_available,
                      'products_weight' =>
  tep_db_prepare_input($HTTP_POST_VARS['products_weight']),
                      'products_status' =>
  tep_db_prepare_input($HTTP_POST_VARS['products_status']),
                      'products_tax_class_id' =>
  tep_db_prepare_input($HTTP_POST_VARS['products_tax_class_id']),
                      'manufacturers_id' =>
  tep_db_prepare_input($HTTP_POST_VARS['manufacturers_id']));
```

Replace with the following code:

```
$products_expires_date =
  tep_db_prepare_input($HTTP_POST_VARS['products_expires_date']);

$products_expires_date = (date('Y-m-d') <
$products_expires_date) ? $products_expires_date : 'null';

$sql_data_array = array('products_quantity' =>
  tep_db_prepare_input($HTTP_POST_VARS['products_quantity']),
                    'products_model' =>
  tep_db_prepare_input($HTTP_POST_VARS['products_model']),
                    'products_price' =>
  tep_db_prepare_input($HTTP_POST_VARS['products_price']),
                    'products_date_available' =>
$products_date_available,
                    'products_expires_date' =>
$products_expires_date,
                    'products_weight' =>
  tep_db_prepare_input($HTTP_POST_VARS['products_weight']),
                    'products_status' =>
  tep_db_prepare_input($HTTP_POST_VARS['products_status']),
                    'products_tax_class_id' =>
  tep_db_prepare_input($HTTP_POST_VARS['products_tax_class_id']),
                    'manufacturers_id' =>
  tep_db_prepare_input($HTTP_POST_VARS['manufacturers_id']));
```

3. A few lines further down, find this in line 299:

```
$product_query = tep_db_query("select products_quantity,
  products_model, products_image, products_price,
  products_date_available, products_weight,
  products_tax_class_id, manufacturers_id from " .
  TABLE_PRODUCTS . " where products_id = '" .
  (int)$products_id . "'");
$product = tep_db_fetch_array($product_query);

tep_db_query("insert into " . TABLE_PRODUCTS .
  " (products_quantity, products_model,products_image,
    products_price, products_date_added,
    products_date_available, products_weight, products_status,
    products_tax_class_id, manufacturers_id)
values ('" . tep_db_input($product['products_quantity']) . "',
  '" . tep_db_input($product['products_model']) . "', '" .
    tep_db_input($product['products_image']) . "', '" .
      tep_db_input($product['products_price']) . "', now(), "
        . (empty($product['products_date_available']) ?
```

```
            "null" : "'" .
        tep_db_input($product['products_date_available']) . "'")
    . ", '" . tep_db_input($product['products_weight']) . "',
        '0', '" . (int)$product['products_tax_class_id'] . "',
    '" . (int)$product['manufacturers_id'] . "')");
```

Add the new columns to the *select* and *insert* statements, so products that are copied carry that information over to the new product:

```
$product_query = tep_db_query("select products_quantity,
    products_model, products_image, products_price,
    products_date_available, products_expires_date,
    products_date_status_change, products_weight,
    products_tax_class_id, manufacturers_id from " . TABLE_PRODUCTS
    . " where products_id = '" . (int)$products_id . "'");
$product = tep_db_fetch_array($product_query);

tep_db_query("insert into " . TABLE_PRODUCTS . "
    (products_quantity, products_model,products_image,
    products_price, products_date_added, products_date_available,
        products_expires_date, products_date_status_change,
    products_weight, products_status, products_tax_class_id,
    manufacturers_id)
values ('" . tep_db_input($product['products_quantity']) . "', '"
    . tep_db_input($product['products_model']) . "', '" .
    tep_db_input($product['products_image']) . "', '" .
    tep_db_input($product['products_price']) . "', now(), " .
    (empty($product['products_date_available']) ? "null" : "'" .
        tep_db_input($product['products_date_available']) . "') .
        ", " . (empty($product['products_expires_date']) ? "null" :
        "'" . tep_db_input($product['products_expires_date']) . "'")
        . ", " . (empty($product['products_date_status_change']) ?
        "null" : "'" .
        tep_db_input($product['products_date_status_change']) . "'")
        . ", '" . tep_db_input($product['products_weight']) . "',
        '0', '" . (int)$product['products_tax_class_id'] . "', '" .
    (int)$product['manufacturers_id'] . "')");
```

4. In the section for new or edited products, find this in line 379:

    ```
    'products_date_available' => '',
    ```

    Replace with the following code. This code adds the declaration for the products_expires_date variable for new product creation or editing. There is no need of the products_date_status_change column here as that column will not be filled in the admin front end, but by the function that checks for expiry.

```
'products_date_available' => '',
'products_expires_date' => '',
```

5. Find the product query for editing products in line 388:

```
$product_query = tep_db_query("select pd.products_name,
   pd.products_description, pd.products_url, p.products_id,
   p.products_quantity, p.products_model, p.products_image,
   p.products_price, p.products_weight, p.products_date_added,
   p.products_last_modified,
   date_format(p.products_date_available,
   '%Y-%m-%d') as products_date_available, p.products_status,
   p.products_tax_class_id, p.manufacturers_id from " .
   TABLE_PRODUCTS . " p, " . TABLE_PRODUCTS_DESCRIPTION .
   " pd where p.products_id = '" . (int)$HTTP_GET_VARS['pID'] . "'
   and p.products_id = pd.products_id and pd.language_id = '" .
   (int)$languages_id . "'");
```

Replace it with this query. Add just the new products_expires_date
column here, as in step 4:

```
$product_query = tep_db_query("select pd.products_name,
   pd.products_description, pd.products_url, p.products_id,
   p.products_quantity, p.products_model, p.products_image,
   p.products_price, p.products_weight, p.products_date_added,
   p.products_last_modified,
   date_format(p.products_date_available,
   '%Y-%m-%d') as products_date_available,
   date_format(p.products_expires_date, '%Y-%m-%d') as
   products_expires_date, p.products_status,
   p.products_tax_class_id, p.manufacturers_id from " .
   TABLE_PRODUCTS . " p, " . TABLE_PRODUCTS_DESCRIPTION .
   " pd where p.products_id = '" . (int)$HTTP_GET_VARS['pID'] . "'
   and p.products_id = pd.products_id and pd.language_id = '" .
   (int)$languages_id . "'");
```

6. In line 425, find the declaration of the variable dateAvailable using the
   calendar function for products that will be available in the future:

```
var dateAvailable = new ctlSpiffyCalendarBox("dateAvailable",
"new_product", "products_date_available","btnDate1","
<?php echo $pInfo->products_date_available;
?>",scBTNMODE_CUSTOMBLUE);
```

Add a new variable dateExpire for the expiry date, also using a calendar
pop up, right below it:

```
var dateExpire = new ctlSpiffyCalendarBox("dateExpire",
```

```
"new_product", "products_expires_date","btnDate1",
"<?php echo $pInfo->products_expires_date;
  ?>",scBTNMODE_CUSTOMBLUE);
```

7. In line 497, find the input field for products expected:

```
<tr>
  <td class="main"><?php echo TEXT_PRODUCTS_DATE_AVAILABLE;
  ?><br><small>(YYYY-MM-DD)</small></td>
  <td class="main"><?php echo
  tep_draw_separator('pixel_trans.gif', '24', '15') . ' ';
  ?>
  <script language="javascript">dateAvailable.writeControl();
  dateAvailable.dateFormat="yyyy-MM-dd";</script></td>
</tr>
```

Add directly below it the new entry field for expiry date, including a tip text explaining that the field is not mandatory:

```
<tr>
  <td colspan="2"><?php echo
  tep_draw_separator('pixel_trans.gif', '1', '10'); ?></td>
</tr>
<tr>
  <td class="main"><?php echo TEXT_EXPIRES_DATE;
  ?><br><small>(YYYY-MM-DD)</small></td>
  <td class="main"><?php echo
  tep_draw_separator('pixel_trans.gif', '24', '15') . ' ';
  ?>
  <script language="javascript">dateExpire.writeControl();
  dateExpire.dateFormat="yyyy-MM-dd";</script> 
  <?php echo TEXT_TIP; ?></td>
</tr>
```

8. The last section that you have to amend is the default page, which displays the results of a products search. You can modify the information that is shown in the right column when one of the products is highlighted. Find the following queries in line 828:

```
$products_query = tep_db_query("select p.products_id,
  pd.products_name, p.products_quantity, p.products_image,
  p.products_price, p.products_date_added,
  p.products_last_modified, p.products_date_available,
  p.products_status, p2c.categories_id from " . TABLE_PRODUCTS .
  " p, " . TABLE_PRODUCTS_DESCRIPTION . " pd, " .
  TABLE_PRODUCTS_TO_CATEGORIES . " p2c
  where p.products_id = pd.products_id and
```

```
  pd.language_id = '" . (int)$languages_id . "' and
  p.products_id = p2c.products_id and pd.products_name like '%" .
  tep_db_input($search) . "%' order by pd.products_name");
} else {
  $products_query = tep_db_query("select p.products_id,
    pd.products_name, p.products_quantity, p.products_image,
    p.products_price, p.products_date_added,
    p.products_last_modified, p.products_date_available,
    p.products_status from " . TABLE_PRODUCTS . " p, " .
    TABLE_PRODUCTS_DESCRIPTION . " pd, " .
    TABLE_PRODUCTS_TO_CATEGORIES . " p2c where
    p.products_id = pd.products_id and
    pd.language_id = '" . (int)$languages_id . "' and
    p.products_id = p2c.products_id and
    p2c.categories_id = '" . (int)$current_category_id . "'
    order by pd.products_name");
```

Replace them with these queries, adding your two new columns:

```
$products_query = tep_db_query("select p.products_id,
  pd.products_name, p.products_quantity, p.products_image,
  p.products_price, p.products_date_added,
  p.products_last_modified, p.products_date_available,
  p.products_expires_date, p.products_date_status_change,
  p.products_status, p2c.categories_id from " . TABLE_PRODUCTS .
  " p, " . TABLE_PRODUCTS_DESCRIPTION . " pd, " .
  TABLE_PRODUCTS_TO_CATEGORIES . " p2c where
  p.products_id = pd.products_id and
  pd.language_id = '" . (int)$languages_id . "' and
  p.products_id = p2c.products_id and pd.products_name like '%" .
  tep_db_input($search) . "%' order by pd.products_name");
} else {
  $products_query = tep_db_query("select p.products_id,
    pd.products_name, p.products_quantity, p.products_image,
    p.products_price, p.products_date_added,
    p.products_last_modified, p.products_date_available,
    p.products_expires_date, p.products_date_status_change,
    p.products_status from " . TABLE_PRODUCTS . " p, " .
    TABLE_PRODUCTS_DESCRIPTION . " pd, " .
    TABLE_PRODUCTS_TO_CATEGORIES . " p2c where
    p.products_id = pd.products_id and
    pd.language_id = '" . (int)$languages_id . "' and
    p.products_id = p2c.products_id and
    p2c.categories_id = '" . (int)$current_category_id . "'
    order by pd.products_name");
```

9. In line 1002, find the section of the right column where extra information is shown about the date modified and date available for a product:

```
if (tep_not_null($pInfo->products_last_modified))
  $contents[] = array('text' => TEXT_LAST_MODIFIED . ' ' .
  tep_date_short($pInfo->products_last_modified));
if (date('Y-m-d') < $pInfo->products_date_available)
  $contents[] = array('text' => TEXT_DATE_AVAILABLE . ' ' .
  tep_date_short($pInfo->products_date_available));
```

Add information about expiry date directly below it, to be displayed if relevant for the highlighted product:

```
if (date('Y-m-d') < $pInfo->products_expires_date)
  $contents[] = array('text' => TEXT_INFO_EXPIRES_DATE . ' ' .
  tep_date_short($pInfo->products_expires_date));
if (tep_not_null($pInfo->products_date_status_change))
  $contents[] = array('text' => TEXT_INFO_STATUS_CHANGE . ' ' .
  tep_date_short($pInfo->products_date_status_change));
```

10. Open `catalog/admin/includes/languages/english/categories.php` and add the following language file defines:

```
define('TEXT_TIP', 'Leave the expiry date empty for no
  expiration');
define('TEXT_EXPIRES_DATE', 'Expiry Date:');
define('TEXT_INFO_EXPIRES_DATE', 'Expires At:');
define('TEXT_INFO_STATUS_CHANGE', 'Expired:');
```

11. Navigate to **Administration | Catalog | Categories/Products**, edit a product, and choose a future date when you want the product to expire:

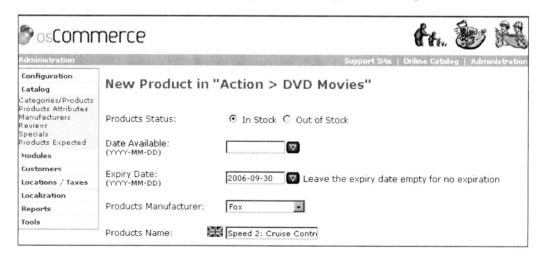

12. Create the new file `catalog/includes/functions/products.php`, responsible for checking if a product needs to be expired, with the following code:

```php
<?php
/*
  $Id: products.php,v 1.00 2006/07/25 00:00:00 mm Exp $

  Module written by Monika Mathé
  http://www.monikamathe.com

  Module Copyright (c) 2006 Monika Mathé

  osCommerce, Open Source E-Commerce Solutions
  http://www.oscommerce.com

  Copyright (c) 2003 osCommerce

  Released under the GNU General Public License
*/

////
// Sets the status of a product
  function tep_set_products_expiry_status($products_id, $status) {
    return tep_db_query("update " . TABLE_PRODUCTS . " set
    products_status = '" . $status . "',
    products_date_status_change = now() where
    products_id = '" . (int)$products_id . "'");
  }

////
// Auto expire products
  function tep_expire_products() {
    $products_query = tep_db_query("select products_id from " .
    TABLE_PRODUCTS . " where products_status = '1' and
    now() >= products_expires_date and
    products_expires_date > 0");
    if (tep_db_num_rows($products_query)) {
      while ($products = tep_db_fetch_array($products_query)) {
        tep_set_products_expiry_status($products['products_id'],
        '0');
      }
    }
  }
?>
```

13. Open `catalog/includes/application_top.php` and find this in line 441:

```
// auto expire special products
  require(DIR_WS_FUNCTIONS . 'specials.php');
  tep_expire_specials();
```

Directly below it add your new function, to be included from its own file, and then called.

```
// auto expire products
  require(DIR_WS_FUNCTIONS . 'products.php');
  tep_expire_products();
```

There's nothing better than keeping a clean fridge! Bon appetit!

65. Limit Also Purchased Products Selection by Date

The Also Purchased infobox shows the customers those products that have been purchased by other customers in addition to the product they are just viewing in the Products Detail page. With large stores and frequently changed or seasonal products, it is reckless to show products that are not relevant to your customer, be it for seasonality or practicality. This recipe shows you how to limit this selection to a specific number of days from the time the last purchase was made.

Presentation

The following screenshot shows **Administration | Configuration | Maximum Values** with the new key **Also Purchased Max Days** edited to limit by the last 60 days:

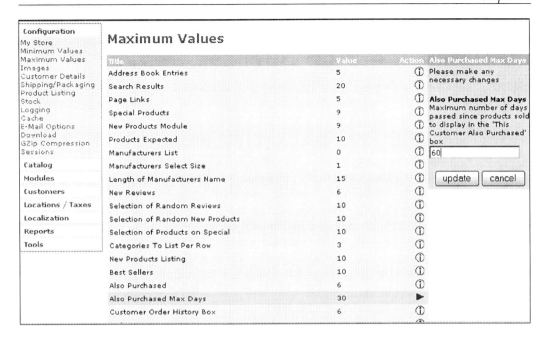

Ready to slice the roast?

Ingredients

New:

database.sql (to be run in phpMyAdmin)

Modified:

catalog/includes/modules/also_purchased_products.php

Cooking

1. Run the SQL statement in phpMyAdmin to create a new key in the **Maximum Values** area of your configuration parameters that will allow you to limit the days since a purchase was made:

```
INSERT INTO configuration (configuration_title,
    configuration_key, configuration_value,
    configuration_description, configuration_group_id,
    sort_order, date_added)
VALUES ('Also Purchased Max Days',
```

```
'MAX_DISPLAY_TIME_ALSO_PURCHASED', '30',
'Maximum number of days passed since products sold to display
in the \'This Customer Also Purchased\' box', '3', '16',
now());
```

2. Open `catalog/includes/modules/also_purchased_products.php` and find this in line 14:

```
$orders_query = tep_db_query("select p.products_id,
    p.products_image from " . TABLE_ORDERS_PRODUCTS . " opa, " .
    TABLE_ORDERS_PRODUCTS . " opb, " . TABLE_ORDERS . " o, " .
    TABLE_PRODUCTS . " p where opa.products_id = '" .
    (int)$HTTP_GET_VARS['products_id'] . "' and opa.orders_id =
    opb.orders_id and opb.products_id != '" .
    (int)$HTTP_GET_VARS['products_id'] . "' and opb.products_id =
     p.products_id and opb.orders_id = o.orders_id and
     p.products_status = '1' group by p.products_id
    order by o.date_purchased desc limit " .
    MAX_DISPLAY_ALSO_PURCHASED);
```

In the *where* clause part of this query, add a statement limiting the results to only those purchases that have been made in the timeframe specified in admin by the parameter **Also Purchased Max Days**, here **60** days :

```
$orders_query = tep_db_query("select p.products_id,
    p.products_image from " . TABLE_ORDERS_PRODUCTS . " opa, " .
    TABLE_ORDERS_PRODUCTS . " opb, " . TABLE_ORDERS . " o, " .
    TABLE_PRODUCTS . " p where opa.products_id = '" .
    (int)$HTTP_GET_VARS['products_id'] . "' and opa.orders_id =
    opb.orders_id and opb.products_id != '" .
    (int)$HTTP_GET_VARS['products_id'] . "' and opb.products_id =
    p.products_id and opb.orders_id = o.orders_id and
    p.products_status = '1' and o.date_purchased >
    SUBDATE( now( ) , INTERVAL " .
    MAX_DISPLAY_TIME_ALSO_PURCHASED . " DAY ) group by
    p.products_id order by o.date_purchased desc limit " .
    MAX_DISPLAY_ALSO_PURCHASED);
```

Cooked to perfection! Bon appetit!

66. Display Full Information for Customer, Delivery, and Billing Addresses at a Glance

Default osCommerce doesn't offer a search function to search within the customers' addresses (either the address used to sign up, or the one for delivery, or the billing address). This recipe adds an address-driven search to your **Orders** page and allows you to view these three addresses at a glance.

Presentation

The following screenshot shows **Administration | Customers | Orders** with the new search option for address data and all address information displayed for a selected order row:

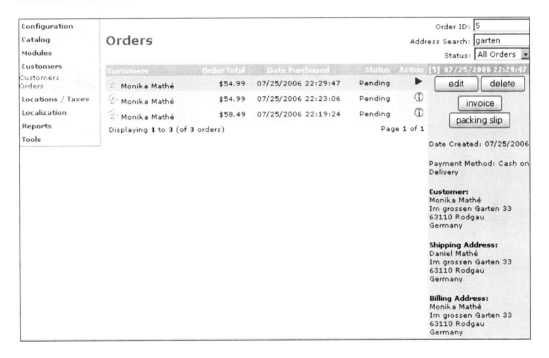

Brisket, Corned, and Jerky… all at hand!

Ingredients

Modified:

```
catalog/admin/orders.php
catalog/admin/includes/languages/english/orders.php
```

Cooking

1. Open `catalog/admin/orders.php` and find this in line 91:

   ```
   include(DIR_WS_CLASSES . 'order.php');
   ```

   Here you will process the new address-search field to find the orders that use the search keyword in one of the order address fields. Replace it with the following code:

   ```
   if (isset($HTTP_GET_VARS['address_text'])) {
   $address_text =
    tep_db_prepare_input($HTTP_GET_VARS['address_text']);
   $orders_query = tep_db_query("
      select orders_id from " . TABLE_ORDERS . "
      where customers_name like '%" . $address_text . "%' or
      customers_street_address like '%" . $address_text . "%' or
      customers_city like '%" . $address_text . "%' or
      customers_postcode like '%" . $address_text . "%' or
      delivery_name like '%" . $address_text . "%' or
      delivery_street_address like '%" . $address_text . "%' or
      delivery_city like '%" . $address_text . "%' or
      delivery_postcode like '%" . $address_text . "%' or
      billing_name like '%" . $address_text . "%' or
      billing_street_address like '%" . $address_text . "%' or
      billing_city like '%" . $address_text . "%' or
      billing_postcode like '%" . $address_text . "%' ");
   $order_exists = true;
   //prefill to limit search results even if no result found
   $orders_array[] = '0';
   if (!tep_db_num_rows($orders_query)) {
     $order_exists = false;
     $messageStack->add(ERROR_ORDER_DOES_NOT_EXIST, 'error');
   } else {
    while ($orders_search = tep_db_fetch_array($orders_query)) {
     $orders_array[] = $orders_search['orders_id'];
    }
   ```

```
  }.
  }

  include(DIR_WS_CLASSES . 'order.php');
  $order = new order($HTTP_GET_VARS['oID']);
```

2. Find the form for order ID search in line 367:

```
<tr><?php echo tep_draw_form('orders', FILENAME_ORDERS, '',
  'get'); ?>
  <td class="smallText" align="right"><?php echo
  HEADING_TITLE_SEARCH . ' ' . tep_draw_input_field('oID', '',
  'size="12"') . tep_draw_hidden_field('action', 'edit');
  ?></td>
</form></tr>
```

Add directly below it a new search input field for address-related entries:

```
<tr><?php echo tep_draw_form('address', FILENAME_ORDERS, '',
    'get'); ?>
  <td class="smallText" align="right"><?php echo
  HEADING_TITLE_SEARCH_ADDRESS . ' ' .
    tep_draw_input_field('address_text', '', 'size="12"');
  ?></td>
</form></tr>
```

3. Find in line 392 the following code, which processes search fields:

```
if (isset($HTTP_GET_VARS['cID'])) {
  $cID = tep_db_prepare_input($HTTP_GET_VARS['cID']);
  $orders_query_raw = "select o.orders_id, o.customers_name,
    o.customers_id, o.payment_method, o.date_purchased,
    o.last_modified, o.currency, o.currency_value,
    s.orders_status_name, ot.text as order_total from " .
    TABLE_ORDERS . " o left join " . TABLE_ORDERS_TOTAL .
    " ot on (o.orders_id = ot.orders_id), " .
    TABLE_ORDERS_STATUS . " s where o.customers_id = '" .
    (int)$cID . "' and o.orders_status = s.orders_status_id and
    s.language_id = '" . (int)$languages_id . "' and
    ot.class = 'ot_total' order by orders_id DESC";
} elseif (isset($HTTP_GET_VARS['status']) &&
  is_numeric($HTTP_GET_VARS['status']) &&
  ($HTTP_GET_VARS['status'] > 0)) {
    $status = tep_db_prepare_input($HTTP_GET_VARS['status']);
    $orders_query_raw = "select o.orders_id, o.customers_name,
    o.payment_method, o.date_purchased, o.last_modified,
    o.currency, o.currency_value, s.orders_status_name,
```

```
      ot.text as order_total from " . TABLE_ORDERS .
      " o left join " . TABLE_ORDERS_TOTAL . " ot on
        (o.orders_id = ot.orders_id), " . TABLE_ORDERS_STATUS .
        " s where o.orders_status = s.orders_status_id and
      s.language_id = '" . (int)$languages_id . "' and
        s.orders_status_id = '" . (int)$status . "' and
        ot.class = 'ot_total' order by o.orders_id DESC";
    } else {
      $orders_query_raw = "select o.orders_id, o.customers_name,
      o.payment_method, o.date_purchased, o.last_modified,
      o.currency, o.currency_value, s.orders_status_name,
      ot.text as order_total from " . TABLE_ORDERS . "
      o left join " . TABLE_ORDERS_TOTAL . " ot on
        (o.orders_id = ot.orders_id), " . TABLE_ORDERS_STATUS .
        " s where o.orders_status = s.orders_status_id and
        s.language_id = '" . (int)$languages_id . "' and
        ot.class = 'ot_total' order by o.orders_id DESC";
    }
```

Replace it with this code, adding the check for address-field related search:

```
$orders_extra_info = '';
 if (isset($HTTP_GET_VARS['address_text'])) {
 $orders_extra_info = " and o.orders_id in (" . implode(',' ,
 $orders_array) . ")";
 }

 if (isset($HTTP_GET_VARS['cID'])) {
   $cID = tep_db_prepare_input($HTTP_GET_VARS['cID']);
   $orders_query_raw = "select o.orders_id, o.customers_name,
   o.customers_id, o.payment_method, o.date_purchased,
   o.last_modified, o.currency, o.currency_value,
   s.orders_status_name, ot.text as order_total from " .
   TABLE_ORDERS . " o left join " . TABLE_ORDERS_TOTAL . "
   ot on (o.orders_id = ot.orders_id), " . TABLE_ORDERS_STATUS .
   " s where o.customers_id = '" . (int)$cID . "' and
   o.orders_status = s.orders_status_id and
   s.language_id = '" . (int)$languages_id . "' and
   ot.class = 'ot_total' " . $orders_extra_info . "
   order by o.orders_id DESC";
 } elseif (isset($HTTP_GET_VARS['status']) &&
 is_numeric($HTTP_GET_VARS['status']) &&
 ($HTTP_GET_VARS['status'] > 0)) {
   $status = tep_db_prepare_input($HTTP_GET_VARS['status']);
   $orders_query_raw = "select o.orders_id, o.customers_name,
   o.payment_method, o.date_purchased, o.last_modified,
```

```
o.currency, o.currency_value, s.orders_status_name,
ot.text as order_total from " . TABLE_ORDERS .
" o left join " . TABLE_ORDERS_TOTAL . " ot on
(o.orders_id = ot.orders_id), " . TABLE_ORDERS_STATUS .
" s where o.orders_status = s.orders_status_id and
  s.language_id = '" . (int)$languages_id . "' and
  s.orders_status_id = '" . (int)$status . "' and
  ot.class = 'ot_total' " . $orders_extra_info .
  " order by o.orders_id DESC";
 } else {
  $orders_query_raw = "select o.orders_id, o.customers_name,
  o.payment_method, o.date_purchased, o.last_modified,
  o.currency, o.currency_value, s.orders_status_name,
  ot.text as order_total from " . TABLE_ORDERS .
  " o left join " . TABLE_ORDERS_TOTAL . " ot on
  (o.orders_id = ot.orders_id), " . TABLE_ORDERS_STATUS .
  " s where o.orders_status = s.orders_status_id and
   s.language_id = '" . (int)$languages_id . "' and
  ot.class = 'ot_total' " . $orders_extra_info . "
  order by o.orders_id DESC";
}
```

4. As a final step, find the code that displays information for each order in the right column. This is the code in line 459, displaying the payment method:

```
$contents[] = array('text' => '<br>' . TEXT_INFO_PAYMENT_METHOD .
' ' . $oInfo->payment_method);
```

Directly below it add the code for display of the customer address as well as the delivery and billing address:

```
if (isset($HTTP_GET_VARS['oID'])) {
  $contents[] = array('text' => '<br><b>' . ENTRY_CUSTOMER .
  '</b><br>' . tep_address_format($order->customer['format_id'],
  $order->customer, 1, '', '<br>'));
  $contents[] = array('text' => '<br><b>' .
  ENTRY_SHIPPING_ADDRESS . '</b><br>' .
  tep_address_format($order->delivery['format_id'],
  $order->delivery, 1, '', '<br>'));
  $contents[] = array('text' => '<br><b>' .
  ENTRY_BILLING_ADDRESS . '</b><br>' .
  tep_address_format($order->billing['format_id'],
  $order->billing, 1, '', '<br>'));
}
```

5. Open `catalog/admin/includes/languages/english/orders.php` and add the following language-file define for your new search box:

```
define('HEADING_TITLE_SEARCH_ADDRESS', 'Address Search:');
```

Hardly any cleanup! Bon appetit!

67. Highlight Orders According to their Order Status

This recipe will be much appreciated by busy stores that require quick references to the status of a recent order without doing a search from the drop-down list. Choosing colors to highlight the status of each order will group your orders visually, so they can easily be distinguished.

Chef's suggestion:

While you can use any color to highlight status, here traffic light colors were selected with **Pending** being red, **Processing** being yellow, and **Delivered** being green.

Presentation

The following screenshot shows **Administration | Customers | Orders** with the order status colored according to its value:

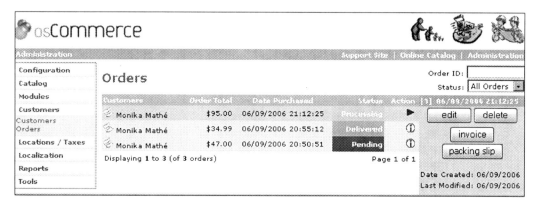

Blue, Medium, or Well Done?

Ingredients

Modified:

```
catalog/admin/includes/stylesheet.css
catalog/admin/orders.php
```

Cooking

1. Open `catalog/admin/includes/stylesheet.css` and add the following classes, one for each order status you want to highlight, specifying a different background color for each:

```
/* status */
.delivered {
  font-family: Verdana, Arial, sans-serif;
  font-size: 10px;
  color: #ffffff;
  background-color: #7ed48a; /* green */

  font-weight: bold;
}
.processing {
  font-family: Verdana, Arial, sans-serif;
  font-size: 10px;
  color: #ffffff;
  background-color: #ffd772; /* yellow */

  font-weight: bold;
}
.pending {
  font-family: Verdana, Arial, sans-serif;
  font-size: 10px;
  color: #ffffff;
  background:  #CC0000; /* red */
  font-weight: bold;
}
```

2. Go to line 376 of the `catalog/admin/orders.php` file. The following code displays each order with its status. As you will see, the current setup uses the default class for table content:

```
<td class="dataTableContent"><?php echo
  '<a href="' . tep_href_link(FILENAME_ORDERS,
    tep_get_all_get_params(array('oID', 'action')) .
```

```
         'oID=' . $orders['orders_id'] . '&action=edit') . '">' .
         tep_image(DIR_WS_ICONS . 'preview.gif', ICON_PREVIEW) .
         '</a> ' . $orders['customers_name']; ?></td>
<td class="dataTableContent" align="right"><?php echo
   strip_tags($orders['order_total']); ?></td>
<td class="dataTableContent" align="center"><?php echo
      tep_datetime_short($orders['date_purchased']); ?></td>
<td class="dataTableContent" align="right"><?php echo
      $orders['orders_status_name']; ?></td>
```

Replace it with the following code that checks the order-status name and assigns a new stylesheet class to the td cell, called instead of the class dataTableContent used for all cells in the default version:

```php
<?php
  $class='dataTableContent';
  if ($orders['orders_status_name'] == 'Processing') {
   $class='processing';
  }elseif ($orders['orders_status_name'] == 'Pending') {
   $class='pending';
  }elseif ($orders['orders_status_name'] == 'Delivered') {
    $class='delivered';
 }
?>
<td class="dataTableContent"><?php echo
 '<a href="' . tep_href_link(FILENAME_ORDERS,
     tep_get_all_get_params(array('oID', 'action')) .
     'oID=' . $orders['orders_id'] . '&action=edit') . '">' .
     tep_image(DIR_WS_ICONS . 'preview.gif', ICON_PREVIEW) .
   '</a> ' . $orders['customers_name'];
 ?></td>
<td class="dataTableContent" align="right"><?php echo
   strip_tags($orders['order_total']); ?></td>
<td class="dataTableContent" align="center"><?php echo
   tep_datetime_short($orders['date_purchased']); ?></td>
<td class="<?php echo $class; ?>" align="right"><?php echo
   $orders['orders_status_name']; ?></td>
```

Chef's suggestion:

For multilingual stores, tweak the query for the table display not only to use the order-status name, but also to include the order-status ID, just as it is stored in the underlying table. Use that value to name your stylesheet classes and for the conditional statements.

No matter the degree of cooking, the meat is excellent! Bon appetit!

68. Sort Your Administration Menu Configuration-Box Entries

This recipe provides you, as the master of the kitchen, the choice of sorting entries in your configuration box. Default osCommerce sorts the parameters by the sort_order column specified in the configuration_group table, which is created during installation. If you do not consider the current sorting method intuitive to use, here you'll find options to create your customized sorting choice, and even divide the configuration-box links into bite-sized sections according to the areas covered by the entries.

Presentation

The following screenshot shows **Administration | Configuration | Minimum Values** with the selected box (**Minimum Values**) highlighted in red:

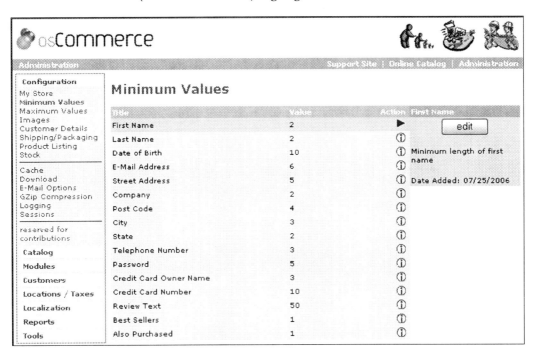

Note that three sections have been created for this screenshot, with the first covering catalog administration and the second covering site administration. A third area (**reserved for contributions**) has been set up to be automatically filled by new groups added to your configuration box during contribution installation.

Sorting for the first area was kept default-sorted by the `sort_order` column, while the other two areas are sorted alphabetically.

Ready to organize the spice cupboard?

Ingredients

Modified:

```
catalog/admin/includes/stylesheet.css
catalog/admin/includes/boxes/configuration.php
```

Cooking

1. Open `catalog/admin/includes/stylesheet.css` and add the following class for highlighted infobox links to be displayed in bold red font:

   ```
   A.menuBoxHighlight:visited { font-family: Verdana, Arial,
      sans-serif; font-size: 10px; color: FF0000; font-weight: bold;
      text-decoration: none; }
   ```

2. Open `catalog/admin/includes/boxes/configuration.php` and find this in line 24.

   ```
   $cfg_groups = '';
   $configuration_groups_query = tep_db_query("select
      configuration_group_id as cgID, configuration_group_title as
      cgTitle from " . TABLE_CONFIGURATION_GROUP .
      " where visible = '1' order by sort_order");
   while ($configuration_groups =
         tep_db_fetch_array($configuration_groups_query)) {
      $cfg_groups .= '<a href="' .
         tep_href_link(FILENAME_CONFIGURATION,
         'gID=' . $configuration_groups['cgID'], 'NONSSL') . '"'
         class="menuBoxContentLink">' .
      $configuration_groups['cgTitle'] . '</a><br>';
   }

   $contents[] = array('text'  => $cfg_groups);
   ```

   In this part of the code, all configuration groups are selected from the database and displayed after sorting, defined by the value for `sort_order`. The query is separated into three parts. The default entries in the `configuration_group` table hold two different topics, namely, catalog administration (ID < 10) and site administration (10 < ID <= 15). The third part is for new entries that you will be adding when installing contributions from the osCommerce website; the ID value is the primary key of the table and hence will be greater than 15. Each part can have the sorting specified as needed, with the default column `sort_order` being kept for the first area and alphabetic sorting for the other two sections of the box.

Note that a placeholder text is provided to show if no new contributions have been added to the `configuration_group` table. When you click on a link, the new class highlights the topic in bold red.

Replace the previous code with the following new module:

```
//catalog area
$cfg_groups = '';
$sort = 'sort_order';//alternative: $sort = 'cgTitle';
$configuration_groups_query =
    tep_db_query("select configuration_group_id as cgID,
        configuration_group_title as cgTitle from " .
        TABLE_CONFIGURATION_GROUP . " where visible = '1' and
        configuration_group_id < 10 order by " . $sort);
while ($configuration_groups =
    tep_db_fetch_array($configuration_groups_query)) {
        $class = 'menuBoxContentLink';
    if ($HTTP_GET_VARS['gID'] == $configuration_groups['cgID'])
    $class = 'menuBoxHighlight';
    $cfg_groups .= '<a href="' .
        tep_href_link(FILENAME_CONFIGURATION,
        'gID=' . $configuration_groups['cgID'], 'NONSSL') .
        '" class="' . $class . '">' .
        $configuration_groups['cgTitle'] . '</a><br>';
}
$contents[] = array('text'  => $cfg_groups);
$contents[] = array('text'  => tep_draw_separator());

//administrating site
$cfg_groups = '';
$sort = 'cgTitle';//alternative: $sort = 'sort_order';
$configuration_groups_query = tep_db_query("select
  configuration_group_id as cgID, configuration_group_title as
  cgTitle from " . TABLE_CONFIGURATION_GROUP .
  " where visible = '1' and configuration_group_id >= 10 and
  configuration_group_id < 16 order by " . $sort);
while ($configuration_groups =
      tep_db_fetch_array($configuration_groups_query)) {
        $class = 'menuBoxContentLink';
  if ($HTTP_GET_VARS['gID'] == $configuration_groups['cgID'])
     $class = 'menuBoxHighlight';
```

```
        $cfg_groups .= '<a href="' .
          tep_href_link(FILENAME_CONFIGURATION,
          'gID=' . $configuration_groups['cgID'], 'NONSSL') .
          '" class="' . $class . '">' .
          $configuration_groups['cgTitle'] . '</a><br>';
    }
    $contents[] = array('text'  => $cfg_groups);
    $contents[] = array('text'  => tep_draw_separator());

    //new contributions
    $cfg_groups = '';
    $sort = 'cgTitle';//alternative: $sort = 'sort_order';
    $configuration_groups_query = tep_db_query("select
        configuration_group_id as cgID, configuration_group_title as
        cgTitle from " . TABLE_CONFIGURATION_GROUP .
        " where visible = '1' and configuration_group_id > 15 order by
        " . $sort);
    while ($configuration_groups =
        tep_db_fetch_array($configuration_groups_query)) {
        $class = 'menuBoxContentLink';
     if ($HTTP_GET_VARS['gID'] == $configuration_groups['cgID'])
        $class = 'menuBoxHighlight';
        $cfg_groups .= '<a href="' .
        tep_href_link(FILENAME_CONFIGURATION,
        'gID=' . $configuration_groups['cgID'], 'NONSSL') .
        '" class="' . $class . '">' .
        $configuration_groups['cgTitle'] . '</a><br>';
    }
    if ($cfg_groups == '') $cfg_groups = 'reserved for
                                contributions';
        $contents[] = array('text'  => $cfg_groups);
```

Chef's suggestion:

Just as sorting alphabetically by configuration-group name and by the `sort_order` column in the `configuration_groups` table is possible, you may want to have your contributions sorted by the date you added them. To achieve this, you will have to write a join query to get the highest date parameter for each configuration group from the configuration table to be able to sort, as the `configuration_groups` table doesn't have its own date column.

All lined up and ready to go! Bon appetit!

69. Allow Entering Products in an Additional Currency

This recipe will be invaluable for you if you purchase some of the products you sell in a currency that differs from the default currency of your shop. You will be able to add products in a predefined secondary currency with prices converted immediately to your default currency during data entry. A link to a synchronizer file has been added to the left column for updating currency via **xe** or **oanda** exchange rate servers, while prices for all products added in your second currency will be recalculated using the latest exchange rates.

Chef's suggestion:

While manual updating is always an option, this synchronizer file should be scheduled as a cron job and executed daily if you are dealing with fast-fluctuating exchange rates.

Presentation

The following screenshot shows **Administration | Catalog | Categories/Products** with the new module that enables you to add products in your second currency:

Note that the label of the entry field displays the three letter code of the currency defined as the second currency of your shop.

Argentinean, American, British, or French Beef?

Ingredients

New:

```
database.sql (to be run in phpMyAdmin)
catalog/admin/synchronize_supplier_prices.php
catalog/admin/includes/boxes/synchronize.php
```

Modified:

```
catalog/admin/categories.php
catalog/admin/includes/languages/english/categories.php
catalog/admin/inludes/column_left.php
catalog/includes/boxes/currencies.php
```

Cooking

1. Run the following SQL statement in phpMyAdmin to create a new key added to the **My Store** configuration-box section called **Second Currency for Data Entry**. The script will also add a new column to your products table, which will store information about products that were entered in your second currency.

    ```
    INSERT INTO configuration (configuration_title,
        configuration_key, configuration_value,
        configuration_description, configuration_group_id,
        sort_order, date_added)
    VALUES ('Second Currency for Data Entry', 'SECOND_CURRENCY',
        'EUR', '3 letter code of the second currency in product
        entry form', '1', '10', now());

    ALTER TABLE products
    ADD products_second_currency decimal(15,4) NULL;
    ```

2. Navigate to **Administration | Configuration | My Store** and edit the new key to reflect the second currency needed for your store. Note that this currency needs to be a valid currency defined in the section **Administration | Localization | Currencies** so that a currency exchange rate can be read from the database for this currency later on:

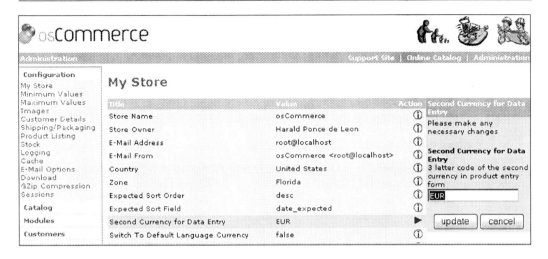

3. Open `catalog/admin/categories.php`. There will be quite a few changes in this file to incorporate the new column into the `products` table insert, update, and select statements. Find the following code in line 217 for the array used to insert products into the `products` table:

```
'products_price' =>
        tep_db_prepare_input($HTTP_POST_VARS['products_price']),
```

Add the new column to the array directly below it:

```
'products_second_currency' =>
tep_db_prepare_input($HTTP_POST_VARS['products_second_currency']),
```

4. The next modification tackles the area where products are copied to be duplicated or linked. Find this in line 290:

```
$product_query = tep_db_query("select products_quantity,
    products_model, products_image, products_price,
    products_date_available, products_weight,
    products_tax_class_id, manufacturers_id from " .
    TABLE_PRODUCTS . " where products_id = '" .
    (int)$products_id . "'");
$product = tep_db_fetch_array($product_query);

tep_db_query("insert into " . TABLE_PRODUCTS .
    " (products_quantity, products_model,products_image,
        products_price, products_date_added,
        products_date_available, products_weight, products_status,
        products_tax_class_id, manufacturers_id)
values ('" . tep_db_input($product['products_quantity']) . "',
    '" . tep_db_input($product['products_model']) . "',
```

```
'" . tep_db_input($product['products_image']) . "',
'" . tep_db_input($product['products_price']) . "',  now(),
 " . (empty($product['products_date_available']) ? "null" :
"'" . tep_db_input($product['products_date_available']) . "'") .
", '" . tep_db_input($product['products_weight']) . "', '0',
'" . (int)$product['products_tax_class_id'] . "',
'" . (int)$product['manufacturers_id'] . "')");
```

Replace it with the following code, adding the new second-currency column:

```
$product_query = tep_db_query("select products_quantity,
  products_model, products_image, products_price,
  products_second_currency, products_date_available,
  products_weight, products_tax_class_id, manufacturers_id from "
  . TABLE_PRODUCTS . " where products_id = '" .
  (int)$products_id . "'");
$product = tep_db_fetch_array($product_query);

tep_db_query("insert into " . TABLE_PRODUCTS .
  " (products_quantity, products_model,products_image,
     products_price, products_second_currency,
     products_date_added, products_date_available,
     products_weight, products_status, products_tax_class_id,
     manufacturers_id)
values ('" . tep_db_input($product['products_quantity']) . "',
  '" . tep_db_input($product['products_model']) . "',
  '" . tep_db_input($product['products_image']) . "',
  '" . tep_db_input($product['products_price']) . "',
  '" . tep_db_input($product['products_second_currency']) . "',
  now(), " . (empty($product['products_date_available']) ? "null"
  : "'" . tep_db_input($product['products_date_available']) .
  "'") . ",
  '" . tep_db_input($product['products_weight']) . "', '0', '" .
  (int)$product['products_tax_class_id'] . "', '" .
  (int)$product['manufacturers_id'] . "')");
```

5. For the new-product section, find this in line 366, setting up the parameters for data entry:

```
'products_price' => '',
```

Add directly below it the new-column definition:

```
'products_second_currency' => '',
```

6. In line 379, find the query that is run when you click on the product-preview button on the category-overview page:

```
$product_query = tep_db_query("select pd.products_name,
    pd.products_description, pd.products_url, p.products_id,
    p.products_quantity, p.products_model, p.products_image,
    p.products_price, p.products_weight, p.products_date_added,
    p.products_last_modified,
    date_format(p.products_date_available, '%Y-%m-%d') as
    products_date_available, p.products_status,
    p.products_tax_class_id, p.manufacturers_id from " .
    TABLE_PRODUCTS . " p, " . TABLE_PRODUCTS_DESCRIPTION .
    " pd where p.products_id = '" . (int)$HTTP_GET_VARS['pID'] .
    "' and p.products_id = pd.products_id and
    pd.language_id = '" . (int)$languages_id . "'");
```

Here also add the new column:

```
$product_query = tep_db_query("select pd.products_name,
    pd.products_description, pd.products_url, p.products_id,
    p.products_quantity, p.products_model, p.products_image,
    p.products_price, p.products_second_currency,
    p.products_weight, p.products_date_added,
    p.products_last_modified,
    date_format(p.products_date_available, '%Y-%m-%d') as
    products_date_available, p.products_status,
    p.products_tax_class_id, p.manufacturers_id from " .
    TABLE_PRODUCTS . " p, " . TABLE_PRODUCTS_DESCRIPTION .
    " pd where p.products_id = '" . (int)$HTTP_GET_VARS['pID'] .
    "' and p.products_id = pd.products_id and
    pd.language_id = '" . (int)$languages_id . "'");
```

7. In line 443 find the JavaScript function that updates the gross price when entering products.

```
function updateGross() {
```

Add directly above it the new updateSecondCurrencyNet() function. This new function converts a price entered into the second-currency input field to your default currency, using the conversion rate for this currency from the database table currencies. In a second step, this function updates the gross price of the product.

```
function updateSecondCurrencyNet() {

<?php echo 'var exchangeRate = ' .
 $currencies->currencies[SECOND_CURRENCY]['value'] . ';' .
 "\n"; ?>
 var netValue =
   document.forms["new_product"].products_second_currency.value;
```

```
if (exchangeRate > 0) {
 netValue = netValue / exchangeRate;
}

document.forms["new_product"].products_price.value =
                doRound(netValue, 4);

var taxRate = getTaxRate();
var grossValue = doRound(netValue, 4);

if (taxRate > 0) {
 grossValue = grossValue * ((taxRate / 100) + 1);
}

document.forms["new_product"].products_price_gross.value =
            doRound(grossValue, 4);
}
```

8. Find in line 543 the code that displays the entry field for the gross price:

```
<tr bgcolor="#ebebff">
  <td class="main"><?php echo TEXT_PRODUCTS_PRICE_GROSS; ?></td>
  <td class="main"><?php echo
    tep_draw_separator('pixel_trans.gif', '24', '15') . ' '
    . tep_draw_input_field('products_price_gross',
    $pInfo->products_price, 'OnKeyUp="updateNet()"'); ?></td>
</tr>
```

Add directly below it the entry field for your second currency. The label uses the currency name for display. While typing in a price, this price will be converted into the net price of your product, using the new updateSecondCurrencyNet() function.

```
<tr bgcolor="#dca944">
 <td class="main"><?php echo sprintf(TEXT_PRODUCTS_PRICE_SECOND,
   SECOND_CURRENCY); ?></td>
 <td class="main"><?php echo
   tep_draw_separator('pixel_trans.gif', '24', '15') . ' '
   . tep_draw_input_field('products_second_currency',
   $pInfo->products_second_currency,
   'OnKeyUp="updateSecondCurrencyNet()"'); ?></td>
</tr>
```

9. Open catalog/admin/includes/languages/english/categories.php and add the following language define needed for the new second-currency column:

```
define('TEXT_PRODUCTS_PRICE_SECOND', 'Price in %s:');
```

10. Navigate to **Administration | Catalog | Categories/Products** and edit the DVD Movie **There's Something About Mary**. Here, you will see a European supplier and **40** as the **EUR** price for recalculating according to conversion rate. **Net** and **Gross** price are calculated in real time.

11. Create the new file `catalog/admin/synchronize_supplier_prices.php` using the following code. This file will synchronize exchange rates via oanda or xe, and recalculate all product prices for products using the second-currency column. If you plan to use cron jobs only, comment out all `echo` statements, which are only used to create a live report of the updating when run manually:

```php
<?php
/*
  $Id: synchronize_supplier_prices.php

  Module written by Monika Mathé
  http://www.monikamathe.com

  Module Copyright (c) 2006 Monika Mathé

  osCommerce, Open Source E-Commerce Solutions
  http://www.oscommerce.com

  Copyright (c) 2003 osCommerce

  Released under the GNU General Public License
*/

include("includes/application_top.php");

echo 'synchronising currency exchange rate' . '<p>';
echo '********************************************************'
  . '<br>';
$server_used = CURRENCY_SERVER_PRIMARY;

$currency_query = tep_db_query("select currencies_id, code,
  title from " . TABLE_CURRENCIES);
while ($currency = tep_db_fetch_array($currency_query)) {
 $quote_function = 'quote_' .
                   CURRENCY_SERVER_PRIMARY . '_currency';
 $rate = $quote_function($currency['code']);

 if (empty($rate) && (tep_not_null(CURRENCY_SERVER_BACKUP))) {

  $quote_function = 'quote_' .
                    CURRENCY_SERVER_BACKUP . '_currency';
```

```
    $rate = $quote_function($currency['code']);

    $server_used = CURRENCY_SERVER_BACKUP;
  }

  if (tep_not_null($rate)) {
   tep_db_query("update " . TABLE_CURRENCIES . " set value = '" .
       $rate . "', last_updated = now() where
       currencies_id = '" . (int)$currency['currencies_id'] .
                                                   "'");

    echo 'successfully synchronised currency exchange rate via ' .
      $server_used . ' (' . $currency['title'] . ', ' .
      $currency['code'] . ', ' . $rate . ')<br>';
  } else {
   echo 'failed synchronizing currency exchange rate via ' .
      $server_used . ' (' . $currency['title'] . ', ' .
      $currency['code'] . ', ' . $rate . ')<br>';
  }
}
echo '*********************************************************'
  . '<p>';

if (tep_not_null($rate)) {

 echo 'the following products will be synchronized:' . '<br>';
 echo '===================================================' .
'<br>';

 require(DIR_WS_CLASSES . 'currencies.php');
 $currencies = new currencies();

 $query_test = tep_db_query("SELECT products_id, products_model,
    products_price, products_second_currency from products where
    products_second_currency > 0");
 while ($query = tep_db_fetch_array($query_test)) {

  $new_price = round($query['products_second_currency'] /
       $currencies->currencies[SECOND_CURRENCY]['value'], 4);

  $new_price_sql = "update products set products_price = " .
  $new_price . " where products_id = '" . $query['products_id'] .
  "'";

  tep_db_query($new_price_sql);

 echo $new_price_sql;
```

```
}

 echo '==================================================' .
'<p>';
 echo '<p>successfully finished synchronizing' . '<p>';
} else {
 echo '<p>synchronizing not possible at this date' . '<p>';
}
?>
<a href="javascript:history.back();">Back</a>
```

12. Create the new file `catalog/admin/includes/boxes/synchronize.php`.
This box holds the link for the file `synchronize_supplier_prices.php`,
which can therefore be called manually from the left column by clicking on
Synchronizer. You will only need to follow steps 12 and 13 if you can not use
cron jobs.

```php
<?php
/*
 $Id: synchronizer.php,v 1.00 2006/07/20 00:00:00 mm Exp $

 Module written by Monika Mathé
 http://www.monikamathe.com

 Module Copyright (c) 2006 Monika Mathé

 osCommerce, Open Source E-Commerce Solutions
 http://www.oscommerce.com

 Copyright (c) 2002 osCommerce

 Released under the GNU General Public License
*/
?>
<!-- synchronizer //-->
     <tr>
      <td>
<?php
 $heading = array();
 $contents = array();

 $heading[] = array('text' => 'Synchronizer',
     'link' => tep_href_link('synchronize_supplier_prices.php',
         'selected_box=synchronizer'));

 if ($selected_box == 'synchronizer') {
 $contents[] = array('text' => '');
```

```
        }

        $box = new box;
        echo $box->menuBox($heading, $contents);
        ?>
            </td>
            </tr>
<!-- synchronizer_eof //-->
```

13. Add the box `synchronize.php` to your left column below the **Tools** box. Find this in line 25 of `catalog/admin/inludes/column_left.php`:

    ```
    require(DIR_WS_BOXES . 'tools.php');
    ```

    Immediately below it, add the following call:

    ```
    require(DIR_WS_BOXES . 'synchronizer.php');
    ```

14. **Optional**: If you are using the currency box in the catalog part of your store and you prefer not to show the currency that is needed in admin as a second currency in the catalog part of your store, open `catalog/includes/boxes/currencies.php` and find the following code in line 25:

    ```
    $currencies_array = array();
    while (list($key, $value) = each($currencies->currencies)) {
      $currencies_array[] = array('id' => $key,
          'text' => $value['title']);
    }
    ```

    Replace it with the following code, excluding the currency used for the second currency entry in admin:

    ```
    $currencies_array = array();
    while (list($key, $value) = each($currencies->currencies)) {
      if ($key != SECOND_CURRENCY) {
        $currencies_array[] = array('id' => $key,
          'text' => $value['title']);
      }
    }
    ```

15. If you would like your file to be automatically executed as a task via cron, enter the data into the cron table of your host. Note that different hosts need different calls for the file to be executed, so check documentation or send in a quick support ticket to your web host to make sure. If you haven't used your crontab yet, your host may need to enable it for you first; or there could be an option in your cPanel FTP manager for you to enable it yourself. The host used here uses the following call for files (replace with your own login and password to admin, and your own admin folder path in SSL mode):

```
/usr/bin/curl -o /dev/null
https://ENTER_ADMINLOGIN:ENTER_PASSWORD_FOR_THIS_USER_HERE
    @www.monikamathe.com/admin/synchronize_supplier_prices.php
```

This is how a cron job is laid out:

```
minute (0-59), hour (0-23, 0 = midnight), day (1-31),
month (1-12), weekday (0-6, 0 = Sunday), command
```

Execution time has been set to once per day at midnight–00:00, and the full cron table looks like that in the following screenshot (numbers are values, * means all possible values). Note that the entry field for **Command** only shows part of the string as a result of limited space.

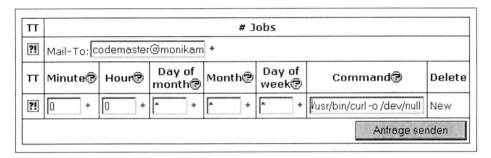

Your roast will satisfy all clientele! Bon appetit!

Summary

A pinch of this, a sprinkle of that, and presto! Your administration area behaves just as you need it to. For the recipes in this chapter, you have used your sharpest knives in the drawer to chop up the default code and achieve outstanding results.

You are no longer tied to the natural sorting of New Products for your catalog display; instead you reset specific products with a simple click of a button to show the focal points of your site at will. Products expire automatically if you decide to set an expiry date, making promotional offers much less of a hassle to schedule and control. The selection for the Also Purchased Products box now only includes purchases from the last "x" days set by you in your **Maximum Values** area.

Your **Orders** screen not only allows you to view all customer, delivery, and billing addresses data at a glance, but also features colored status cells for quick and easy referencing of orders based on processing status.

The **Configuration** box, originally a more or less deliberately sorted list of entries, is now grouped visually into logical areas, even allowing for a new area to be included for contribution-configuration parameters; the selected entry is now highlighted in bold red.

As a very special treat for your shop, you can now choose to enter products you purchase abroad in a second currency. This value is converted to your default currency in real time and updated as often as you wish via a cron job or manually to compensate for currency fluctuation.

That's all; that's it; there is no more! Pull out that chilled bottle of champagne you've saved for that special day–*today's* that day!

Chin chin!

You have earned the *Master Cook Award* for being your own osCommerce Chef. I hope that you thoroughly enjoyed our culinary journey through the topics of this amazing online-shop software. Its framework as an Open Source project makes it possible for us to mix and match, to try and taste, and finally to enjoy the delicious fruits of our labor. Your guests will feel pampered for sure.

Chef's suggestion:

Have fun with your shop and never consider it finished; something hard to do given all these exciting options for modifications just sitting here waiting for your skilled hands to get to work...

Happy cooking, and see you on the forums!

Kindly,

Monika Mathé

Index

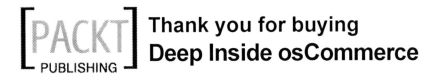

Thank you for buying
Deep Inside osCommerce

Packt Open Source Project Royalties

When we sell a book written on an Open Source project, we pay a royalty directly to that project. Therefore by purchasing Deep Inside osCommerce, Packt will have given some of the money received to the osCommerce project.

In the long term, we see ourselves and you — customers and readers of our books — as part of the Open Source ecosystem, providing sustainable revenue for the projects we publish on. Our aim at Packt is to establish publishing royalties as an essential part of the service and support a business model that sustains Open Source.

If you're working with an Open Source project that you would like us to publish on, and subsequently pay royalties to, please get in touch with us.

Writing for Packt

We welcome all inquiries from people who are interested in authoring. Book proposals should be sent to authors@packtpub.com. If your book idea is still at an early stage and you would like to discuss it first before writing a formal book proposal, contact us; one of our commissioning editors will get in touch with you.

We're not just looking for published authors; if you have strong technical skills but no writing experience, our experienced editors can help you develop a writing career, or simply get some additional reward for your expertise.

About Packt Publishing

Packt, pronounced 'packed', published its first book "Mastering phpMyAdmin for Effective MySQL Management" in April 2004 and subsequently continued to specialize in publishing highly focused books on specific technologies and solutions.

Our books and publications share the experiences of your fellow IT professionals in adapting and customizing today's systems, applications, and frameworks. Our solution-based books give you the knowledge and power to customize the software and technologies you're using to get the job done. Packt books are more specific and less general than the IT books you have seen in the past. Our unique business model allows us to bring you more focused information, giving you more of what you need to know, and less of what you don't.

Packt is a modern, yet unique publishing company, which focuses on producing quality, cutting-edge books for communities of developers, administrators, and newbies alike. For more information, please visit our website: www.PacktPub.com.

Building Online Stores with osCommerce: Beginner Edition

ISBN: 1-904811-88-4   Paperback: 181 pages

A step by step introduction to osCommerce.

1. A step by step introduction to osCommerce

2. Install and configure osCommerce

3. Build your first ecommerce website

4. A special Beginnner's edition of the complete

Building Online Stores with osCommerce: Professional Edition

ISBN: 1-904811-14-0   Paperback: 370 pages

Learn how to design, build, and profit from a sophisticated online business.

1. Install, configure, and customize osCommerce

2. Enhance and modify osCommerce

3. Learn from a sample, fully functional site packed with useful features such as gift certificates and discounts, cross- and up-selling, RSS feed aggregation, enhanced product image handling and bug fixes.

Please check **www.PacktPub.com** for information on our titles

AJAX and PHP: Building Responsive Web Applications

ISBN: 1-904811-82-5   Paperback: 275 pages

Enhance the user experience of your PHP website using AJAX with this practical tutorial featuring detailed case studies

1. Build a solid foundation for your next generation of web applications

2. Use better JavaScript code to enable powerful web features

3. Leverage the power of PHP and MySQL to create powerful back-end functionality and make it work in harmony with the smart AJAX client

cPanel User Guide and Tutorial

ISBN: 1-904811-92-2   Paperback: 190 pages

Get the most from cPanel with this easy to follow guide

1. Everything you need to manage files, email, and databases using cPanel

2. Organise your web siteâ€¦ create subdomains, custom error messages, and password protected areas

3. Analyse site logs, ensure your site and data remain secure, and learn how to create and restore data back upst

4. Use advanced features, find powerful cPanel add ons, and install web scripts from within cPanel: osCommerce, Mambo, phpBB, and more.

Please check **www.PacktPub.com** for information on our titles

Printed in the United Kingdom by
Lightning Source UK Ltd., Milton Keynes
142422UK00001B/91/A